New Perspectives on Gillian Clarke

WRITING WALES IN ENGLISH

CREW series of Critical and Scholarly Studies
General Editors: Kirsti Bohata and Daniel G. Williams (*CREW*, Swansea University)

This *CREW* series is dedicated to Emyr Humphreys, a major figure in the literary culture of modern Wales, a founding patron of the *Centre for Research into the English Literature and Language of Wales*. Grateful thanks are due to the late Richard Dynevor for making this series possible.

Other titles in the series
Stephen Knight, *A Hundred Years of Fiction* (978-0-7083-1846-1)
Barbara Prys-Williams, *Twentieth-Century Autobiography* (978-0-7083-1891-1)
Kirsti Bohata, *Postcolonialism Revisited* (978-0-7083-1892-8)
Chris Wigginton, *Modernism from the Margins* (978-0-7083-1927-7)
Linden Peach, *Contemporary Irish and Welsh Women's Fiction* (978-0-7083-1998-7)
Sarah Prescott, *Eighteenth-Century Writing from Wales: Bards and Britons* (978-0-7083-2053-2)
Hywel Dix, *After Raymond Williams: Cultural Materialism and the Break-Up of Britain* (978-0-7083-2153-9)
Matthew Jarvis, *Welsh Environments in Contemporary Welsh Poetry* (978-0-7083-2152-2)
Harri Garrod Roberts, *Embodying Identity: Representations of the Body in Welsh Literature* (978-0-7083-2169-0)
Diane Green, *Emyr Humphreys: A Postcolonial Novelist* (978-0-7083-2217-8)
M. Wynn Thomas, *In the Shadow of the Pulpit: Literature and Nonconformist Wales* (978-0-7083-2225-3)
Linden Peach, *The Fiction of Emyr Humphreys: Contemporary Critical Perspectives* (978-0-7083-2216-1)
Daniel Westover, *R. S. Thomas: A Stylistic Biography* (978-0-7083-2413-4)
Jasmine Donahaye, *Whose People? Wales, Israel, Palestine* (978-0-7083-2483-7)
Judy Kendall, *Edward Thomas: The Origins of His Poetry* (978-0-7083-2403-5)
Damian Walford Davies, *Cartographies of Culture: New Geographies of Welsh Writing in English* (978-0-7083-2476-9)
Daniel G. Williams, *Black Skin, Blue Books: African Americans and Wales 1845–1945* (978-0-7083-1987-1)
Andrew Webb, *Edward Thomas and World Literary Studies: Wales, Anglocentrism and English Literature* (978-0-7083-2622-0)
Alyce von Rothkirch, *J. O. Francis, realist drama and ethics: Culture, place and nation* (978-1-7831-6070-9)
Rhian Barfoot, *Liberating Dylan Thomas: Rescuing a Poet from Psycho-Sexual Servitude* (978-1-7831-6184-3)
Daniel G. Williams, *Wales Unchained: Literature, Politics and Identity in the American Century* (978-1-7831-6212-3)
M. Wynn Thomas, *The Nations of Wales 1890–1914* (978-1-78316-837-8)
Richard McLauchlan, *Saturday's Silence: R. S. Thomas and Paschal Reading* (978-1-7831-6920-7)
Bethan M. Jenkins, *Between Wales and England: Anglophone Welsh Writing of the Eighteenth Century* (978-1-7868-3029-6)
M. Wynn Thomas, *All that is Wales: The Collected Essays of M. Wynn Thomas* (978-1-7868-3088-3)
Laura Wainwright, *New Territories in Modernism: Anglophone Welsh Writing, 1930–1949* (978-1-7868-3217-7)
Siriol McAvoy, *Locating Lynette Roberts: 'Always Observant and Slightly Obscure'* (978-1-7868-3382-2)
Linden Peach, *Pacifism, Peace and Modern Welsh Writing* (978-1-7868-3402-7)
Kieron Smith, *John Ormond's Organic Mosaic* (978-1-7868-3488-1)
Georgia Burdett and Sarah Morse (eds), *Fight and Flight: Essays on Ron Berry* (978-1-7868-3528-4)
M. Wynn Thomas, *Eutopia: Studies in Cultural Euro-Welshness, 1850–1980* (978-1-78683-614-4)
Linden Peach, *Animals, Animality and Controversy in Modern Welsh Literature and Culture* (978-1-78683-937-4)

New Perspectives on Gillian Clarke

Community, Cosmology, Climate and Conflict

WRITING WALES IN ENGLISH

Linden Peach

UNIVERSITY OF WALES PRESS
2025

© Linden Peach, 2025

All rights reserved. No part of this book may be reproduced in any material form (including photocopying or storing it in any medium by electronic means and whether or not transiently or incidentally to some other use of this publication) without the written permission of the copyright owner. Applications for the copyright owner's written permission to reproduce any part of this publication should be addressed to the University of Wales Press, University Registry, King Edward VII Avenue, Cardiff CF10 3NS.

www.uwp.co.uk

British Library CIP Data
A catalogue record for this book is available from the British Library.

ISBN: 978-1-83772-279-2
e-ISBN: 978-1-83772-281-5

The right of Linden Peach to be identified as author of this work has been asserted in accordance with sections 77 and 79 of the Copyright, Designs and Patents Act 1988.

For GPSR enquiries please contact:
Easy Access System Europe Oü, 16879218
Mustamäe tee 50, 10621, Tallinn, Estonia.
gpsr.requests@easproject.com

Typeset by Marie Doherty
Printed and bound by CPI Group (UK) Ltd, Croydon, CR0 4YY

Contents

Series Editors' Preface		vii
Acknowledgements		ix
Introduction and Overview		1
1	Emotional Communities	11
2	Cosmology in a Planetary Age	35
3	Climate and Weather in the Anthropocene	65
4	Sound, Water, Blackness and Cosmogenesis	93
5	Geology, Human Development and the Anthropocene	115
6	War and Peace (Part One)	133
7	War and Peace (Part Two)	159
Afterword		179
Notes		183
Select Bibliography		211
Index		219

Series Editors' Preface

The aim of this series, since its founding in 2004 by Professor M. Wynn Thomas, is to publish scholarly and critical work by established specialists and younger scholars that reflects the richness and variety of the English-language literature of modern Wales. The studies published so far have amply demonstrated that concepts, models and discourses current in the best contemporary studies can illuminate aspects of Welsh culture, and have also foregrounded the potential of the Welsh example to draw attention to themes that are often neglected or marginalised in anglophone cultural studies. The series defines and explores that which distinguishes Wales's anglophone literature, challenges critics to develop methods and approaches adequate to the task of interpreting Welsh culture, and invites its readers to locate the process of writing Wales in English within comparative and transnational contexts.

Professor Kirsti Bohata and Professor Daniel G. Williams

Founding Editor: Professor M. Wynn Thomas (2004–15)

CREW (*Centre for Research into the English Literature and Language of Wales*)
Swansea University

Acknowledgements

Like all books by teachers in higher education, this work has benefited from discussions with students and colleagues and my participation in conferences and research seminars. My ideas about Gillian Clarke's perspectives on cosmology and a relational universe were first mooted in *Animals, Animality and Controversy in Modern Welsh Literature and Culture* (2022), also published by the University of Wales Press, which includes a chapter on her sequence of poems about a year on a sheep farm on Yr Wyddfa. As I extended my thinking about the environmental turns in Clarke's poetry, journals and reflective essays, I benefited from the opportunity to be able to present a paper on Clarke at the Association of Welsh Writing in English 2023 conference. I am especially grateful to my Doctoral students and colleagues at the King's School of Traditional Arts, London, who have contributed to the development of my thoughts and arguments in ways in which some of them may not even be fully aware.

Over the last decade, I have been inspired by colleagues and scholars who have argued for, and have demonstrated in their own works, an interdisciplinary approach to the literature, history and geography of Wales and especially by those who have pursued relationships between Welsh- and English-language writings. My own Welsh has provided me, as was the case with my recent books, *Pacifism, Peace and Modern Welsh Writing* (2019) and *Animals, Animality and Controversy in Modern Welsh Literature and Culture*, with fresh insights into the history and culture of Wales without which this book would not have been possible, and, once again, I am conscious of my debt to tutors in Welsh at the Open University and Welsh for Adults, Bangor University.

I am grateful for the encouragement and support of the University of Wales Press and especially Dr Llion Wigley (commissioning editor, Welsh Language and Topics) and his colleagues in the production and marketing divisions.

Like many authors I am indebted to the patience and support of my family who are up to their necks in their own lives and projects.

i Angela, Kate a Matthew

Introduction and Overview

Gillian Clarke is one of the most significant and respected contemporary Welsh poets. As a writer and teacher, she has inspired generations of readers. In mapping her achievements as a writer, it is impossible to overlook her appointment, in 2008, as the third National Poet of Wales, a position she held until 2016. Her appointment surprised no one. In 1999, she had received the Glyndŵr Award for her 'Outstanding Contribution to the Arts in Wales' presented during the Machynlleth Festival and shortly after was chosen as the inaugural Capital Poet for Cardiff 2005–6. But her achievements do not stop there. In 2010, she was awarded the Queen's Gold Medal for poetry, only the second Welsh person to receive this honour. In 2011, she was elected to the Gorsedd of Bards, while, in 2012, she received the Wilfred Owen Association Poetry award. Three of her works have been Poetry Book Society Recommendations. She has given poetry readings and lectures in Europe and the United States; her work has been translated into ten languages including Chinese.

Clarke's writings have been the subject of reviews and chapters in books on poetry and Welsh writing in English and discussion online. However, this is the first book to take an overall view of her work from her first publication in *Poetry Wales* in 1970 to her most recent volume of poetry published in 2024. As such, it traces key themes in her work which have been generally overlooked by scholars and reviewers but which unveil her significance as a contemporary poet and her relevance to our times. The basic facts of Clarke's early life are fairly well known, having been recorded in her many books and mentioned regularly in reviews of her work. However, the tensions within her family when she was a child are not often discussed in depth. Households are hardly ever coherent, singular units. This was certainly the case in Clarke's family, and it enabled her to approach the communities in south and west Wales in which she lived with her own family in ways that anticipated a new field of academic study, the history of emotions.

Born in Cardiff in June 1937, she was brought up there and in the middle-class, seaside enclave of Penarth, although for part of the Second World War she spent time in Pembrokeshire to which her widowed grandmother had moved from Carmarthenshire and, postwar, in a Catholic boarding school, St Clare's Convent, Porthcawl. These experiences revealed for her the way in which our emotional lives, as discussed in Chapter 1, are often formed by different kinds of communities simultaneously and in movement between them. As she admitted in one of her reflective, autobiographical essays, 'For seven years Cardiff became The Weekend and The Holidays.'[1]

As Clarke reminds us in her essay 'Beginning with Bendigeidfran', her parents came from families with roots in rural west and north Wales and in Welsh-language communities.[2] Her mother was a tenant farmer's daughter, one of ten children in a Welsh-speaking family in Denbighshire, who left Grove Park Grammar School in Wrexham at the age of fourteen and eventually became a nurse, a life which Clarke imagines in her poem 'The City' (1998). Her father, the son of a rural railwayman, also left school – Llanelli Grammar School – at the age of fourteen but having been a wireless officer with the Marconi company, travelling the world with the merchant navy, by the time Clarke was born he was a broadcasting engineer at the BBC in Wales.[3] Her mother taught her to read before she started school and, with her, she learned all the English nursery rhymes. But Clarke came to feel, very early in her life, that her mother had given her 'a mixed bag of gifts and deprivations' because 'she banned Welsh'.[4] She was fonder of her father, who died unexpectedly when she was a teenager, than her mother. She enjoyed a kind, close relationship with him and remained grateful for the way in which he opened her eyes to nature, the countryside, the skies and the weather around them – some of the themes which this volume develops from new perspectives.

Although neither parent encouraged Clarke as a Welsh speaker, her father did introduce her to aspects of the Welsh language and to its myths and stories. By contrast, her mother seemed better adjusted to anglicised Wales than her father and sought to guide Clarke's emotional development according to her own, anglicised aspirations. But in her work published in the 1990s and in the early 2000s, Clarke depicts her mother more sympathetically. Her journal in 2019 exemplifies how, as the years passed, she came to appreciate her mother as a person, and especially a woman, in her own right, defined and exhausted by the roles and lack of opportunities for women in the 1930s and 1940s.

In her essay 'Tramp. Nothing is until it has a word', Clarke gratefully remembers that 'we had books at home'.[5] As she recalls, this aspect of her childhood home helped to create its particular emotional identity. Not untypically of the time, all the books were in English, which reflected her mother's attitude toward the Welsh language. Welsh, Clarke quickly realised, was the absent presence in their domestic library.

The divisive nature of her family is disclosed in her account of a visit with her aunt to see *King Lear*: 'There, in the theatre, where the characters were live people, my whole body listened. I was eavesdropping on the grown-ups, as I did all the time at home. I'd learned to read their white lies, their whispers, their "not in front of the child!"'[6] This is an important insight not only into Clarke's own childhood home but domestic environments generally, which, even from childhood, she saw with the heightened emotional intelligence that informs her poetry and her autobiographical essays.

From the childhood home and family that I have outlined here, Clarke – not surprisingly given her love of books – went on to study English at the University College in Cardiff. But, in her essay 'Cardiff', she stresses not the difference in the level of work between the University and the sixth form at St Clare's but the different community in which she now found herself. As she says, 'I was in love with the very idea of university, and relished my new life.'[7] Rather than her studies, she focuses in the essay on the transformative effect of being at university, of its physical presence and surroundings, of its contrast as a community with Penarth and how 'Cardiff was suddenly glamorous'.[8] On graduating, she continued to live in different communities simultaneously. Moving between them constituted the rhythm of her life. After a year working with the BBC in London, she returned to Cardiff and the anglicised suburbs with which she was most familiar, which meant that her children, a daughter and two sons, were to be born in Wales. For a while, she lived in the south-Wales port and seaside town of Barry, in a house on the Parade that constituted its own kind of enclave within the larger society with which it rubbed shoulders, and worked as an English teacher in two very different educational environments: Reardon-Smith Nautical College and, later, Newport College of Art.

When Clarke studied English at Cardiff University, language and literature, as in the discipline of English studies as a whole, were approached largely through a frame of close critical reading, literary history and an emergent interest in literary theory. But from the 1980s, creative writing began to assume a more significant place in higher education, initially as modules within an otherwise academic curriculum and eventually constituting a degree programme in its own right. English became a more creative, and it has to be said more affective, discipline, encouraging a different kind of discourse – as in Clarke's 'Why I Write' (2021) – compared with a decade or two earlier.

New undergraduate and post-graduate programmes in creative writing recruited writers as part-time and eventually full-time tutors and, several years after moving to Ceredigion, Clarke was appointed a tutor on the MPhil in Creative Writing at the then University of Glamorgan, now the University of South Wales, led by well-recognised writers Tony Curtis, Christopher Meredith and Sheenagh Pugh. Teaching writing has been an important part of Clarke's life; she has often run classes for adults and is President of Tŷ Newydd, the writers' centre which she co-founded in 1990 in north Wales.

From the 1960s, Welsh writing in English – initially Anglo-Welsh Writing – developed as an important field of literary study and works by English-language Welsh writers were studied in schools, colleges and in higher education. Clarke made her mark in this area through her own inspirational role as a teacher and as a writer, editor and translator – she was a successful editor of the influential *Anglo-Welsh Review* from 1975 to 1984. Her poetry is studied by GCSE and A-level students throughout Britain and a considerable number of her poems are included in the GCSE AQA Anthology.

BECOMING A PUBLISHED WRITER IN THE 1970s

When Clarke first began writing and thinking about publishing poetry as a woman and as a Welsh writer, in the 1970s, the publishing world in Wales was on the cusp of an important transformation from one type of regime, which did not reflect these priorities, to another quite different kind of publishing community which soon began providing women and Welsh writers with new opportunities to see their work in print.⁹ Clarke has said of her own first attempts at writing: 'I threw my first poems in the bin because I was unaware they were poems ... I think we all need models, and I was both Welsh and a woman ... Have you noticed how late in their careers women get published?'[10] How she was first published is a well-known but still an interesting story: her first husband sent some of her poems to *Poetry Wales*, which was edited at the time by the journalist and literary scholar Meic Stephens, and, unbeknown to her, he accepted them. And four of her poems – 'Beach Buds', 'Nightride', 'Sailing' and 'The Fox' – appeared in the magazine.[11] But it is not often stressed that this enabled Clarke to join, and experience, publishing as a 'community'. *Poetry Wales* had a pivotal role in publishing new, and especially women, poets, including Alison Bielski, Ruth Bidgood and Sally Roberts (Jones). As Clarke also recognised, the nature of the global publishing of poetry was changing through the reputations that international, and especially American, women writers such as Sylvia Plath, Anne Sexton and Anne Stevenson, were rapidly acquiring.[12]

From the late 1960s and 1970s especially, the emergence of a different publishing environment in Wales was characterised, as Clarke herself has acknowledged, by the increased availability of literary magazines:

> I began to write and to post poems because of the existence of the Welsh magazines written in English, like the *Anglo-Welsh Review*, *Poetry Wales*, and others. Those magazines gave me a sense of my own ability to join the ranks of the writers within them, writers who seemed to be giving me, written down, my own world.[13]

The publication of Welsh women writers and the beginning of a new publishing community of women authors brought about a profound change in the publishing world of poetry in the 1960s and 1970s, and, with it, a greater awareness of the scope of Welsh society and culture – the importance of which Clarke herself has drawn attention. 'Feminine values', to use Clarke's own term, which has always been a deep-rooted characteristic of her work, had begun to be 'noticed and admired'.[14] This had a considerable impact on men's writing and publishing as well as that of women. As a result, male writers were able to associate themselves with a community that included, and was respectful of, women writers and male writers sympathetic with feminism and 'feminine values' who in turn reflected this in their work. Clarke, like many new writers at this time, found inspiration in charismatic male poets like Seamus Heaney, Ted Hughes and R. S. Thomas. New writers and readers – mainly but not exclusively women – found themselves able to bond with this work and this was especially true of Heaney, a crucial influence on contemporary poetry and for Clarke herself who admitted finding in his work 'a tremendously feminine sensibility'.[15]

HOW WELSH IS WELSH?

Clarke says in an interview published in the mid-1980s: 'My loss of Welsh has been a very strong tension in my writing ... I didn't begin writing properly until I was thirty, by which time I had long been learning Welsh.'[16] This journey is not surprising because, despite her mother's reluctance for her daughter to become a Welsh speaker and her father's failure, if that is not too harsh, to be a stronger advocate for the Welsh language in the family, she was not completely removed from Welsh as a child. As she says in her essay 'Voice of the Tribe': 'The Welsh language, like the landscape, is always on the skyline or at the end of the street in a name';[17] and, as she reminds us in another essay, 'Beginning with Bendigeidfran', 'Our placenames and our English speech are haunted by Welsh'.[18] Moreover, there were Welsh-speaking communities in and around Cardiff and at the time that she lived there it was impossible not to be aware of the burgeoning campaigns to restore the Welsh language in Wales as a living and legal entity. But the real emotional turn as far as her Welshness was concerned came in the mid-1980s when she moved to rural Ceredigion in west Wales with her second husband.

In her poem 'Language Act' from *Five Fields* (1998), published after Wales had voted for a Welsh assembly in 1997 and a year before the Senedd was established in Cardiff, she remembers herself as an English monoglot speaker but now sees herself as a developing Welsh-language speaker. Living, from the 1980s onward, in a community where Welsh was the everyday language, and there was a Welsh-language heritage, provided Clarke with access to a richer Welsh culture than had been available to her in south Wales. In her writings, she began to look at Welsh history, not as something outside her, a backcloth on which events were projected, but as something lived from within. As she says in 'Beginning with Bendigeidfran': 'We share history, ancestral connections with Nonconformism, farming, heavy industry, and even an enduring respect for and ambition for education.'[19]

One of the key themes in Clarke's writings about her childhood – that we inhabit more than one community simultaneously – has a strong bearing on her work rooted in west Wales: 'Two sea-sounds, two languages, two versions of the world, of myself, of history, of what should be valued, of what culture and civilisation are.'[20] She comes to realise more strongly that Welsh- and English-language writers are connected by 'the sound of two drums speaking'.[21] Some literary scholars, such as M. Wynn Thomas, have argued that Clarke came 'to realise that to belong to a Welsh-speaking community is to belong to a permanently beleaguered remnant'.[22] But, given the success of Welsh medium education, Welsh media and national and community-led initiatives to encourage Welsh speakers, others, such as the writer and scholar Mary-Ann Constantine, argue for the significance of a new generation in Wales that 'feels more culturally resilient, more confident – and, yes, more visible'.[23]

Clarke had no reservations in saying that 'to be female is to live a woman's life, an essentially seasonal, physical, rhythmic, body-conscious life form'.[24] She has sought – as an adult immersing herself in Welsh-language culture – to achieve a similar physical, rhythmic, body-conscious Welsh. This concept is encapsulated by the contemporary Welsh-language folk-music group, Pedair: 'The Welsh language is an integral part of our whole being. We feel, think, and dream in Welsh and looking forward, our precious and ancient language will continue to thrive and keep the heart of our nation beating for centuries to come.'[25] This is an inspiration behind, and to an extent realised in, much of Clarke's life and work even though this is never as completely achieved for Clarke as for Pedair.

RESIDENCIES AND COMMISSIONS

One aspect of Clarke's career as a writer that has been overlooked, but is one of the reasons why she is such a relevant and 'contemporary' voice, is the impact on her creativity of the residencies and commissions that she has undertaken. These external opportunities enabled her to extend her creativity into new forms related to subjects and interests that she was already exploring, albeit in more embryonic form, and to link her writing with contemporary issues. It is impossible to mention all of them but those responsible for significant turns in her work cannot be ignored.

'Letter from a Far Country' was commissioned as a half-hour radio play in 1978 (and published four years later)[26] and writing for radio rather than the page gave Clarke the opportunity to create a poem of reverberations and silences and to indulge her ear for sound in the expression of women's frustrations in the 1970s over the restrictive nature of norms and codes that determined women's expression of their emotions even thirty years after the Second World War (discussed in Chapter 1). An equally innovative work, this time a sequence of short poems, written with the requirements and expectations of another media, 'The King of Britain's Daughter: an Oratorio', was commissioned by the Director of the *Sunday Times* Hay-on-Wye Festival of Literature, 1993.[27] It provided Clarke with an opportunity to work with the composer Adrian Williams on the story of Branwen and to pursue her interest in poetry as song. Two subsequent ambitious works relating poetry with music, 'Concerto' and 'The City'[28] (discussed in Chapters 2, 4 and 6), were commissioned by the Bridgewater Hall, Manchester, during a residency in May 1997.

Poetry Live and the British Council enabled Clarke to spend a week in India in 2007, on which she based her poem sequence 'Mumbai', a key text within the collection *A Recipe for Water* (2009) (discussed in Chapter 4).[29] An equally significant poem sequence 'One Year' (2017), charting twelve months on a north Wales sheep farm but also drawing on her own experience of rearing sheep, was commissioned by the National Theatre of Wales and performed in association with the National Trust on Yr Wyddfa (referred to as Snowdon in the book). The poem sequence, 'Behind Glass' (discussed in Chapter 5), published in the same volume as 'One Year', arose out of a different type of residency at the Museum of Zoology, Cambridge, which enabled her to develop fresh perspectives on fossils, the bones and skeletons of animals and birds, and insects preserved as fossils or 'pinned' as part of someone's private collection.[30]

A commission for *The National Botanic Garden of Wales* (2000), edited by A. Sclater,[31] provided Clarke with an opportunity to return to her long-standing interest in science and geology that enabled some of her most significant environmental writing. As a consequence of this commission, Clarke was able to complete the poem sequence 'The Stone Poems' published in *Making the Beds for the Dead* (2004) (discussed as part of her wider interest in geology in Chapter 5) and one of her most compelling reflective essays 'The Poetry of Stone: Pentre Ifan' (2008).[32]

OVERVIEW

As mentioned at the outset, this book begins with a discussion of Clarke's work in the context of the new and burgeoning field in historical studies – the history of emotions. Although a fast-developing field, it has yet to make its full mark on the study of Welsh history and this book examines how Clarke's poetry, essays and journals offer new ways of looking at Wales in terms of its communities and revises some of the ways in which internal differences in Wales in terms of geography, historical, cultural and linguistic differences are usually discussed. It examines how, through her poetry from the 1970s to the 1990s, Clarke began to invest herself emotionally and creatively in the different communities that constituted south and west Wales. Through close analysis of Clarke's understanding of emotional communities, Chapter 1 provides fresh insights into the controversial, and much discussed, long poem 'Letter from a Far Country' (1982) before turning to one of her later sequences of poems, 'Making the Beds for the Dead' (2004).

Chapters 2 and 3 are an extended analysis of how the 'emotional turn' which led to the history of emotions as an academic discipline resonates with similar developments in other areas of thought – not least the natural and physical sciences and cosmology. Drawing on this work, and a close reading of Clarke's environmental writing, including her ambitious poem 'Concerto' (1998), the chapters argue that while Clarke's poetry suggests that there is a central order at the heart of nature which inspires wonder and beauty, this is frequently juxtaposed with a less reassuring view of the cosmos which presents us with an impending sense of extinction. How Clarke's poetry negotiates this apparent contradictory cosmos and its impact on her well-being and the human psyche generally is the focus of Chapter 3 in particular. Chapter 4 develops the discussion of cosmology in Clarke's work through the concept of 'cosmogenesis', which acquires greater emphasis in her post-1990 poetry and journals. Selecting three phenomena – sound, water and blackness – the chapter argues that, while her work retains its immediacy, sensuousness and proximity to the natural world, from 1990 onward, it displays a deeper interest in its origins. The discussion of sound is based on an analysis of

Clarke's rather overlooked but important long poem 'The City', while her interest in connecting cosmogenesis with rivers and water is part of a wider discussion of themes such as the sensuous experience of water, the trauma triggered by flooding and the pollution of natural resources. This discussion of Clarke's engagement with environmental issues around water, not least the interconnectedness of all living and non-living forms, includes a detailed reading of the poem sequence 'Mumbai' from *A Recipe for Water*. The chapter turns to examine Clarke's interest in what she calls 'the deepening geography', and the psychology, of snow introducing a new profound and discomforting 'blackness' into her work. This preoccupation with black(ness) is analysed in her recent poetry, including *Ice* (2012), with reference to the work of the artist and colour theorist Kathryn Simon.

Chapter 5 explores Clarke's interest in geology, focused on what is now seen as a 'human turn' in the science. The chapter is based on an analysis of Clarke's well-researched, geologically based sequences 'The Stone Poems' (2014), reflecting her interest in geology, time and cosmic energy, and the sequence of fossil poems, 'Behind Glass' (2017), which revises conventional ways of looking at human and non-human evolution through moments of 'wonder'.

The book concludes with two linked chapters on war and peace which constitute another theme that runs throughout Clarke's work but which, like her engagement with cosmology and climate change, shifts in focus from the 1990s onwards. The first of these chapters examines the influence on Clarke and her poetry of her wartime childhood and the 'mediatisation' of a more diffused warfare in the later decades of the twentieth century, suggesting that 'The City', which is read in relation to cosmogenesis in Chapter 4, should also be read as a 'war poem'. The second linked chapter examines Clarke's version of Aneirin's *Y Gododdin* in the context of her long-standing interest in war and the Welsh tradition of pacifism and peace. Clarke's *The Gododdin: Lament for the Fallen* (2021) is seen as bringing together her interest in war and conflict, cosmology and emotional communities.

1

EMOTIONAL COMMUNITIES

The way in which Gillian Clarke thinks of community resonates with ideas and concepts in historical studies – the history of emotions.[1] As emotions historians Barbara Rosenwein and Riccardo Cristiani observe:

> Now everyone – novelists, journalists, psychologists, neuropsychologists, philosophers and sociologists – thinks and writes about emotions, each for his or her own purposes, each taking a different direction. Historians are no exception.[2]

One of the key themes in this field is the way in which an individual's experience of emotional expression and behaviour is guided by the codes and norms within particular societies and communities which Rosenwein encourages us to think of as 'groups in which people adhere to the same norms of emotional expression and value – or devalue – the same or related emotions'.[3] This takes us to the heart of Clarke's writing about Wales and her historical perspectives.

Clarke found, as noted in the Introduction, that as she moved between different parts of south and west Wales, to use Rosenwein's words, 'more than one emotional community may exist ... contemporaneously, and these communities may change over time'.[4] In her historicised texts, as in the history of emotions generally, two areas of interest come to the fore: the way in which the articulation of emotions – such as love, fear and anger – changes across cultures and over time; and that states of emotion consist of an experience but also the expression/utterance of that experience acting together in ways which are culturally influenced and governed by social norms and rules.[5] In the history of emotions, the latter has led to recognition of what has come to be called 'emotional regimes' and 'emotional communities'. The American historian William Reddy first distinguished them by seeing emotions in the former as determined and controlled by overt concentrations of power and in the latter as being influenced more subtly through normative behaviour within a community which might be a village, a society of like-minded individuals, a family or even a household. In both cases, emotional forms of expression are inculcated and determined by customs, rituals and practices.[6]

Although the history of emotions has yet to impact fully on Welsh history, it resonates with the community-based approach to social history developed in the 1980s by the distinguished Professor of Welsh History Ieuan Gwynedd Jones. Rather than seeing Wales as one social structure, Jones's approach to Welsh history, which he applied like Gillian Clarke to industrial, urban and rural Wales alike, conceived of communities which 'differed substantially from place to place and from time to time ... [and which] nourished a strong individuality'.[7] To fully appreciate Clarke's writing about Wales in terms of different communities, it is useful to look through Jones's lens to locations where 'joint concerns and common interests on social and political questions were invariably friable and grew longitudinally'.[8]

The following sections examine the ways in which Clarke began to see Welsh history and culture from the perspectives of emotional history, drawing on three principal genres: her diary poems about south Wales communities, published in the 1970s and early 1980s; the long poem 'Letter from a Far Country' (1982) concerned with the history of the parish in west Wales to which she moved in the mid-1980s; and a sequence of poems, 'Making the Beds for the Dead' (2004), focused on the impact of the foot-and-mouth pandemic on farming communities in north Wales.

THE ENCLAVES OF SOUTH WALES

Clarke's poetry of the 1970s and 1980s examines south Wales as a series of social, economic and cultural communities – some principally middle-class, but the majority more overtly working-class and industrial areas – that were all separate from each other in some respects yet connected in others. In 'East Moors' (*Letter from a Far Country*, 1982), a poem referring to the closure in 1978 of the steelworks in Cardiff – opened by the Dowlais Iron Company of Merthyr Tydfil in 1891 – she acerbically comments that at least the washing strung along the narrow gardens of two middle-class communities, Roath and Rumney, will stay clean.[9] Peter Finch, the Cardiff poet and psychogeographer, remembers the demolition of the houses about which Clarke writes: 'A whole block of Splott terracing here has vanished. Built in the armpit of the East Moors Steelworks with blast furnace black smog billowing through their gardens daily they are no more.'[10] But in 'East Moors', the extent of the pollution from the steelworks' chimneys serves as a metaphor as to how everyone at the time lived in more than one emotional community. As Dennis Morgan says, 'For nearly 90 years the great furnaces and chimney stacks of the East Moors Works, casting their red glow at night, were a familiar part of the skyline in Splott and Tremorfa.'[11]

In the 1970s and 1980s, Clarke began to invest herself creatively and emotionally in the different communities that constituted south Wales which she saw as defined by their contexts. In this regard, many of her early short poems may be approached as creative expositions of the emotional reality that originates in, and develops with, particular communities as in the psychological dilemmas, entanglements and changed domestic relationships within families affected by the demise of heavy industry. As noted in the Introduction, as a child Clarke eavesdropped on her parents at home,[12] experiencing herself the fractious nature of households – 'I'd learned to read their white lies, their whispers, their "not in front of the child!"'[13] – a perspective which she brought to bear on the households of 'East Moors' as emotional communities where the unemployed men are confined to their sitting room and invested with a lethargy unbroken by the little jobs which their wives find for them. Her poem reminds us that the East Moors was more than an industrial plant. In the steelworks, like Jones's collieries, 'the work itself encouraged a sense of community' and, due to its brutally hard and dangerous nature, workers 'could survive only in co-operation with his fellows'.[14] What Jones says of the collier is true also of the steelworker, there cannot be individualised workers but only a community of workers, 'all inter-dependent, breathing the same inadequate air, relying upon their joint skills, all subject to the same instantaneous disaster'.[15]

'East Moors' provides an introduction to the nature of emotional communities and the different micro-communities within them.[16] The steelworks determined the nature of working-class culture and the emotional lives of the workers and their families that were dependent upon them. As Jones, in his approach to history from a community perspective, observes of life in colliery villages, 'the activities of the household likewise revolved around the imperious note of the colliery hooter, the wife as subject to it as her husband and working children'.[17] The Welsh social historian Dan Evans stresses how 'new communities clustered around these new industrial workplaces' with corner shops, pubs, churches and sporting teams – and 'a whole new way of life was born'.[18]

The nub of Clarke's 'East Moors' and Jones's community perspective is an insight that is crucial to the history of emotions: 'Inner disciplines may in the final analysis be more important in explaining the inner life of a community than externally imposed disciplines.'[19] Ultimately, Clarke's poem is about the way in which the demise of the steel plant changed the emotional dynamics of domestic life within the tightly knit community of the workers' families – reflected in the poem in the altered function of the kept-for-best 'front room' – and the creation of emotional subcommunities within the rows of small terraced houses constituted of the women, the men, and (implicitly) the younger adults and children. The sense of isolation and personal psychological pain that can be experienced in emotional communities whose codes inhibit their full expression is a strong motif in several of Clarke's early poems. 'Suicide on Pentwyn Bridge' (1982), for example, concerns a woman unable to fully express her grief for her husband who is slowly dying after jumping from a bridge – the 'long-drawn out falling in the brown / eyes of his wife week after week / at the supermarket cash-out'[20] – and for whom the local store becomes an emotional community in which people enquire about him and listen to the latest hospital news. In what is a recurring characteristic of the short poems from the 1970s and 1980s, different emotional communities are contrasted: in this poem, the store and the hospital – where the doctors had 'no words' and 'no common supermarket women's talk'.[21]

Emotional communities in many of Clarke's poems written in the 1970s and 1980s are defined by the traditions and rituals which guide the expectations and emotional expressions of women within them. 'Taid's Funeral' (*Letter from a Far Country*, 1982) closes poignantly with an image of how women in rural societies had to assume responsibility for family deaths: 'There are dark incisions in the stalks / of the daisies made by a woman's nail. / A new dress stains green with their sap.'[22] But it goes without saying that these are feminist poems which redefine 'feminine values', question the ways in which the normative values have shaped women's lives in families and unveil some of the emotional strategies by which women coped with the expectations placed on them, as in 'Sunday' (*Letter from a Far Country*, 1982):

> Getting up early on a Sunday morning
> leaving them sleep for the sake of peace,
> the lunch pungent, windows open
> for a blackbird singing in Cyncoed.[23]

The assumption that it is the role of the wife/mother to prepare the family meals is contrasted with women's desire for peace and, as signified by the open window and the singing birds, freedom – anticipating the longer poem 'Letter from a Far Country' to which I will turn in a moment. The house and the family in both poems are perceived as emotional communities centred up-to-a-point around love but also selfishness, control, frustration and unfulfilled desires.

As these short poems express greater interest in the emotive communities of women and how women are defined by the wider communities to which they belong, like the suburbs of Cardiff, they locate different emotional communities inside one another like a set of Russian dolls. The opening line of a poem set in west Wales, 'Blaen Cwrt' (*The Sundial*, 1978) – 'You ask how it is. I will tell you.'[24] – encapsulates the tone of many of the poems of the 1970s and 1980s including those rooted in south Wales. 'Death of a Young Woman' (*The Sundial*, 1978) opens in a characteristically unguarded voice – 'She died on a hot day'[25] – and does not mince its words as the narrative moves from one emotional community to another: the emotional life she shared as part of a couple – 'He wept for her and for the hard tasks / he had lovingly done, for the short, / Fierce life she had lived in the white bed'[26] – albeit determined by the wider conventions that defined the roles of men and women in their particular community; the larger society of family and friends in which they participated as a married couple; and emotional communities centred on places like pubs where different emotional expressions would be encouraged or discouraged according to their nature.

The very title of 'St Augustine's, Penarth' (*The Sundial*, 1978) suggests the extent to which different emotional communities which developed around church or chapel embedded themselves in different types of societies: 'From everywhere / You can see Top Church, remote / As high church is from chapel.'[27] St Augustine's Church – Eglwys Sant Awstin – was a Gothic revival nineteenth-century Parish church in Penarth. Penarth itself became, like Splott, an imaginary community but, centred on its church, promenade and pier, it was a very different kind of hypercentre. As Finch points out, promenading on what he calls 'Las Ramblas' was carefully controlled and had its own codes of emotional expression. It had to be undertaken slowly, in a mannered fashion, with ice creams, walking sticks, and cigars in hand and well-shined shoes.[28] But the Penarth to which Clarke refers is more than its promenade. She uses the steep nature of the town, with streets wonderfully described as 'tilted chutes / Of grey sliding on all sides',[29] as an example of how, when she lived there, she moved through different types of community and micro-communities, each with its implied set of codes, practices, rituals and permitted expressions of emotions: 'From the church, to sea and dock, / To shopping streets and home.'[30]

FAMILIES AND HOUSEHOLDS

How closely Clarke's early writing was tied to family as the principal emotional community to which she belonged is evident in the importance to her of keeping a diary from which her poetry evolved. In fact, she has kept a journal since she was given a five-year diary at the age of 15 and even in this century most mornings, as she says in 'Why I Write', still begin with her journal.[31] In many respects, her generally short poems published in *The Sundial* (1978) and *Letter from a Far Country* (1982) – which constituted most of her first *Selected Poems* (1985) – read as if they are entries in a diary. In her essay 'Beginning with Bendigeidfran' (2008), she remembers the origins of these 'diary' poems and how at first 'it was the living moment and the present tense' that informed them.[32]

Important for the 'drama' in her domestic poems were the internal divisions within families. This was especially true, as was observed in the Introduction, in the case of her parents who each guided Clarke in different emotional directions and permissible modes of emotional expression. Her thinking about her mother during her childhood and adolescence brings to the fore the concept of households, as Rosenwein says, as 'communities formed by a shared identity or goal (or aspiration towards these), practised through a specific set of emotional expressions, acts or performances, and exercised in a particular space or site'.[33] In Clarke's case, for example, as noted in the Introduction, while each of her parents could speak Welsh, neither of them encouraged her to do so and they bought her English-language books. However, as also suggested in the Introduction, her understanding as to where these emotional guidelines came from changed and developed in the course of her life. Her enriched understanding of Welsh history in terms of emotional communities, especially after her move to west Wales, enabled her to appreciate more fully not only Welsh-language communities per se but her mother's background.

During the closing years of the twentieth century and the arrival of the new millennium, Clarke revisits her mother's attitudes to the Welsh language with more understanding and a much sharper political focus than in the 1980s. In 'Not' (*A Recipe for Water*, 2009), she sees her mother as the victim as much as the purveyor of English contempt for the Welsh people and their language. The poem's title alludes to the Welsh 'Not' used in schools in the nineteenth century – although probably not as extensively as some histories would have us believe – whereby a pupil who spoke Welsh and was reported to their teacher for doing so would be forced to wear this word on a piece of wood around their neck until the end of the day when they would be beaten. They might only avoid punishment by reporting another child and thereby passing on the 'Not'. As the daughter of a tenant farmer, Clarke's mother felt deeply the shame inflicted on her by the landlord's agents who, through clenched teeth, would dismiss her as 'Welsh'. Moments when she found herself being on the receiving end of this racial slur hung like a curse around her neck which she sought, in a misguided but well-intentioned way, not to pass on to her children. Clarke returns to this subject in her poem 'The City' (1998), to which I will now turn, and over eighty years later in a 'cofiant', or biography, of her mother in *The Silence* (2024) discussed in Chapter 7.

In his study of communities in Wales, Jones links Welsh-language speakers and the emotional community to which they belonged quite deftly: Welsh 'represented the essence of community to them at the critical periods in the histories of these communities'.[34] As a child, despite her mother's attitude to the Welsh language, Clarke felt that she belonged to the Welsh-speaking Wales of her father and of her grandparents, especially her Nain – grandmother – with whom she associated warmth and kindness. She remembered, long into her life, being sent to sleep as a child on a soothing boatful of her Nain's

Welsh vowels while her father, encapsulating the community in which he was brought up, taught her the onomatopoeia in the Welsh words for water, wind and waves which brought her closer to nature, a subject to which I return in Chapter 5.

Clarke's 'Phoning Home', published in *Five Fields* (1998), is based around a telephone conversation with her then elderly mother, a picture of her mother as a child and reflections on old age. The relationship between daughter and mother is reversed. Her mother now is the one who is small and frail and she speaks to her as her mother might have spoken to Clarke when she was a child, telling her to be careful not to fall, take time to sit in the sun and walk on the green and make sure that she eats properly. The photograph depicts her mother as a child in an emotional community which was much closer to the one to which Clarke herself moved in rural west Wales where harvest time meant something to the community: 'She leans in muslin against barley stooks / singing with ripe seed and I'm not born.'[35] 'Phoning Home' recalls the photograph of her mother invoked in the poem 'Siege', from *Letter from a Far Country*, in which she remembers seeing her 'posing in a summer dress / in the corn at harvest time'.[36]

But in *Five Fields*, 'Phoning Home' is juxtaposed with the poem sequences 'The City' and 'Glass' and in some respects serves as their preface. Unlike her daughter in the home that she established for her in Cardiff, her mother in her childhood had little opportunity (as suggested in 'The City') to escape the noisy business of much of her life. She had to struggle, as Clarke now appreciates, to find the time and peace to read a book or to complete her homework. But called by her mother to assist with the smallholding and its animals, she enjoyed a soft-sounding closeness to nature, which she might not have fully appreciated at the time – 'She saw beasts born in meadow-grass, carried / new-born lambs to a shippon and clean straw'[37] – and which Clarke herself really only found in west Wales and what had been her grandmother's home. The language of domestic life which characterised her mother's less affluent childhood – 'hand-me-downs' and 'make-do's'[38] – draws Clarke emotionally closer to her. But it is the interplay of the different aspects of rural cottage life – snatched periods of peace, the robust noisiness of her mother's brothers, tasks like churning butter, and the quiet care of newborn animals – which, in this poem, transforms economic history into lived experience. Most important to Clarke, like the birdsong which opens 'The City', is the sublimity in being part of the natural order that comes in the vision of her mother sleeping 'to the sound of water turning the mill-wheel'.[39]

In the poem sequence 'Glass', from *Five Fields* (1998), Clarke's mother is remembered for her life in a different kind of emotional community. In fact, a point that this sequence makes is not that her mother enjoyed life in an urban, wartime and a post-war community but that she was in many respects an outsider to them. The social behaviours which she appropriated in order to be accepted in anglicised south Wales determined her everyday routines and the enjoyment which she derived from shopping and taking afternoon tea in one of Cardiff's principal hotels. In her daughter's memories, she is perpetually associated with cut-glass, brass ornaments and well-polished furniture. In a companion poem to her 'elegy' for her mother in *The Silence*, Clarke remembers clearing her mother's possessions after she had passed and drawing from the glove box a pair in 'exquisite suede, / she'd have paid with sacrifice, coupons saved / to impress her sisters'.[40] As Rosenwein and Cristiani observe, 'when words do not exist, objects themselves may be considered "bodies" that interact with other (human) bodies on an emotional level'.[41] Most of the poems in this sequence extend from a specific memory to which others then attach themselves: the tables that her mother laid for meals, her habit of switching off lamps, her Saturday shopping, her mother nurturing her through a migraine, helping her mother plant a quince tree and being handed her favourite cut-glass after her mother's death.

As a sequence of poems, 'Glass' reads as if the poet is turning the pages of a family album and reminds us that, although, as children, we grow up in 'our' time, we also belong to the period in which our parents grew up, handed down to us through their language – in 'Shopping', 'brought up with make do and mend'[42] – as well as their behaviours, as in 'The Habit of Life': 'She'd come through the bean rows in tottering shoes, / her pinny full of strawberries.'[43] The place of Clarke's mother in the home, like that of her grandmother, revolved around parenting skills which Clarke gratefully and lovingly remembers in her poem 'Migraine'. She recalls her mother treating 'a sick headache',[44] as it was called in her day, lovingly with hot and cold flannels. By contrast, Clarke as a modern mother relies on over-the-counter medicines. But she also enjoys the comfortable domestic life that she describes in 'Letter from a Far Country' – 'In the kitchen, saucepans danced their lids, the kettle purred / on the Aga, supper on its breath and the buttery melt / of a pie'[45] – in which the language sometimes conveys a child's emotional worldview.

In 'Glass', Clarke acknowledges the comfort that she took for granted as a child but also the pleasure that her mother derived from status symbols that defined the emotional community beyond their home in which she sought to establish herself. Her Aga, cut-glass and polished furniture were not simply objects, as those mentioned in 'Letter from a Far Country', but signifiers of a middle-class lifestyle. But in time, as the social community in which the Clarkes lived and the family they constituted changed, all these signifying objects lost their meanings. The kitchen table is left standing on linoleum that they cannot afford to replace and much that Clarke's mother valued become signifiers of the endless destruction of war, reflected at one point in the repetition of 'after' across three lines: 'after melting glass, / after biting a hole in the dining room window, / after burning a hole in the rust carpet.'[46]

WELSH HISTORY THROUGH EMOTIONAL COMMUNITIES

In *At the Source*, Clarke dwells on the lives of the previous inhabitants of the parish in west Wales to which she moved:

> Other ghosts have left their traces and their names. Some are benign ghosts whose lost habitations are marked only by the nettles and gooseberry bushes that show they were ever there. Ysgol Pwll-y-Pwdel, the old school by the river Glowan; Cae Gwreichion, the field of sparks where the plough still turns ashes and horseshoes from the black soil of a long-vanished forge; harp-shaped Cae Delyn. And Marged, Blaen Cwrt's last long-term inhabitant, who took her own life one bleak winter in the 1930s; Mamgu, my grandmother-in-law, walked with Marged past the old school, up the lane, past Blaen Cwrt and over Allt Ddu to the Capel Cynon fair a hundred years ago, wearing, she told me on her hundredth birthday, her best button boots.[47]

Such snapshots have a poignancy which scholars and critics have overlooked. The Icelandic writer Andri Snær Magnason, in speaking of his own past relatives, provides an insight into Clarke's work: 'As I listen to their stories and look at their pictures, I don't know if I'm trying to preserve their stories for the stories' sake or whether I'm trying to preserve my grandparents and their lives, to somehow mute an inevitable loss.'[48] This resonates with an entry in Clarke's 2019 journal about Marged in which Clarke appears to be muting the emotional impact of a significant family loss from before she was born. After the death of Marged's grandfather and her aunt, Clarke describes how Marged found herself, as did many women from rural Wales at that time, 'middle-aged, defeated by poverty and loneliness'.[49] Clarke conjures the land around Blaen Cwrt as it was in Marged's day where 'hens pecked and the house pig snouted the earth for whatever it could find' and the one tree that now survives seems in her imagination a reflection of the elderly person who lived there, 'leaning and shapeless, still producing its small, dark-purple fruit'.[50]

WELSH HISTORY IN EMOTIONAL COMMUNITIES

Initially perceived as 'geographical', the division of Wales by social historians into enclaves came to be seen as embracing, as M. Wynn Thomas has said, 'historical, social, cultural [and] linguistic differences'.[51] However, valid as this analysis might be, Rosenwein and Cristiani maintain that contemporary historians are increasingly inclined to 'think about the meanings of place and space in creating, shaping, and expressing emotions'.[52] As a result of their new-found emphasis on emotional communities, historians – albeit largely outside Wales at the moment – and writers of new literature, both within and outside Wales, examine societies and social change through the lens of emotional expression, emotional regimes, emotional communities, and emotional performances. This is an approach which has roots, at least as far as Wales is concerned, in the country memoir. In *Welsh Country Upbringing* (1948), D. Parry-Jones recalls the nature of the emotional community in which he was brought up, where farms were part of a close-knit local enclave exemplified in the hay harvest which he remembers as 'the happiest and gayest of all seasonal activities by reason of the big, merry and animate company that came together'.[53] Such occasions brought together not only individuals but communities, each with their own character:

> These intervals gave the older folk who had seen the world the opportunity to tell their tales and give of their experience. The miner described life underground. He told of accidents and disasters in pits – and carried evidence of them; of trips to Cardiff; of jolly days in the Rhondda before he knew the dole. The soldier – this was rare – regaled us with stories of

marches and scraps, of dusty roads and thirst, of the ways and customs of the East. The majority would join in, adding from their own stock of knowledge and experience.[54]

One of Parry-Jones's most profound regrets was the way in which many of the networks to which farms and farming families belonged disappeared: 'The communal character of the hay harvest has disappeared with the introduction of machinery of all kinds. The single farm is a self-contained unit now, to the great social loss of the people and the undermining of the solidarity of the rural community.'[55] His grief at the demise of traditional rural communities resonates with the sense of loss that Clarke feels over the collapse of the steel industry in south Wales and the communities associated with them: 'Demolition gangs / erase skylines whose hieroglyphs / recorded all our stories.'[56] For both writers, the loss of emotional communities and the stories that bound them together create an overwhelming emptiness, as Clarke describes:

> I am reminded of that Sunday
> years ago when we brought the children
> to watch two water cooling towers
> blown up, recall the appalling void
> in the sunlight, like a death.[57]

In Clarke's poetry, such emotions are felt in the body itself as it deals with pain, plays out its gender, and becomes involved in the production of words and the 'performance' that they imply.[58] To fully appreciate the importance of this corporeal dimension of Clarke's poetry, it is necessary to turn, as I do now, to her long poem about 'feminine values' 'Letter from a Far Country', written, as noted in the Introduction, for a thirty-minute radio broadcast in the early 1970s. Clarke herself said of this poem that it is 'an imagined day in the life of one, fictional woman ... based on all the women I know'.[59] It begins at 8.00 a.m. when her children leave for work and school and ends when they return from 4.00 p.m. onwards. But it is also the history of the parish, drawing on the 1870 census and the parish records, where Clarke has spent most of her adult life. The people's names, their farms and cottages are all real, as are the stories about the people who lived in them in so far as Clarke has recorded them 'just as I heard them'.[60] In many respects an original work, the way to the creation, broadcast and eventual publication of 'Letter from a Far Country' was paved by the publication/republication of historical accounts of women's day-to-day lives in the mid-twentieth century, one of the most widely known of which dated from a similar rural parish in the eighteenth century, *The Diary of a Farmer's Wife 1796–1797*. Written by Anne Hughes, a farmer's wife, it was passed down through her daughter, compiled by Jeanne Preston, first published in *Farmer's Weekly* 1937 and thereafter republished by *Countrywise Books* (1964) before becoming a popular Penguin publication in 1981.

As is now widely understood by historians of emotion, the word 'regime' might be used effectively in relation not only to political regimes but to particular institutions such as schools, churches, parliaments and prisons. As Clarke makes clear in 'Letter from a Far Country', expectations of emotional behaviours are often enforced through verbal and physical communication: 'Gossip, / whispers, lowing sounds. Laughter.'[61] She thinks about the way in which the snide remark operates in this context: 'Here's a woman who ought to be / up to her wrists in marriage.'[62] And, although a piece for radio, the poem makes much of the way in which words in performance, through gossip, whispers and laughter, as Rosenwein and Cristiani maintain, move 'in spaces and places, giving them meaning' as, at the same time, they 'assume cultural and individual meanings that affect people in turn'.[63] In this context, what Clarke says about the community, the way in which people interact and talk acquires a deep significance beneath its surface meaning:

> The landscape collects conversations
> as carefully as a bucket,
> gives them back in a concert
> with a wood of birdsong.[64]

This is evident in different cases, from different social strata touched upon in the letter, such as the unsupported woman with pauper written against her name in the black book of the parish; the numerous women relying on the parish for want of work and the woman who appeared to have everything but nevertheless took her own life. But it is not just talk that controls emotional expression and behaviour. The graveyard fulfils this purpose, too, reinforcing the distinction between the men and the women: 'On the graves of my grandfathers / the stones, in their lichens and mosses / record each one's importance.'[65]

However, the stones do not only record their achievements but the expectations of them – 'Three times at chapel on Sundays' – while making clear their impact on the women whose 'simple names' are only recorded.[66] Even deeper than the feminist, social critique in these lines is the sense of the codes and norms that determine the contours of women's lives and often also curtailed their emotional development, expression and behaviour:

> It has always been a matter
> of lists. We have been counting,
> folding, measuring, making,
> tenderly laundering cloth
> ever since we have been women.[67]

As Clarke says, the subject of 'Letter from a Far Country' is a woman who 'is fed up with housework and the family taking her for granted, and she feels like running away'.[68] She will 'tidy the house, leave notes and lists everywhere to help the family survive, then set off on an adventure to a far country'.[69] It is a poem which, as with a number of Clarke's poems, involves anger but, as she herself explains, this poem has a special kind of exasperation:

> Really the anger arose because of the difficulty of actually writing the poem ... The anger eventually was against those who assumed I had all the time in the world and that all women have all the time in the world to do things simply because they live in a house and work in a house which is clearly a place where nothing goes on. It was also to do with the low valuation that is given to what women do.[70]

However, this is not to say that women, despite their oppression by men – and, not to be coy about it, by other women too – have not found in domestic life at least some satisfaction – even a pleasure – which has not been available to men. Clarke admits that 'in a way ["Letter from a Far Country"] is a political poem written from a feminist, socialist viewpoint' but that it was written 'absolutely without bitterness'.[71] At its heart is an examination of the nature of what the environmental writer Samantha Walton, drawing on the work of the psychologist Donald Winnicott, calls the 'true' and 'false' self.[72] A question that is central to his work and Walton's own writings – 'why some people feel grounded and happy, while others feel uncertain about their place in the world and desperate for answers'[73]

– is relevant also to Clarke's work. For both Clarke and Walton, this question has to be understood psychologically and emotionally and not only socio-politically. In this regard, 'Letter from a Far Country' can be seen as interweaving the true self which, to use Walton's words, 'acts spontaneously making us feel fully alive and "real"' and the self that lives behind a façade which 'might project a convincing mask of realness, but living with it leaves us feeling hollow, unreal and never absolutely alive'.[74]

Some of the men in 'Letter from a Far Country' might have acquired a particular social status but, against the stony silence of their graves, it amounts to little. On the other hand, women have some compensation for their limited social opportunities and emotional expression in a deeper sense of contact with nature than is allowed the men in the stubbled fields:

> Familiar days are stored whole
> in bottles. There's a wet morning
> orchard in the dandelion wine;
> a white spring distilled
> in elderflower's clarity;
> and a loving, late, sunburning
> day of October in the syrups
> of rose hip and the beautiful
> black sloes that stained the gin to rose.[75]

Despite their importance to gathering the harvest, many of the men in 'Letter from a Far Country' who do not acquire civic influence pass silently from time. This is suggested, too, in the photograph in 'Siege', a short poem from the same volume as 'Letter from a Far Country', in which Clarke's mother as a child stands in the foreground but her brothers are only 'shadowy middle distance figures'.[76]

The difference between the roles that men and women have in rural communities is the result of the ways in which traditional agrarian societies defined, and guided, emotional expression in relation to nature along gender lines. Thus, rural communities were as much emotive regimes as emotive communities, within which women were repressed in one respect but acquired power in another. Throughout 'Letter from a Far Country' what society defined as their difference from men, men came to envy but also resent. As the anthropologist Karen Armstrong explains: 'women were the source of new life; it was they – not the expendable males – who ensured the continuity of the tribe'.[77] The silhouette of the men in the fields in 'Letter from a Far Country' suggests how, in themselves, the generations of farmers like worker ants do not have the same involvement in the cycle of birth, life and death as women who bring it into being.

In 'Letter from a Far Country' men within their respective communities have acquired social importance but are also rendered more disposable than the women on whom the life of the community is dependent. In this respect, the agrarian sections of the poem anticipate the concluding three verses in italics concerned with how it is mainly the men who from ancient times have been sacrificed to war. Interestingly, Clarke herself says of these verses – which as she admits some readers may find uncomfortable – that she intended them as 'something that plays in our heads whether we like it or no'.[78] However, one of the recurring themes in Clarke's poetry is the offsetting of the fact of death with creativity and language. She captures this in a wonderful quotation in her journal in 2019 from the African-American novelist Toni Morrison: 'We die. That may be the meaning of life. But we do language. That may be the measure of our lives.'[79]

Creativity is recognised as the meaningful measure of life in Clarke's later poem 'The Lacemaker', from *Five Fields* (1998), which further develops her interest in her rural, women ancestors and the hardships which they had to endure. The poem takes the reader back to a period when lacemaking in west Wales was a cottage industry. The poem does not mention the imperialism and slavery that brought the cotton and lace industry into existence, or the hard life based around the cotton mills, but focuses on a different sphere of hardship at the boundary of two types of domestic life for women. The lacemaker lives in the shadow of the prosperity of the towns and of those enjoying prestigious positions in the country signified by tablecloths, petticoats and clean linen. By contrast, her own home is dependent upon flickering oil-lamps and unreliable 'primitive' electricity while all the time she is vulnerable to the power of nature which is everywhere present – in the waterfalls, the westerly winds and the wild winters brought about by Atlantic storms. The image of the lacemaker greeting the poet as a child with the eggs of two wild birds in her hands breaks down the boundary between genteel domesticity signified by the lace and the 'wilder' domesticity which the lacemaker knows. As in histories of the emotions, and Jones's historiography based on communities, the emphasis falls on the inner life within them and forces which are in control of them emotionally.[80]

Clarke's 'Letter from a Far Country' is a coherent and tightly structured poetic 'essay' based on her experiences, and those of other women, in male-dominated communities. But there is no more outspoken a sequence of poems in Clarke's oeuvre, or stronger representation of emotive communities in Wales, than 'Making the Beds for the Dead' (2004), rooted in the impact of the foot-and-mouth pandemic at the beginning of the twenty-first century. Individual poems are integrated with each other through shared themes, recurring images and emotive experiences resonating one with another. However, there is a greater degree of fragmentation and a more pronounced sense of Otherness in this sequence than in 'Letter from a Far Country'. Its structure candidly reflects the way in which emotive communities of upland Wales themselves became fragmented during the pandemic by, for example, the differing extent to which different parts of the community followed, or opposed, the imposition of restrictions and the mass slaughter of animals, participated in an illegal market for animal products, and defined themselves as micro-emotive communities in opposition to the emotive regime which the ministry, and officials from within but largely from outside the area, instigated. It is to this sequence of poems, as an analysis of a north Wales community in crisis, that the discussion now turns.

BEDS FOR THE DEAD

A central theme in 'Making the Beds for the Dead' is how the horrors of the foot-and-mouth pandemic at the beginning of the new millennium tore farming communities apart and what farmers and animals experienced broke the normal boundaries of emotional discourse – as in 'Plague' which looks back to the Black Death:

> Stiff-legged chairs, the animals burn,
> Old furniture on a bonfire, not flesh and bone,
>
> Thrown upside-down and awkward to the flames
> A pedigree Holstein with a fancy name
>
> Hangs grotesque from the JCB hook
> Against an inferno of flame and smoke.[81]

Clarke capturers the horror in lines that recreate rather than report it and images in which *rigor mortis* turns the animals into wood.

The graphic quality of the writing, unusual for Clarke but always something of which she has been capable, exploits metaphor as transformation, in order to convey the deep impact of these experiences on the communal as well as the individual psyche. As I have pointed out in *Animals, Animality and Controversy in Modern Welsh Literature and Culture* (2022), there are many rural areas still haunted by the foot-and-mouth crisis of 2000; in Wales, one million animals were slaughtered, with the army being drafted in to help with the culling which wiped out generations of cattle and sheep breeding.[82] But Clarke's sequence of poems focuses as much on the concept of crisis as the specific details of what occurred and how it transformed long-established emotional communities. It examines how the definition of the pandemic by the Westminster government as a crisis determined particular kinds of decision making, redefined the relationship between authorities and farmers and permitted behaviours – allegedly in the national interest – that rode roughshod over the rights that ordinary people thought they possessed.

One of the worst aspects of the foot-and-mouth pandemic, managed as a crisis, in 'Making the Beds for the Dead' is the eradication of 'difference' so that there is no distinction between 'the sick, the healthy, the rag-tag, the beautiful'.[83] But in some respects, this is only a reversal of the importance of difference in the selection and separation of sheep for breeding and an extended life on the hills from those destined for more immediate slaughter which Clarke confronts in 'One Year', another sequence of poems in a later collection, *Zoology* (2017), which is discussed in *Animals, Animality and Controversy in Modern Welsh Literature and Culture*.[84] At one level, the indifference to the individuality and sentience of animals much in evidence during the foot-and-mouth culling is ironically an intensification of the emotional hardness required to work in farming as an industry which comes to the fore strongly in Clarke's poem 'Blackface', from the same volume as the sequence 'Making the Beds for the Dead': 'So it's come to this. / Just a sheep. Blackface / "Never name them," they warned.'[85] The poem contrasts the loving care shown to a ten-year-old favourite, as it dies having had a forced pregnancy, with the indifference of the ministry employees to the culled animals – 'the millions they threw on the pyres'.[86]

This contrast is central to the poem 'The Vet' which juxtaposes the closeness between those who care for, and have cared for, animals all their lives, as part of an emotional community based around human and animal relations, with the wider indifference to animals as sentient beings in the government ministry and in the language spawned by the slaughter instigated by the foot-and-mouth crisis: '[The Vet's] been up all night committing / the new-born to death, four to a sack.'[87] The poem's participant narrator describes how 'we watched them die, / beasts thrown to the flames'.[88] But what is thrown into the fires, too, is the emotional commitment of farming communities to their animals, especially in the smaller, traditional farms. The poem begins with the way in which each of the sheep is perceived callously as a number on a job specification: 'Number eighty's going nowhere.'[89] But in the course of the poem's narrative, the individuality of the sheep is made clear through their different responses to their death: 'The last lamb's quiet for the needle' while 'some shuddered as they fell. / Some stood still, surprised, and folded in a river of blood.'[90]

In order to place Clarke's farming poems in a wider context and examine the 'contemporaneity' of the issues which they pursue, I shall compare her work for a moment with that of her contemporary Ilse Pedler, herself a vet working in the English Lake District in a similar physical environment to north Wales. In Pedler's poetry a central theme, too, is the extent to which vets move between different emotional communities and regimes, between large farms that 'industrialise' their animals' lives and smaller farms with closer relationships with their animals. In *Auscultation* (2021), Pedler records moments when she is caught off-guard and sees animals as less than sentient beings: 'Each cow / a collection of monumental bones in a predetermined order / covered over with stitched hide.'[91] At such times, she catches sight of herself as a cog in the machine of modern industrialised farming: 'In the morning, the stockman gives the order to hold the cow / and before she can turn, the calf is gone. Her udder swells, heavy / with milk but he'll be back to take her to the parlour before long.'[92] However, in Pedler's 'Culling' and 'Castrating Calves', as in Clarke's 'Making the Beds for the Dead', the vet is never wholly emotionally distant from animals:

> One by one the sweet-breathed calves – so
> innocent – are held as much
> as is needed, which depends
> on the sharpness of her knife upon
> their soft hairless pouches of skin.[93]

In 'Making the Beds for the Dead', the emotions involved in caring for animals during the culling process is traumatic, as when Clarke's vet allows himself to experience 'the body quivering warm against his chest'.[94] On such occasions, Clarke unveils the love for animals, and the commitment to animal welfare, that is behind innocuous phrases, such as 'the farm-child's pet', which have been developed in and reflect small farms as emotional communities.[95] The attitudes toward animals, the human behaviours and the language which have developed in these emotionally close communities is contrasted with their equivalent in different farming regimes in which 'the ministry men, / the vets, the slaughtermen'[96] have a must-be-done attitude to the cull. The inclusion of the vet at two contrasting moments in the sequence of poems reflects the complex and contradictory nature of farming and the ambivalent position of vets within it, being responsible for animal care but also supporting the meat industry and all its attendant cruelties.

But the work of both Clarke and Pedler examine not only vets as liminal figures but veterinary medicine as a complex and contradictory business. It is a profession, as Clarke and Pedler realise, in which there is a permeable boundary between learned knowledge and intuition, as in discovering when to use 'a gypsy twitch to calm a fractious mare', where 'to find the sweet spot behind an old boar's ears' and which 'voice to use to soothe a fearful dog'.[97] Both poets bring to the fore how, ultimately, veterinary medicine can be about killing – in the animal's or the industry's interests – and even 'routinises' killing, as Pedler realises in her training: ' Teach me to kill in the smallest lecture theatre / with the unmarked door. Teach me the tricks / of the trade, how to kill and then carry on.'[98] Clarke's creative reflections on how the foot-and-mouth pandemic has been conceived – and acted upon – as a crisis similarly involves her imaginatively entering situations in which the 'gun' replaces caring hands and medical instruments. But what separates vets, who are pulled emotionally in different directions, from the ministry people who belong to a more singularly focused occupation is that the caring does not stop at the end of the vet's arm. Pedler describes responding to an injured horse in a road accident: 'his heat / and the pulse of him that I can feel still / through the rigid cold of the gun.'[99]

Recognising that farming, like veterinary medicine, involves having a foot in more than one emotional community, 'Making the Beds for the Dead' pulls no punches in drawing attention to the realities of animal agriculture, emphasising, for example, the psychological as well as the physical pain that animals sent over long distances to their slaughter suffer:

> the flock
> tumbrelled down the motorway,
> fleece to fleece in the tiered truck
> rocking the road, sipping drips
> from oil-slicked rain on the slats, then blood and blunder
> in a strange country.[100]

It is not simply the level of detail that drives the emotion in these lines, but the uncompromising language – 'tumbrelled', 'fleece to fleece', 'tiered truck', 'sipping drips', 'blood and blunder' – that captures the way in which the status of the sheep has been transformed from living, sentient beings by their despatch to slaughter. The language depicts the cruelties which the animals endure, their desperation for even the smallest relief, and anticipates the chaos that characterises their eventual moment of death. There is no solace to be derived from much of this poetry. It is a somewhat naked presentation of what animals bred to meet human needs have to suffer and the indifference of which humans are capable.

The image of 'a strange country' is an allusion to the animals being moved away from their home hills but also to the slaughterhouse itself. Within the context of the poem as a whole, it also signifies the way in which the animals' home territory has changed because of the foot-and-mouth virus and the way crisis has redefined that homeland. Beside the ecstasy of animals, and of their owners, experiencing birth in 'First Lamb' is the grim reality of what the definition of the crisis means: 'For a moment we forget / the lorries and the fires, / the hooded men, the smell ...'[101] The reference to 'blood and blunder' invokes the confusion, incompetence and cruelty – intentional or unintentional – that will greet the flock at the slaughterhouse. But it also draws attention to the additional stress arising from the panic in the definition of foot-and-mouth as a crisis – 'A man in a field with a rifle, / firing at sheep, hit and miss'[102] – and the way in which farming as a series of emotional communities is susceptible to unregulated and illegal practices. This happens through farmers avoiding the regulations implemented during the crisis in order to protect their animals from the ministry vets while attempting to safeguard their livelihoods, but also through the activities of unscrupulous meat dealers who themselves constitute once again a different type of emotional community in which animals find themselves 'trucked from the north / to an Essex slaughterhouse, / bought cheap, sold dear'.[103] The virus creates an illegal meat industry where strangers acting on the word of a friend try 'trading / *traed a genau* / in a layby on the M4'.[104]

The crisis generated by the foot-and-mouth pandemic transforms Clarke's poetic discourse, making it somehow more urban and gritty as in her description of 'in the slipstream of trucks, / the meat dealers banking the profits'.[105] Clarke insisted in one of her essays that she is 'careful' with her words for 'they are my tools, my art, my truth …'.[106] Thus we cannot glance over the fact that beside the glimpses of rural beauty in some of the images and in some of the language in 'Making Beds for the Dead', there are words that are not often found in Clarke's work that come from an outside, almost alien, world and one that, as she says, is 'on the run', exemplified by phrases such as a 'theatre of death', 'hooded men', 'strangers dressed to kill', 'cooped up, captive', 'atoms of bone', 'particles of blood', 'barricades of disinfected straw', 'festering waste', 'putrefying meat' and a 'soup of chemicals'. There are echoes of the World Wars in the fear of 'loose talk' and the images of festering waste, howls of pain, 'muffled drums', and 'blood and blunder'. These resonances enhance the verisimilitude of the impact of foot-and-mouth on farming communities, but they also extend our understanding of how crisis transforms ordinary life and pushes back the boundaries of the extraordinary.

The quietest 'poetic' language in 'Making the Beds for the Dead' originates in the bond between the poet-participant as a smallholder and her sheep: 'my fingers deep in her wool / till the pulse in her neck / fades to a flitter'.[107] By contrast, the harshest language is reserved for the circumstances that arise as a result of the virus outbreak being defined as a crisis and the overlooked suffering that occurs as a consequence: 'Then, that October ram raid, the broken gate. / A gang of males penned a year too long / by Livestock Movement Restrictions.'[108] But another level of plain speaking enters the poem in the description of the process of burial and the transformation in the ewe's body after death – 'swollen and slippery, stiffening already'[109] – and the glimpse of the dead lamb inside the corpse. Although 'realistic' in terms of the physical facts of death, the poem is careful to respect not only the integrity of what has happened but the love that the poet feels for both the ewe and the lamb: 'like a sanctuary lamp /

at the door of the vulva, / and the lamb dead in the boat of her body.'[110] That said, the most 'matter-of-fact' voice is determined by the cyclical nature of the farm as a business and of life in rural Wales more generally: 'There's a pen to be cleaned, / fresh straw to be laid. Hay. Water.'[111] The syntax of the lines reflects, and encapsulates, the way in which, at this point, action takes priority over analysis and reflection. The farmer finds a sanctuary in the tasks which she undertakes and in ordinary objects. Sometimes the 'realities' of animal farming elbow sensitivities aside as Pedler makes clear in 'Castrating Calves': 'The / woman straightens and with a flick of her white / thin wrist throws the last of them to the chickens.'[112] In another of Pedler's poems, 'All this Accumulation of Knowledge', one of the most important lessons that a vet has to learn is 'why looking away is sometimes the best option / how life leaves through the backs of eyes / when to tighten a grip – when to let go'.[113]

'Making the Beds for the Dead', like 'Letter from a Far Country', is about emotional communities. Although very different in genre and content, they share an interest in the way in which social norms and codes bring emotional communities into being, shape the emotions and determine emotional expression and behaviour. 'Making the Beds for the Dead' provides us with new insights into the impact of foot-and-mouth on Welsh farming communities but also into agricultural practices, recognising that they are informed by the ways in which we see ourselves and the extent to which we see planetary life as part of a wider relationality.

Thus, in summary, learning Welsh and moving to a Welsh-speaking community in west Wales was a turning point for Clarke in many ways. It enabled her to read the geographical and cultural landscape of Wales from different perspectives and in more depth than had previously been possible. It afforded her access to the deep time of Welsh history and enabled her to get closer to contemporary Welsh rural communities. But Clarke's work also unveils how Welsh society and culture are best understood through the history of emotions with its corresponding focus on emotional communities and the norms which determine emotional behaviours. However, while the concept of emotional communities provides interesting insights into how Gillian Clarke thought of Wales, there has been a comparative emotional turn in other areas of thought and philosophy – not least science and cosmology. Clarke, like many of her generation, has an interest in, and an understanding of, science and cosmology which may be traced to the mid-twentieth century and especially to the decades following the Second World War. The impact of her engagement with them on her work is the subject of the following chapters, beginning with her much overlooked interest in cosmology.

2

Cosmology in a Planetary Age

As discussed in Chapter 1, the concept of emotional communities, as developed in the history of emotions, provides interesting insights into how Gillian Clarke thought of Welsh history, society and culture. But this kind of emotional turn is to be found in other areas of late-twentieth-century thought in addition to history including the natural and physical sciences, astronomy and cosmology. In these areas, it is possible to trace a trajectory that – as in Clarke's poetry – points toward a deeper emotional engagement with the cosmos, which has even caused some leading cosmologists and philosophers, such as Noel Cobb to whose work I shall turn later, to begin to think in terms of an 'emotional' cosmos.

While talk of an 'emotional' cosmos may seem somewhat puzzling, the linking of emotions and cosmology is neither new nor unsurprising. Cosmology, as Audra Mitchell points out, concerns those 'images of the universe which shape the beliefs of a particular group of people'.[1] Thus, cosmology determines not only how we see the world but how we live in it and relate to it. From this perspective any cosmology must be emotive. But cosmologies, embedded in particular historical epochs, change over time and with cultures, and Clarke's lifetime has corresponded with a spectacular period of cosmological change. Her poetry reflects the way in which the natural and physical sciences of the late twentieth and early twenty-first centuries have redefined, and are redefining, the way in which we see the cosmos as a 'relational' universe. This concept, developed by physicists Lee Smolin and Carlo Rovelli in conjunction with social theorists such as Roberto Mangabeira Unger, has been neatly explained by Milja Kurki, a professor of international relations: 'At the core of relational cosmology, is an extension, if you will, of what it means to think relationally ... understanding the universe as bound together, through networks of relations which bring it into being, and through which it unfolds.'[2]

In spelling out how the new physics sees the universe, Smolin argues that the cosmos cannot be 'grasped *solely* by the discovery of a perfect and eternal mathematical law' but has to be understood as having arisen 'just as the beauty of the living world came to be: through a process of self-organization, by which the world has evolved over time to become intricately structured'.[3] This universe, he maintains, 'is not eternal. Nor is it static ... rather than living in an eternal cosmos, we live in a young world, the story of whose maturation we see spread out before us as we look out with our telescopes and antennas.'[4] And the way in which the new physicists such as Smolin write about the relational universe is often resonant of poetry and tinged with emotion:

> The discovery of a unification represents a great step in our understanding of nature. Each time it happens, it reassures us that our hubris that nature is understandable continues to be answered with comprehension. Furthermore, when some beautiful idea is found to be at the core of the unification, we see again at work the mysterious power we human beings seem to have to imagine what is behind the appearance of nature.[5]

The relational universe in effect deconstructs, and displaces, the cosmological model that has dominated our thinking, our planetary awareness and the way in which we have perceived our relationship to nature over the last four hundred years. During this period, the emphasis in Newtonian physics upon the rational order of the universe, its mechanistic assumption of the laws of motion and its way of looking at everything as operating in a universal empty space sidelined more relational ways of looking at the cosmos.

The profound poetics of the new relational vision of the universe, which has inspired Kurki as a political scientist, underpins an optimistic way of thinking about the cosmos and the prospects for life on earth in the future. But, as Kurki demonstrates, it is important to go further than this, for it is not enough simply 'to critique our own cosmological assumptions but for us "to think creatively" about cosmology and to do so with new constituencies in order to help us think about the international, the global, and the planetary in some new ways and as such to be able to open up different political imaginations'.[6]

CLARKE'S COSMOLOGY AND ITS ORIGINS

As we contemplate the hierarchal nature of the cosmos of astrophysics – planets, stars, solar systems, star clusters, milky way, galaxy clusters, super clusters, universe, multiverse – it is increasingly beyond our comprehension. And so far beyond human contemplation, that in most cultures and religions we continue to rely on using circles and stars in hierarchies to describe it. As such, the cosmos of astrophysics seems to have little impact on our planetary, let alone our individual, life. To identify with it, we have to think in terms of the microcosmos with which Clarke engages.

Pierre Joris, in his introduction to the recent collection of essays by the avant garde poet and visual artist Allen Fisher, reminds us, quoting Robin Blaser, that the 'real business of poetry is cosmology' and, turning to the work of Margaret Mead, that the cosmic sense involved here is a 'human instinctual need for a perceptual relation to the universe'.[7] Cosmology – or microcosmology – has always been at the centre of Clarke's work. As she says in her essay 'Something Understood' (2021): 'My key words are wonder, worship and story ... Wonder is what our ancestors felt, worship arose from it ... [and] it is no surprise to know that our ancestors worshipped the heavens, and the earth, and that we are inclined not to worship anything. Yet we do feel wonder, don't we?'[8] This essay offers a succinct explanation of how she thinks cosmologically in terms of 'Earth's mysterious relationship, with the sun and moon, stars and planets, seasons and the weather, and of our subordinate placing in it'.[9] But her work is more than an expression of wonder and awe at the cosmos, important to her poetry as these emotions are. As she explains: 'Wonder is a questing, questioning word.'[10] This 'questing' informs the 'politics' of her oeuvre and its 'urge to follow the thrill of wonder by wanting to save the planet'.[11]

While cosmologists and physical and social scientists argue for a relational view of planetary life, Clarke lives it:

> Sometimes you stand still, stunned by the beauty of it all, as if something had been started from its lair right there in your ribcage. You're in love with the planet and with life itself. It is the life-urge. It's what may save

the planet ... A flash of joy that keeps hope burning, makes being alive worthwhile.[12]

The image of the universe as a network of relations can be traced back centuries in literature, often characterised by a 'theocracy' of nature and couched in biblical language. But in the 1940s and 1950s, the decades of Clarke's childhood, nature writing became caught in a dialectic between theologically inspired, contemplative traditions and scientific appreciation of the universe. W. P. Hodgkinson, the wartime nature writer of the Severn valley, for example, wished to believe, anticipating the relational science of half a century later, that 'birds, like trees and flowers, are part of that great theocracy which is Nature'.[13] The theological themes in his writing are unmistakable. Echoing the seventeenth-century Welsh poet Henry Vaughan, he held that 'every simple action was a sacrament', that 'the roots of eternity are in the now' and that 'all things meet together in God'.[14] But he also felt that the contemplative tradition in nature was slipping away in mid-twentieth-century Britain. Alongside the mystical, theological insights to be found in his work, there is a grasp of, for example, 'the laws of cosmic perspective', 'void', 'space and time being one' and 'atoms'.[15] However, it is not simply new scientific concepts but the new language in which they are couched that enters, and at times take over, his writing so that he talks of what is 'at the back of time, in the void, in the impenetrable world'.[16] As such, it is possible to locate Hodgkinson on a trajectory in nature writing that can be carried forward to R. S. Thomas. In 'Bravo!', from *Frequencies* (1978), Thomas contemplates the science of human life and wrestles with its wider impact on human philosophy:

> Oh, I know it and don't
> care. I know there is nothing in me
> but cells and chromosomes
> waiting to beget chromosomes
> and cells. You could take me to pieces
> and there would be no angel hard
> by, wringing its hands over
> the demolition of its temple.[17]

This poem is rooted not simply in the dialectic between two ways of perceiving the cosmos – Thomas's initial theocracy and the science which the concept of cells and chromosomes ushered in – but in the tension between the language of science and that of traditional theology, speaking of 'temple' and 'angel' and alluding to specific events in the Bible. The notion of the new language of science entering philosophy and theology and disrupting, if not displacing, them is one to which Thomas returns several times in *Frequencies* as in 'At It' in which he contemplates the God which science is bringing into being:

> I think he sits at that strange table
> of Eddington's, that is not a table
> at all, but nodes and molecules
> pushing against molecules
> and nodes;
> ...[18]

The discovery of cells and chromosomes has distant origins in the late seventeenth century with the development and refinement of the microscope but it was in the late Victorian period that Walter Sutton and Theodor Boveri were responsible for identifying chromosomes as the hub of hereditary – the subject of Thomas's 'Bravo!' – and further developed in the twentieth-century by the work of James Watson and Francis Crick on the structure of DNA and later by James Thompson's discovery of stem cells. All of this influenced, and changed, the way in which Thomas, as in 'Bravo!', saw humanity and its relationship to the cosmos and to 'God'. But with the new science came a new, or non-Newtonian, perception of matter which challenged the Newtonian conception of materiality whereby matter appears inert and passive. In the 'old materialism', as Kurki points out, matter is 'somehow an inanimate, meaningless context for actions of "humans"' but the new thinking 'emphasizes the vitality of matter and the ways in which "we" and all life and non-life are part of processes of moving together'.[19] This transformation in the way in which matter is perceived is an important dimension of both Thomas's and, under his influence to some extent, Gillian Clarke's work. As the literary scholar, and one of the most perceptive critics of R. S. Thomas, J. P. Ward said of *Frequencies*,

> the poet enters the vocabulary and language of our scientific apprehension, and lets them play over his responses to which he becomes attached. It is as though, in surrendering to a new science's way of seeing things, R. S. Thomas has experienced a certain sense of wonderment now gone

calm, such that human calamity and ignominy may be seen in more serene perspective.[20]

However, while Thomas allows the new vocabulary of scientific apprehension – cells, chromosomes, molecules and nodes – to 'play over his responses' as Ward maintains, it is not a matter of Thomas 'surrendering to a new science's way of seeing things' but – like Hodgkinson and certainly Clarke – being inspired to see the cosmos with a new sense of awe and wonder.

Smolin maintains: 'It is a cliché to say that in the twentieth century science has replaced religion as the dominant cosmological authority ... physicists are the official makers and keepers of the story of the cosmos.'[21] But, perhaps, more than anything else, it is the view of the universe 'as a coherent whole, in relationship only to itself, without need of anything outside itself to give it law, meaning and order'[22] which most inspired and challenged R. S. Thomas. His work, which had an impact on most late-twentieth-century Welsh writers, exemplifies how this new scientific thinking permeated contemporary Welsh poetry in English. In an interview, demonstrating his interest in the cosmic revelations of contemporary physical science, Thomas admitted: 'I wouldn't say that I'm an orthodox Christian at all and the longer we live in the twentieth century the more fantastic discoveries are made, the more we hear what the universe is like I find it very difficult to be a kind of orthodox believer.'[23]

As Ward points out, *Frequencies* clearly demonstrates that Thomas is 'in line with late-twentieth century positivistic science, which can no longer easily postulate either the detached observer, nor dead and meaningless matter as the basis of all that is observed.'[24] But Hodgkinson defines the position in which theologically inclined writers with an interest in the new science like himself found themselves somewhat differently from Ward: 'I stand like some bewildered star that finds itself at break of dawn half-in, half-out of Heaven.'[25] His pithy, poetic phrase – 'half-in, half-out of Heaven' – encapsulates the intellectual world into which Thomas and Clarke were born. As Ward says, in Thomas's work 'the cosmos itself is peered into as though space itself defines the greatest absence of all' – referring to God – yet 'it also takes us out of the everyday on track of, perhaps, the infinite.'[26] However, while Clarke's work, too, takes us on the track of the infinite, it does not lift us out of the everyday. Rather it imbues the everyday with the wider sense of wonder that she, like the new natural science, finds in the cosmos. Her work explores nature and the cosmos, as redefined in the work of Smolin and the new scientists and revels – admittedly as does Thomas's 'Frequencies' – in the newfound vitality of matter of which all life and non-life are a part.

As the scholar and historian Nicholas Campion, specialising in astrology and cosmology, points out, 'cosmos' is a word of Greek origin which translates as 'beautiful order' but goes beyond this as 'a conception of the universe'.[27] Thus, as he observes: 'For pre-modern cultures, the cosmos was interior as much as exterior; it was inside as much as outside us.'[28] Such has it been for Clarke. Her strongest expression of the internalisation of the cosmos comes through her poetry based on north Wales upland sheep farms where it is connected with the Welsh concept of *cynefin*:

> laid down in the brain, blood, belonging,
> belief, tribal memory, and land,
> heft, habit, *hiraeth* and hearth,
> passed through generations.[29]

Her poetry increasingly focuses not only on how one conceives of the cosmos but how one *feels* one's place within it. In her poem 'Labour', this rests on an image of a sheep understanding the connection between its heart beat and 'the sounding waters in the earth / drumming the rock beneath her feet', suggesting that the cosmos enters not so much our cerebral understanding but our bodily consciousness.[30]

Clarke's younger contemporary Ilse Pedler, discussed in Chapter 1, who lives and writes among the hill farms of the English lake district, also uses the image of a ewe to foreground how cosmology is something that animals and humans feel at the core of their beings – especially through ewe and lamb, mother and daughter – and in doing so raises questions about nature, knowledge and different kinds of 'intelligence':

> imprinted by what she knows
> and is part of. She is hefted to this
> mountainside, passing the knowledge on through
> umbilical cord and thick milk, mother
> to daughter to daughter – home.[31]

The anthropologist Karen Armstrong pithily summarises the implications of this argument:

we need to learn not only how to act differently but also how to think differently about the natural world. We need to recover the veneration of nature that human beings carefully cultivated for millennia ... We should consciously develop this remnant of our primordial link to nature in our struggle to save the planet. It is essential not only to our well-being but to our humanity.[32]

In the wake of the new scientific thinking of the late twentieth century, the works of many nature writers and poets engage with the environment and other-than-human life in fresh and exciting ways. They open our eyes to how many of our assumptions about, and attitudes toward, our planet and the cosmos are based on outmoded cosmological conceptions, scientific discourses and sociocultural modelling which have been discredited and/or surpassed. In a cosmology inherited from Newton, life forms – including animals, birds, insects and plant life – have too often been seen as part of a world of things in which spatial and temporal boundaries have been defined according to our image of ourselves as special, intelligent and superior to other life on the planet. In thinking about the world around us from a relational cosmological perspective, Clarke's work challenges and critiques our cosmological, scientific and sociocultural assumptions – the subject of the next section.

BIO-COSMOLOGY

The profound sense of the interconnectedness within nature and the cosmos inspires us, as Thomas and Clarke suggest throughout their work, to cast aside our human exceptionalism – our assumption of our importance as humans – and see the world in less destructive and more harmonious ways. For Clarke, cosmology is both a spiritual and political undertaking, resonating with the way in which contemporary cosmologists such as Richard Tarnas lament 'the alienation of the modern self in a cosmos that has no coherence with our inner spiritual aspiration, with our psychological nature'.[33] Similarly regretting the loss of a cosmic foundation and the motivation and values that it provides, Clarke mounts a fierce opposition to the way in which political power and technological prowess shape cosmologically alienated societies and determine environmentally hostile behaviours.

This kind of emotive cosmology is central, for example, to Clarke's poem 'Blue Sky Thinking', a reflection on the impact of the grounding of planes across Europe in April 2010 due to the eruption of the Icelandic volcano at Eyjafjallajökull. The events of that year, she suggests, brought people closer to nature, curtailed the continuous pollution of the atmosphere and reawakened the ways in which the human psyche reads the sky and sees a connection between the visibility of the heavens – now left to 'Venus and a moon / so new it's hardly there'[34] – and a self-fulfilling life on Earth: 'Nothing's overheard but pure blue silence / and skylarks spiralling into infinite space, / a pair of red kites flaunting in the air.'[35] While the poem looks back to 2010, it looks forward to a future in which humans and animals share a different kind of relationship in the image of the red kites – birds that were reduced to a few breeding pairs but (protected under the Wildlife and Conservation Act of 1981) are now one of the most successful conservation stories in contemporary Wales.

The cleansing silence of 'Blue Sky Thinking' is a theme to which Clarke returns in her later writing about the impact of the regulations restricting human gatherings and movement during the Covid-19 pandemic, from January to June 2020. In a journal entry for August that year, she refers to the resulting silence as 'The Great Silence' and describes how 'It is unprecedented in my lifetime: theatres, pubs, shops, offices all closed, cities and towns silent, empty, and people under order to stay home.'[36] But, like the silence of 'Blue Sky Thinking', Clarke with the advantage of living in the Welsh countryside – unlike those confined, say, to a small flat in a built-up environment – welcomes it: 'We relish the silence, the empty roads and clean clear skies. Every dawn is the earth's first morning.'[37] However, self-isolating in Blaen Cwrt's 'green acres', she begins naming, or renaming – conceiving, for example, of 'The Lawn', the 'Middle Lawn', and the 'Orchard Lawn' – a process which she calls, the 'naming of parts', remembering Henry Reed's poem 'Lessons of the War: 1: Naming of Parts' (1942) in which a lecture on the parts of Enfield rifles is juxtaposed with observations on springtime.[38] The allusion to this wartime poem in the 2020 journal entry on 'The Great Silence' links it with a journal entry for August 2019 remembering 'The Great Silence' of 1941: 'There are no cars. Birds are singing.'[39]

Two key poems about the Covid-19 pandemic – 'Spring Equinox, 2020' and 'Spring Equinox, 2021', published in *The Silence* (2024) – develop Clarke's journal entries in overlapping but contrasting ways.[40] 'Spring Equinox, 2020' is set in a moment of transition: 'In dusk's / deepening blues stars prick the dark.'[41] The structure of the line, in which the repetition of 's' and the way in which the absence of a pause enables a lift between 'blues' and 'stars', gives the moment a sublime totality. As in the Second World War, much of life – through short phrases which encapsulate and at the same time emphasise different endings – is entering lockdown: 'Doors are closing, festivals folding their tents. / Music is silenced. The lights are going out.'[42] The last phrase alludes to the well-known quotation attributed to Sir Edward Grey, the British Foreign Secretary, on the eve of the First World War in which he is alleged to have said that 'the lamps are going out all over Europe, we shall not see them lit again in our lifetime'; a warning commemorated in lights going out in the UK on 4 August 2014 between 10 and 11 p.m., 100 years to the day on which war was declared.[43] The poem links its emphasis on the fear of the pandemic and the insurmountable number of deaths which it brought about with The Great Silence of the Second World War through the image of 'radio-waves in the air / the transmission of fear / through a darkening sky'.[44] However, as in 'Blue Sky Thinking', the grounding of international flights during the pandemic – 'empty skies unscarred / by transatlantic planes'[45] – brings a fresh, penetrating sense of colour such as deep blues, rose-beige, jet and silver.

The sense of what Clarke in 'Spring Equinox, 2020' calls 'the world in remission'[46] is developed in the companion poem 'Spring Equinox, 2021' in *The Silence* (2024), which contrasts two cosmologies: the dramatic and fiery cosmos created by Satan in Book 1 of Milton's *Paradise Lost*, invoked in Clarke's phrase 'vault of heaven', borrowed from Milton as the poet Carol Rumens points out,[47] and a new paradisiacal cosmology in which the ozone layer is 'cleared / of particulates, of nitrogen dioxide'.[48] The poem opens in the state of being that the restricted human activity in the pandemic created. The streets are 'carless' – as she said of them in her description of The Great Silence of 1941 – a word that conjures also 'careless', which reflects how many people in the pandemic (unlike in the Second World War) were freed of their usual busyness and anxieties. In this new bodily condition, people are said to be able to breathe again as the poem's last line – 'your breath, mine'[49] – suggests and see, hear and feel with an intensity that many of us have lost. The poem, like 'Blue Sky Thinking', reclaims a new awareness of nature and the cosmos, evident in the rediscovery of the emotional value of birdsong and, in the newfound silence, in the capacity to hear petals falling and a leaf opening. A red kite – the bird mentioned earlier that became almost extinct in Wales but then recovered through human intervention and protection – enters this poem, too, in lines which, through the repetition of 'fl' and the presence of carefully stressed vowels, slip subtly between each other and between the kite's own sense of self and the magnificence which the observer perceives:

> Flamboyant, a kite
> floats flame on blue,
> flexes wings and the fork of its tail
> and turns on a breath.[50]

The bird brings a new form of energy from that which fuelled what William Blake in his poem 'Jerusalem' referred to as satanic industries and allows us to see, once again, the awe and beauty in nature – and the cosmos. For, as Rumens notes, with the kite soaring above other birds and cities, 'the reader's eye is led higher and higher'.[51] The reference to the blue sky recalls 'Blue Sky Thinking' and the new relationship with the heavens in that poem, while the kite's magnificent energy is encapsulated in 'flamboyant', 'floats' 'flame', 'flexes' and 'fork'. 'Flame' might recall the fires of Satan's cosmos, and our world of heavy industry that did so much damage to the environment in what geologists call the Anthropocene, an epoch during which humans have acquired the dominant influence on climate and environment. But the lines are transformed by the key word 'floats' that reflects not only the bird attuned to the blue skies and its silent movement but also our own new-found attunement to this new, less noisy world.

Attentiveness to colour, detail and time characterise many of Clarke's poems about silence and the Great Silence brought about as a consequence of the Covid-19 pandemic. This is especially true of *The Silence* (2024) in which, for example, in 'Wild Laburnum' there is 'A month to breathe yellow' and in 'The Breath of Trees' there is an image of 'lifting leaves / in a golden silence'.[52] 'Red', from the same volume, links past and present through the red body of a hare and of a fox – 'flaming as rage' – with her mother's red hair. In 'Bluebells', in which the hitherto unappreciated intensity of colour again links the present with her childhood, Clarke remembers running as a child through bluebell woods. But colour in nature, most often associated with sight, becomes as much associated with the other senses. In addition to recalling the intensity of the blue in the flowers, she remembers their scent and how this perfume arose from the warmed earth. In 'Bluebells, the primary senses are smell and touch. Running in the bluebell woods is one of the moments in which, as she says, she 'learnt the cool sweetness of blue / with my whole waking self'.[53]

Maybe inspired by the pandemic and the many deaths it brought about, there is a religious refrain in *The Silence*, for example in 'Sext' (part of the poem sequence 'The Hours') when Covid changed the nature, and the meaning, of the seasons – 'Silence in the first spring leaves / is prayer, last rites, and requiem'[54] – and in 'Song', from the same poem sequence, 'Water tells its rosary'[55]. Lines such as these that link sacred activities and highlight a single religious word give a religious aura to the silence that the pandemic brought about but, as throughout *The Silence* as a whole, point beyond specific religious connotation to something deep in cosmology.

In many respects, 'Song' brings together the key themes in Clarke's writing about the pandemic, opening with birdsong that can be heard in the new silence, conjuring with the sacredness of water, as in Clarke's *A Recipe for Water* (2009), discussed in Chapter 4, and turning, with the empty lanes and roads, toward Eden – 'the world's first day / ... before the first sin, / before the machine'.[56] This glimpse into a pre-lapsarian, pre-industrial and pre-Anthropocene world is maintained also in the recurring motif of gold – which is traditionally associated with the highest spiritual qualities, spiritual perfection and the divine – as in 'A Spring Morning', in which the poet watches her husband on a step-ladder carrying out repairs, 'climb gold stairs to the sky' and notes a vase of tulips where 'in every purple throat / is a cross of gold'.[57] In 'Wild Laburnum', in an image bringing gold and paradisical environments together, 'the garden is ringed with gold'.[58]

It is not that Clarke's work, especially during and after the Covid-19 pandemic, takes a stronger religious turn per se. But that one of the key questions in contemporary cosmology comes to the fore, which is summarised pithily by Smolin who asks, 'Could this beautiful universe be the result of the construction of a single planner? Certainly, it is difficult to imagine any human planner choosing the laws of nature carefully enough to result in a universe with such a variety of phenomena.'[59] Unconvinced, he suggests a model of the cosmos that has emerged (is emerging) from contemporary natural sciences which underpins much of Clarke's works:

For is it conceivable that the universe is as we find it to be because it made itself; because the order, structure and beauty we see reflected at every scale are the manifestations of a continual process of self-organization, of self-tuning, that has acted over very long periods of time?[60]

TURNING TO A DIFFERENT STORY

As the historian Dipesh Chakrabarty argues, 'human institutions and practices are geared to a human sense of time and history. But we now have to use these institutions to address processes that unfold over much larger scales of time.'[61] Clarke's work is innovative, challenging and exciting philosophically because, like Chakrabarty, she sees the great challenge of the Anthropocene as the need 'to decipher a new universal history' because we now 'encounter a set of planetary forces and temporal scales that could not be a direct object of experience in our lives yet will be a determining factor for them'.[62] Turning on its head jargon employed by business people who are deemed to have largely created the process of environmental destruction, Clarke's 'Blue Sky Thinking' is a gravelly voice of protest: 'Let's do this again, ground the planes for a while'; 'the sky's not been this clean since I was born'; and 'No mark, no plane trail, jet-growl anywhere.'[63]

The cosmology – how we envisage the universe – underpinning Clarke's 'Blue Sky Thinking' can be traced to her work of the early 1990s and its interest in the importance of a people's relationship with their sky to their sense of home. The central point in 'A Russian Woman in Tashkent, 1979', published as part of *The King of Britain's Daughter* (1993), is that the spirit of place, as the award-winning author Cherry Gilchrist says, is an essential part of Russian culture.[64] Neither the Russian woman nor Clarke is able to feel at home under the hot sun, among the men of the desert and even among the women selling braids of silk. It is this shared absence of home – each knowing their own lands were far from there – that causes the Russian to embrace the Welsh poet. Like the descendants of those who followed the silk roads west, the two women have no knowledge of the future. The poem impresses on us the present in an alienated location – composed of sand, heat and only snaking water – compared to the sense of coherence between the cosmos and the spiritual aspirations of the silk traders of the past who 'slept easy then in their encampments, / glimmering under starry desert skies, earth's skin / twitching harmlessly beneath them'.[65] When the Russian whispers, 'All we women want is peace',[66] a sense of place and a sense of bonding with the cosmos become political.

In Clarke's more overtly cosmological poems of the 1970s and 1980s, a fulfilling relationship with the planet is contrasted, as in 'Scything', with the way in which humans in the Anthropocene try to shape nature to their will. Introducing his view of what he calls 'mutuality' (to which Chapters 6 and 7 will return in a discussion of Clarke's 'war' poems), Chakrabarty, drawing on the philosopher Kant's *Critique of Judgment*, advises that 'the word *striving* – with its connection, in English, to the word *strife* – acts as a reminder that the relationship of mutuality between individual humans and the earth *was not necessarily one of harmony* and would include moments of "equipmental breakdown" ... anxiety or dread'.[67] In 'Scything', Clarke admits acting out of harmony with the natural world in a single image, 'I wade forward with my scythe'.[68] The scythe as an image of death anticipates the accidental, possibly careless, killing of the willow warbler's young. While there are those who might discard the killing of the bird as 'collateral damage', to employ a military term, Clarke, as a mother herself, in a moment of regret, feels for the bird.

It hardly needs pointing out that a recurring theme in Clarke's poetry is how her status and experience as a mother enables her to identify with mothering among animals and birds and participate in the relationality of the cosmos. Thus, unsurprisingly, some of the most haunting and distressing images in her writing are of the accidental violation of the planetary mesh which humans and other forms of life share. It is hard to find a more disturbing image in her work than that in her journal when her husband accidentally mows the top of a nest of bumblebees:

> They'd nested in a burrow hidden between the hedge bank, an acer and an old rose where we rarely manage to mow. The terrible blades of the ride-on mower make a hurricane of steel and air. In a moment all they had built has gone, their citadel roofless, a ruined city, with a pathetic cluster of cells revealed, primitive and vulnerable – not at all like the grand wax palaces of honey bees, whose well-stocked larder must keep them alive through the winter.[69]

How this incident and the event on which 'Scything' is based seems to have troubled Clarke is betrayed by the inclusion in *The Silence* of a poem, 'The Starling', in which she seems to appease her guilt by rescuing a bird from her cat: 'It trembles in your cupped hands, its heart wild, / beak parted, a star in its black eye.'[70]

In 'The Honey Man', from *Five Fields* (1998), Clarke watches a hive taken over by a wild swarm, which she should have arranged to be moved in the winter when the bees slept. The poem opens with an image of an old, rusting frame that has been discarded – the wings of bees from previous summers still cling to it – but closes with the 'rewilded' hive in which 'a million cooling wings beat / like a city in a box'.[71] Her journal suggests that this poem has several sources including 'The Laws of Hywel Dda' which declared that 'the lineage of bees is from paradise'[72] and *The Life of the Bee* by the Belgian poet Maurice Maeterlinck. She quotes an extract from Maeterlinck's observations of bee hives that serves as a gloss on her poem: 'For we are in the abode of life that goes before life. On all sides asleep in their closely sealed cradles, in this indefinite superposition of marvellous six-sided cells, lie thousands of nymphs.'[73] But perhaps the most positive aspect of the poem is the bio-cosmological frame in which it places the children's attraction to the hive: 'At moonrise, before bed, they take turn / to press their ears against the hive.'[74] At the centre of the text is the beauty in a relationship between humans and bees and the closeness which they can assume – the honey man is said to charm them with smoke. This line resonates with an entry in her published journal in which she describes how if at dusk 'you put your ear to the hive you can hear a million wings keeping the temperature just right. This was a fierce colony when it first arrived a few years ago.'[75]

The children's running to the hive betrays their instinctual recognition of the shared energy in which humans, insects, animals and birds participate. The linking of insects with high levels of unrelenting activity entered the popular imagination with books and articles about them in the first half of the twentieth century intended for a general readership. E. F. Linssen, for example, describes how 'the mysterious force of instinct is shown by the classic example of the hive bee which on leaving the hive for the first time performs all the duties of an expert forager.'[76] Of insects more generally, he says that what strikes us 'must surely be their energy, especially the persistence with which they apply it'.[77] This energy is best described by the Greek word *energeia* from the ancient Greek philosophers which, unlike the English word, refers to a vitality or presence that surges from within nature – living and non-living – and provides the basis of a deep, spiritual connection between humans and the cosmos.

Such encounters between humans and animals, reaching almost the level of an epiphany, entered early twentieth-century Welsh-language poetry with R. Williams Parry's well-known poem 'Y Llwynog' (The Fox) (1924) in which the poet and his friend, climbing a mountain side, suddenly encounter a fox – 'Llwybreiddiodd ei ryfeddod prin o'n blaen' – and are held transfixed by the animal's eyes – 'dwy sefydlog fflam / Ei lygaid arnom' – which possess the *energeia* and fire of the cosmos itself.

In Clarke's *Five Fields*, 'The Honey Man' is juxtaposed with a poem, 'Architect', that alludes to the concept of earth's energies running through ley lines, which creates a fissure between 'rationalism' and mysticism. The poem opens with an architect who, in an ellipse, sits under a black plum cherry tree – *Prunus nigra* – in the long grass in an area of the Dordogne in France, known for its Roman sites. The architect takes up his best stance at Perigord, 'all earth's lines come running to him',[78] reminding us of the ethnographically recorded beliefs in the importance of lines running through landscapes in various communities around the world, especially those connected to ancient – and often sacred – sites. The apparent human preoccupation with trying to get lines straight – exemplified in the poem by the mumbling tractor on the hillside – is contrasted with 'the swallow's tangled airy latitudes'.[79] The juxtaposition of human interest in ley lines with birds who in some respects have biological capacities that exceed those of humans implies that they share a planet in which lines of energy and magnetism are important. In the closing image of the poem, a 3H pencil sits all day 'on its compass turning'.[80]

The migration of birds and their associated capacities which humans do not possess – what Clarke calls in *Ice* (2012) the 'secret life of birds'[81] – have fascinated Clarke, as R. S. Thomas, throughout her life. This aspect of her work may have been inspired not only by Thomas's work generally but one poem – 'The Place' – in particular: delighting in the small migratory birds such as martins that summer brings, Thomas admits 'my method is so / To have them about myself / Through the hours of this brief / Season and to fill with their / Movement …'[82] Taking a latitudinal or longitudinal migration, birds orientate themselves by the earth's magnetic field through specialised chemicals and compounds in their eyes, bills and brains.[83]

The complexity of bird migration is a subject to which Clarke returns in one of her poems from the twenty-first century, 'Osprey' – from *Ice* (2012) – in which a bird breaks its migration from Lapland to Africa. It is a poem not so much about the bird as its deep and instinctual understanding of the cosmos encapsulated in 'the latitudes / sliding beneath its heart'.[84] The poem interleaves the mystery of bird migration with the awe in which the planetary system and the influence which one planet in particular has been perceived as having on human psychology: 'It stayed three weeks / like the moon roosting in an oak.'[85]

SKY HOUSEHOLD

As the astronomer and award-winning science writer Stuart Clark reminds us, human kind has long sought a connection with the sky 'through the action of gods, or through mysterious influences that predict future events, or as a means of moulding our personalities'.[86] This may have been among the first pieces of evidence of 'an emotional connection with the stars' which was probably eroded by a 'scientific emphasis on measurement and precision'.[87] Reclaiming an emotional connection with the sky which, as Clark suggests, has been eroded is a developing theme throughout Clarke's poetry. It can be traced to her first published collection of poems, *The Sundial*, and has become fairly dominant in her work of the first two decades of the twenty-first century.

At one level, Clarke's reclamation of a diminishing emotional connection with the sky resonates with the beliefs of ancient peoples that there was, in Stuart Clark's words, 'something magical driving nature' and that there is something 'operating beyond the normal confines of cause and effect'.[88] But in her poetry Clarke moves beyond this to examine the cosmic sublime as part of 'the paradox of seeing something yet believing it to be different'.[89] Both writers find themselves having to make sense of competing ideas, one that is 'very large and intellectually defined, the other subjective and personal'.[90]

A conflict between ideas that are large and intellectually defined and others that are subjective and personal comes to the fore in Clarke's poetry of the late 1990s and the early years of the twenty-first century. Her poem 'Snow' (1998), from *Five Fields*, reflects, for example, contemporary science's argument that when we gaze into the night sky 'we subjectively feel that we are looking at a black dome with twinkling stars' but 'objectively we are looking into a mostly empty void'.[91] However, like Clarke's poetry during this period about winter skies generally, 'Snow' reverts this proposition. In the way in which she writes about the sky we can see a strain of thought that runs through the twentieth century and the Victorian period. As the Victorian nature writer John Lubbock says, reflecting the cosmology of his day, 'For, in addition to the luminous heavenly bodies, we cannot doubt that there are countless others invisible to us, some from their greater distance or smaller size, but others, doubtless, from their feebler light.'[92]

Other trends in Clarke's work reflect attitudes toward the night sky which emerged much more recently, in the decades before and during her childhood. In the absence of official meteorological information during the Second World War, as George Kimble and Raymond Bush pointed out at the time, the majority of people had to rely on the sky and learn to read, or re-read in many cases, the 'weather processes'.[93] Clarke's poetry and personal relationship with the sky, on which much of her own cosmology depends, is indebted to this rejuvenation of interest in reading the weather during the war and her childhood. The extent to which relying on one's own readings of the sky without the benefit of forecasting from the Meteorological Office entered the popular imagination is evident from publications at the time about the weather. A notable example is Sverre Petterssen's *Introduction to Meteorology* (1955) which was a revised version, to meet the needs of a wider readership, of an introductory text commissioned for wartime training programmes.[94] It exemplifies the extent to which meteorology developed in the immediate post-war period and reflects post-war thinking that was to permeate successive decades about the interaction between the earth and its atmosphere in areas that permeate Clarke's poetry, especially the ways in which weather and climate are affected by mountain ranges, oceans and continents.

Weather lore, based on reading the sky with the naked eye, began, as Petterssen says, when people 'noted the characteristics of the seasons, and tried to arrange their activities as well as they could according to the changing weather'.[95] Clarke, no doubt like all of us, feels closest to the cosmos and a part of it when it is most hospitable to life on Earth. In her poem, 'Cae Delyn' from the sequence 'December' in *A Recipe for Water* (2009), a ram left behind in winter is rescued and brought inside where 'set free the locked-in summer camomiles / vanilla, mint, wild thyme, sorrel, / wake in the creature's skull / a memory of grass, / of flock and field, / of being alive'.[96] Awaking to a sense of connectivity with the cosmos of which we are all a part leads to a particular perspective on language as in 'Cae Delyn'. In 'Quayside', a poem almost juxtaposed with 'Cae Delyn' in the volume, Clarke remembers her great-great-grandfather for songs that brought a living relationship with 'the salt psalm of the sea and the wind's hymn / in the tug and thrust of the tide'[97] which Cae Delyn seeks to reflect in its musical list of summer plant smells. As she goes on to say, anticipating the way in which life turns on breath in 'Spring Equinox, 2021' in *The Silence* (2024), recreating the cosmos in language results in 'Words, made of breath, our chain of DNA'.[98] In 'Library Chair', which is juxtaposed in the collection with 'Quayside', this realisation connects her words and breath with the cosmos through the wood craft of John Brown and the writing of the Welsh-language poet Waldo Williams: 'Our songs are worked from the wood and the wheat. / Your work or mine, when art is at the helm / There's vertigo as mind and matter meet.'[99]

The concept of relationality underpinning the way in which the new science conceives of the universe is something Clarke experienced through her reading and involvement in discussions about nature but also grasped intuitively. Perceiving the cosmos as an integrated, interdependent whole, her poetry frequently suggests that the movement of the heavenly bodies is a manifestation of universal order and sustainable change. The writer and lecturer on mythology Jules Cashford observes that 'living time' for earlier peoples was determined by the moon which made time measurable and enabled growing and diminishing things to achieve an eternal rhythm.[100] In 'Foghorns', published in *The Sundial* (1978), Clarke remembers that her daughter believed that the foghorn was the moon moaning, the heat haze becomes rain and the foghorns 'moan, moon-Lonely and the dry lawns drink'.[101] In 'Death of a Cat', from the same volume, Clarke's son watches the family cat's funeral from his window and sees 'the dawn moon dissolving / its wafer on the tongue'.[102] In fact, the moon is one of the recurring images in Clarke's poetry which frequently reflects on how it has been central to the relation between the sky and the human psyche.

In her essay 'Something Understood' (2021), Clarke reflects not only on her regular study of the sky but the deep history of humanity's interest in it: 'We have evidence that our early ancestors were as watchful of the sky above them as they were of the earth they walked on.'[103] Not only in her writing but, as her journal suggests, in her life generally, she reclaims the sense of wonder that the moon held for so many ancient peoples: 'A supermoon, closer and seeming larger than any seen for years, rising like a warning beyond the beech trees, lighting the night.'[104] Imagining the observation of the sky that impelled the lives of ancient peoples, Clarke associates what she has gleaned from her deep scrutiny of the cosmos with them: 'Observation of the moon and stars, of sunrise and sunset, the change of seasons, the weather, were all they knew of science, and of worship.'[105] As the cosmologist Neville Brown points out, the moon has assumed a significant degree of leverage in cosmology because of its larger size than planet Earth and its part in moderating temperature fluctuations and seasons.[106] 'Foghorns' and 'Death of a Cat' reflect a long-standing human interest in the way in which, as Jules Cashford says, 'earthly life took its story from the Moon's story' and earthly affairs 'share the quality of the time, as they are implicated in the character of the Moon at "any one time"'.[107]

In Clarke's poetry of the 1970s and 1980s, life is lived with constant reference to the sky, the passage of seasons and the processes of nature. This is especially evident in the collection *Letter from a Far Country* (1982). The poem 'Scything', for example, announces that 'It is Blue May' and, responding to the year's rhythms, that 'There is work / to be done'.[108] Equally conscious of the seasons and the value of the extended daylight, 'Siege' observes how 'The fallen sun lies low in the bluebells',[109] and Clarke opens it on a note of regret: 'I waste the sun's last hour, sitting here / at the kitchen window.'[110] In 'Miracle on St David's Day', it is nature outside the window that awakens her to the year's movement and the coming of spring as she imagines: 'the first bird / of the year in the breaking darkness'.[111] However, the sense of an alternative way of thinking about the cosmos from that which pervades everyday life comes to the fore in *Letter from a Far Country* in 'The Water-Diviner' which celebrates the awe-inspiring, ever present rhythms in the earth of which most of us have lost our awareness.[112] It is a consciousness which in 'Siege' – in which thrushes 'eavesdrop for stirrings'[113] – connects humans and non-humans.

While observation of the sky might have a long history that can be traced back to the earliest peoples, Clarke, like R. S. Thomas, acknowledges its more immediate origins in the deep interest in the night sky which emerged during the air raids of the Second World War. Again, W. P. Hodgkinson captures the mood of the times when he describes his own passion for the night sky: 'Below me it seemed as though the trees were reaching up to the stars in prayerful attitudes. I was bathed in the silence of the night – a night full of stars and mystery.'[114] In one of his more spiritual moments, as he watches the hills of the Severn valley darken in twilight, he can only wish that he might be as they were 'filled with eternal peace – and emptied of that self-knowledge which alone divides us from God, and which hangs like a veil between us and Heaven'.[115] And it would have been impossible for Clarke and Thomas not to have been aware, too, of the wonder revealed through the new telescopes and the reuse of space technology during the Second World War.

Not coincidentally, the revised edition of Reginald Lester's *The Observer's Book of Weather* (1955) drew extensively on post-war technical and scientific developments and the passion in the 1960s for aeronautic technology and the exploration of space. At the outset of his book, Lester points out that when the Second World War ended, V2 rockets 'were turned to constructive use' and were 'sent into the higher altitudes to collect valuable information about the atmosphere at those great heights'.[116] The capacity to look at the earth from outer space is one of the wonders of late-twentieth-century space technology as is the launch of rockets to other planets. As Stuart Clark maintains: 'It is no longer space that is the awesome thing: it is the fragile balance of Earth.'[117] This is akin to an experience which Clarke had on a mountain in Sweden in August 2019. In her journal, she is overwhelmed by the new perspective: 'We see our earth, our planet, huge and luminous hanging in space.'[118] The event inspires her to read a poem and her companions to chant in an African language. She remembers the whole episode as 'spiritual, beautiful, thrilling, standing in the pitch darkness, seeing our earth as if from space.'[119]

This shrewd observation as to the impact of contemporary space technology on our wider understanding of the planet underpins Clarke's oeuvre, but especially her poetry of the late 1980s and the following decades. In the aptly entitled 'Looking' from *Letting in the Rumour* (1989), Clarke compares the night sky as seen through a telescope – 'the fuzzy dust of stars' – with the skeleton of a woman discovered in an archaeological excavation of a Roman settlement:

> Imprint of bones is a constellation
> shining against silence, against darkness,
> and stars are the pearly vertebrae
> of water-drops against the drought, pelvis,
>
> skull, scapula five million light years old
> wink in the glass …[120]

The cosmos is as baffling a manifestation of space and time as the past which has been created and eroded through generations and generations of births, lives and deaths. But the apparent nothingness of cosmic blackness becomes, through its myriad of galaxies, an image of the vibrancy which led to life on earth, a subject which is discussed more fully in Chapter 5. In this respect, Clarke's poetry frequently alludes to the contemplation of the origins of the cosmos in modern science. As the renowned physicist Dennis W. Sciama pointed out, a perpetual puzzle is 'how the galaxies themselves managed to form in an expanding universe', suggesting that 'even in its early stages large density fluctuations were present' which might have arisen spontaneously or be a 'a consequence of a previous phase of the Universe'.[121]

The revised view of the Roman woman's body in cosmic terms in 'Looking'– as a 'constellation' – offsets her death against the 'vibrancy' of her skeleton as a sophisticated creation which is seen in forensic terms: pelvis, skull, scapula. Although the poem is entitled 'Looking', its subject is really the wonder in looking and how this transforms the seeming blackness of death and space: 'and stardust is all we hold / of the Roman lady's negative / in the infinite dark of the grave'.[122] For Clarke, as in her early poems in which she is absorbed by the blackness which she discovers in the skulls of long-dead sheep, the blackness with which life through death is associated symbolises the way in which being always carries non-being within it.

In juxtaposing observation of the night sky with the excavation of a Roman settlement, Clarke brings together the detailed careful observation of two sciences – astronomy and archaeology – and the extent to which each is infused with emotion. But in doing so, she points toward the primary richness of the unity which anthropologists such as Armstrong suggest earlier peoples found in the cosmos. This notion of the possibility of a deep richness between people and the sky has been developed by Cobb in his concept of the 'ensoulment' of the sky and it provides a frame within which to understand the different perspectives on the relationship between the human psyche and the sky in Clarke's poetry. Cobb emphasises, as does Clarke, recognition of the 'innerness' of sky imagery, that is to say not only our capacity to personify the sky but to sense its own theatre of emotions and also to feel as if we are a part of it.[123]

In Clarke's poem 'Winter', published as part of *Ice*, 'Voyager crosses the far shores of space'[124] and, against this background, the river freezes, breaks and refreezes. The voyager seems a distraction

– 'leaving us lonely, / stirred by story'[125] – from appreciating the wonder and enchantment of the season: 'In winter's cold eye, a star.'[126] As Cobb explains, and Clarke presses home in this poem, 'the soul of the world ... is not perceived unless we give it emotional attention, and turning that attention away from it to "line and rule" is one way of destroying the bridge which unites above and below and whose magical outcome is the world's enchantment.'[127] In its contrasting of the space craft with the poet's emotional appreciation of the cosmos, 'Winter' encapsulates a binary which is important also to Cobb. Recalling the 'innerness', the two-way emotional correspondence between the sky and ourselves, and implicitly reflecting on the American space project, Cobb argues, as noted at the outset of this chapter, for what he calls an 'emotional sky', stressing that 'this is no sentimental projection. It is an essential countermeasure to the ... drive to soar away from "our" world ... whether literally or in the deadly glamorization of science and the hubris of its belief in a scientifically objective world.'[128] In 'Winter', the deep-felt unity of which Cobb speaks is encapsulated in the image of the river freezing and unfreezing invested with the 'innerness' which is fundamental to Cobb's concept of ensoulment: 'its heart slowed in its cage, / the moon a stone / in its throat.'[129] In *Ice*, as a whole, there is a recurrent – almost new age – realisation of the cosmos as an ever turning entity in which moments of transition between light and dark, the seasons and the year are probed for their mystical relevance to life on earth and to reading the future.

Again, Clarke's work might be said to resonate with Cobb's appreciation not simply of 'ensoulment' per se – important as this is – but its 'magical outcome ... the world's enchantment'. As Cobb explains in a development of this argument – in a voice that sounds remarkably like Clarke's in her post-millennial writings: 'The sky – our sky – with its "greatest and lesser lights", its moods, its stars and planets, its mists and clouds and rainbows, is our best teacher of Awakening.'[130] In 'The Year's Midnight', which concludes *Ice*, Clarke suggests, as does Cobb in drawing his essay on 'Soul of the Sky' to a conclusion,[131] that although our planet and cosmos threaten to dissolve into nothing, attachment to the beauty of the world offers us hope:

> Every leaf-scar is a bud
> expecting a future.
> The earth speaks in parables.

> The burning bush. The rainbow.
> Promises. Promises.[132]

In Clarke's earlier poem, 'The Hare' (published in *Letting in the Rumour*, 1989), her friend confides in her how she has spent the night 'sleeping in the clams of a bad dream' and of how physical pain is as 'nothing / to the mental pain'.[133] But the blackness of mental suffering is linked to a cosmological perspective in which, as Cobb's concept of 'ensoulment' suggests, the cosmos seems to have empathy for human suffering: 'In the last heavy nights before the full moon, / when its face seems sorrowful and broken, / I look through binoculars.'[134] However, Clarke develops Cobb's notion of ensoulment from the perspective of what she referred to as 'feminine values' (discussed in Chapter 1) and women's experiences. The alignment of a womanly consciousness with the tides of the moon is a recurring theme in Clarke's poetry from the 1970s and 1980s. As Cashford observes: 'Perpetually moving – from crescent to full to crescent – the moon tells one fundamental story: birth, growth, fullness, decay, death and rebirth.'[135] In many of Clarke's poems what Cobb calls the 'innerness' of the sky and its imagery is experienced in the body. The perception of the cycle of the moon corresponding to the monthly rhythms of women's bodies is very significant to Clarke's cosmology.

THE PRE-MODERN COSMOS

Central to Clarke's cosmology is not only her physical and bodily awareness of it but her fascination with light and dark. It is no coincidence that the interplay of light and shade is the subject of the titular poem of her first collection of poems, *The Sundial* (1978). As the nature writer Rob Cowen has pointed out, 'we live in a world where the shift from dark to light is nothing remarkable' and this makes it difficult 'to conceive of the impact of the spring equinox held in earlier times'.[136] He maintains that 'to eyes long tired of a merciless winter, a strengthening sun returning to banish the darkness was a supremely powerful moment. As the icy crust split, destruction gave way to re-creation. Land was miraculously fertile, fecund and full of energy.'[137]

Clarke's 'The Sundial' hints at how earlier peoples regarded the sun – as a resurrecting light on which the earth, plant forms and animals were dependent – which is developed more explicitly in some of her later poems. Sundials, which date back to 3500 BCE, and probably in a simpler form much earlier, work on the principle that where there is light, there is also dark. Her feverish son constructs his sundial from a circle of white paper, twelve fragments of stone and a broken bean stick for the *gnomon* – the stick whose shadow, when it is properly aligned with the points of the compass, passes over the clock face throughout the day. The shadow's progress around the dial – created in Clarke's poem by the fragments of stone – corresponds with the sun's position in the sky. The poem has two dimensions: the measurement of time – 'calculating / The mathematics of sunshine'[138] – which led to the creation of more sophisticated time pieces but also the experience of planetary time in which Clarke and her son indulge themselves as they spend an entire day together in nature and under the sky: 'All day he told the time to me. / All day we felt and watched the sun.'[139]

In effect, Clarke and her son seek to recreate the experience of the sky and its impact on the human psyche before more sophisticated sundials constructed of obelisks, pillars and other megalithic structures came into being. They position themselves before regulated time – even before the adjustment of adding an hour in summer to mean time – when people experienced the earth's daily rotation, different views of the night sky each evening as the sun completed its elliptical orbit, and a deeper sense of local time, before people realised that away from local time days lengthened or shortened with direction of travel.

In embryonic form, 'The Sundial' introduces what becomes a key source of tension, if not conflict, in Clarke's poetry which Armstrong pithily identifies as the difference between the cosmology of ancient peoples – with an archetypal and mystical sense of unity and timelessness – and the modern world falling away from this 'primal richness' and 'back into the world of time'.[140] In *Letter from a Far Country* (1982) and in some of the new poems published alongside it in *Selected Poems* (1985), Clarke is excited by the mystical qualities that have remained in everyday life, for example, with the water-diviner whose 'fingers tell water like prayer' and a mountaineer who knows the mountain with his body.[141] Through a bodily awareness, they seem to have retained something of the 'primal richness' of which Armstrong speaks which others, including to some extent Clarke herself, have lost through their over-reliance on the cognitive faculties.

Armstrong laments that 'in the modern world we rarely express the gratitude that our ancestors felt for the natural rhythms of nature'.[142] From one perspective, the modern concert venue Bridgewater Hall in

Manchester – designed by Arup in conjunction with the University of Salford – where Clarke spent some time in May 1997 as a writer-in-residence, epitomises the modern disconnection of human beings from the primal richness which Armstrong envisages in the lives of earlier peoples. The building is unconnected to the surrounding ground to alleviate noise from the nearby tramline. As Clarke observes in her poem 'Concerto' from *Five Fields* (1998), 'the building treads on springs, / resting its weight a wafer above ground'.[143]

However, while the venue seems 'unconnected', from another perspective it is connected to a wider cosmos. This different but connected thinking is embraced by Kate Egan's 'Space Piece', a sky-map hanging in the Hall's foyer which, as Clarke writes, pointedly creates 'broken ripples of comets on floating white' that net 'sunlit water falling straight to the earth, like rain'.[144] Egan's work of art reflects the relationship between the mind, the psyche and the sky, which has been central to western philosophical and theological thinking, as Campion stresses, for thousands of years.[145] The installation unveils what Campion has identified as 'that residual impulse which drew humanity to search the sky for meaning and inspiration'.[146]

Clarke's 'Concerto' examines examples of late-twentieth-century cosmological thinking, beginning with the monolith, created by the Japanese sculptor Kan Yasuda, which during the period of Clarke's residency stood in the piazza outside the Bridgewater Hall. To her mind, it brought together key elements from her own developing cosmological thinking as well as his own: 'Stillness of stone in the street, Yasuda's monolith / asleep on limestone, white marble veined with silver.'[147] It resonates with the stone features before which ancient peoples stood in awe and which they invested with their cosmological meaning. But, from another point of view, it is part of the spectacular nature of post-industrial/post-modern society in which things acquire meaning not from their origins as such but their relationship with other objects. It causes those who encounter it to behave differently in its presence, the poet touching it and children including it in a new kind of play. Invoking monoliths as they appeared to ancient peoples, Clarke uses the notion of the sublime to disrupt and/or extend what we experience in the everyday. The sublime is a difficult concept to define precisely because its meaning has changed over time. But the philosopher Robert Clewis offers us a useful, working definition: 'a complex feeling of intense satisfaction, uplift, or elevation, felt before an object or event that is considered to be awe-inspiring'.[148]

Appreciating the cosmologically sublime in Yasuda's monolith in 'Concerto' is dependent upon touch – Clarke touches the stone in the morning and at night – and upon an unleased imagination, exemplified by the children who share stories about it. They see it as 'animal, egg, thing from the depths of the sea' and, becoming 'giddy', are inspired to dance – an acknowledgement of the way in which ancient peoples expressed their awareness of the cosmos and were thus able to 'crack it open for its soul'.[149] Clarke reinforces the cosmological significance embodied in the stone and the children's reactions to it through references to the sun and moon, carried through the streets in a carnival atmosphere and hoisted with the drum beat into the sky above the street musicians. Invoking the rhythms of the music and dance, aligned with the cosmos, the poem seizes upon the musicians' celebration of the cosmos which Armstrong argues ancient peoples understood. Clarke is interested in the cosmological awareness that she witnesses, and experiences, herself, not as something which is beyond community, but which is contained within it: 'The streets are a dazzle of day-glo police jackets, / drummers, magicians, stilt-walkers, jugglers and jazz.'[150]

As its title suggests, 'Concerto' is not simply a verbal narrative but one shaped by musical composition. The choice of concerto is appropriate in this respect, for as the eminent twentieth-century musicologist Reginald Morris pointed out, the concerto was originally a 'motet' – a vocal musical composition in diverse forms and style with an organ accompaniment.[151] While Clarke's poem is a composition based on thought in language, it draws on music as a creative process which, like the cosmos itself, unfolds with the laws of its own nature. The philosopher Tom McLeish suggests that the combination of poetry, music and cosmology is itself unsurprising for music 'was a mathematical discipline from antiquity to the early modern era, and joined astronomy, geometry and arithmetic in the "quadrivium" of higher disciplines.'[152] The poem, drawing on the structure of a concerto, begins with an 'exposition' that distributes contrasting 'tonalities', but then develops them, through repetition and recapitulation, into much quicker parts. As such 'Concerto' seems to act out in modern contexts, the principles of cosmological, mythical thinking to which Armstrong draws attention. In descending to the undercroft, where the Hall rests its weight on springs, Clarke experiences descent into an underworld epitomised in the tunnels and labyrinths of earlier times which she describes as earlier peoples may have thought of them without necessarily having the appropriate language to express their emotions: 'the ghost / of world under world'.[153]

Clarke's account of her journey into the Hall's 'underworld' subtly picks out some of the elements which for peoples of earlier times would have constituted their 'reality', exemplifying her skill in effortlessly merging contemporary and ancient cosmological thinking: sloping outcrops of earth, gravel and sandstone, animal skins, petrified forests, enchanted woods, husks used as great instruments and the merging of human breath through instruments with the sighs of hurricanes. The extent to which wind breathes through the pipes of the organ leads Clarke to think about the distant origins of music in which there is a deep-rooted cosmology:

> Is that how music began?
> A woman singing in a cave
> to the airs of the sea
> as if it's inside her?[154]

In the Anthropocene epoch, we have come to realise, as the environmentalist Timothy Morton says, that we 'are not running the show despite our "most powerful" technical mastery on a powerful scale'.[155] Discussing 'sound' and 'music', he maintains that 'humans are not the conductors of meaning, not the pianists of the real' and, following John Cage's work, that piano strings are not meant simply to express our inner being but 'show the shadow side of the human self' and have 'their own anarchic autonomy'.[156] Throughout the 'Undercroft' section, a persistent sense of descent leads the poet down through the music to a place deep inside herself where she finds: 'I have become the instrument. / Like a gate with the wind in it.'[157] In this spiritual/psychic space the difference between the inner and outer worlds, body and nature disappears. Reminding the reader of 'The Sundial', the poem concludes with the movement from light to dark and the intensity which light can assume in the summer prior to darkness: 'The city glows in the last light of the sun. / Glass walls are touched by its batons of fire.'[158] In 'Concerto', the experience of the longer-lasting summer sky acquires something of the spiritual significance that it had for ancient peoples: 'A month from midsummer, / and the sky still blue in the long evening light.'[159]

As Campion observes, 'most cultures share the notion of the sky as a theatrical device'.[160] In a poem, 'Estuary', from *Five Fields*

(1998), Clarke seems much more ready than in her earlier poems to enjoy the kind of cosmic energy of which Campion writes, observing: 'Skies were thunder / before jets cracked clouds / before the rent skin of sound.'[161] Armstrong, noting that 'nearly every pantheon has its Sky God',[162] effectively summarises how ancient peoples had an emotional grasp of the sky which modern societies seem to have lost. For them, as Armstrong says, the sky seemed 'inconceivably immense, inaccessible and eternal' providing a kind of 'religious' experience.[163] Clarke's 'Concerto', developing the cosmological themes of *Five Fields*, merges the organ, the Hall's auditorium and undercroft with the planets, as did the sky-pieces hoisted by the street musicians and Egan's installation in the foyer. But one of the differences between the cosmology in *Five Fields* – apart from a brooding uncertainty turned to in Chapter 3 – and Clarke's poetry of the 1970s and 1980s is the pronounced sense of the 'innerness' of which Cobb writes and her sense of not only perceiving but being perceived by the cosmos: 'I'll think of the organ's ghost in the undercroft, / and the stone in the white stare of the moon, / in thrall to each other's gravity, like love.'[164]

But, for Clarke and Armstrong, the way in which contemporary western society has removed itself from a close connection with the sky is linked to another loss – the part played by symbolism in our lives. As Armstrong says, 'For us moderns a symbol is essentially separate from the unseen reality to which it directs our attention.'[165] Integrated with the suggestion throughout Clarke's poetry that we have lost the capacity to feel the primary richness of the cosmos is a lament for the loss of our ability to think symbolically. Clarke and Armstrong share an interest in the symbolic value of non-living forms, especially stones. Thinking of ancient peoples, who to her mind enjoyed a universe of unity, Armstrong believed, like Clarke, that they saw, for example, not an 'inert, unpromising rock' but an 'embodied strength, permanence, solidity and an absolute mode of being that was quite different from the vulnerable human state'.[166] 'Chalk Pebble', published in *Letter from a Far Country* (1982), is an intriguing earlier poem from this perspective that contrasts the mutability of a sedimentary rock, prone to erosion over time, with the vulnerability of non-human life captured within a fossil – 'The cicatrice of a flower'[167] – that, at one level, is outside time and dependent for its permanence on its embodiment within a piece of rock, a subject discussed further in Chapter 5.

Clarke's poetry suggests that there is a central order at the heart of nature which inspires wonder and beauty. But this is frequently juxtaposed with a view of the cosmos that is less coherent and presents us, as the sky did for ancient peoples, with a theatre of drama, movement and change which often brings with it a sense of impending destruction and chaos. How Clarke's poetry negotiates this apparent contradictory cosmos and its impact on her well-being and the human psyche generally – themes which bring the intense, emotional cosmos experienced by ancient peoples into our present – is the subject of the next chapter.

3

CLIMATE AND WEATHER IN THE ANTHROPOCENE

As observed in Chapter 2, there are many examples in Clarke's poetry of a reassuring cosmology which – to import the words of the meteorologist and physicist Tim Palmer – 'most of us believe to be the epitome of order and predictability: the motion of the planets'.[1] At times, her post-millennial poems bring a fresh immediacy to the joy derived from contact with nature as in 'Harvest Moon' from *Ice* (2012): 'You called me out to the lane – come quick! – / when the red moon rose in a smoking cloud over Pisgah / like a house on a far mountain helplessly burning.'[2] While invoking the long-held connection in the human psyche with the moon, the poem is a window to the excitement she and her husband felt in nature in their first spring together in west Wales, as in 'Wild Plums', too, from the same collection: 'starbursts of petals / from stubborn wood that April, / and every September' and 'sweet nameless plums / to pick from the air as we pass'.[3]

In these poems from Clarke's later work, seeing and touching nature brings the vast, distant cosmos nearer and allows it to become part of her life's rhythm: 'At night fruit thudding in grass / is the drumbeat of dreams.'[4] But, as they also suggest, beauty in Clarke's poetry is bound up, as in the contemporary natural sciences, with, in the words of the contemporary physicist Lee Smolin, 'the cosmology of an interesting universe': 'So part of the beauty of the scene is that over every scale, from the majestic to the tiny, and over any interval of time, from the second to the year, there is something happening, some harmony to notice or some structure being formed or erased.'[5]

However, despite the beauty and wonder in the order of nature that runs throughout her work, Clarke is drawn, as contemporary physics, to a profound unpredictability and uncertainty in the cosmos. As the *New York Times* writer James Gleick openly acknowledges, contemporary physicists seemed to have found themselves with 'a taste for randomness and complexity, for jagged edges and sudden leaps'.[6] One of the books which had a powerful impact on Clarke in the 1970s, when she had just begun her career as a writer, was Annie Dillard's *Pilgrim at Tinker Creek* (1975) with its view of emotional skies and the Earth as a planet where the cosmos dramatically 'broods, spins, and lurches down'.[7] Anticipating Clarke's view of the cosmos, she observes: 'The planet whirls alone and dreaming ... The planet and the power meet with a shock. They fuse and tumble, lightning, ground fire; they part, mute, submitting, and touch again with hiss and cry.'[8] Similarly, alongside its reflection of the beauty of nature and the environment, Clarke's work invokes a more dramatic and less reassuring cosmos, emphasising that we live in a world of complex, ever changing planetary systems that are connected, for example, to extremes of weather and climate in destructive storms, severe flooding, extreme ice and melting snow caps.

As the mathematician Leonard Smith maintains, the notion of chaos amplifies instability and confounds stable systems.[9] But it poses the question, how stable is stability? There is an increasing sense in Clarke's work of our lives, to use Palmer's words, being 'disordered and confused'.[10] As such, despite its presentation of the wonder and beauty in nature, it reflects the distinction to which late-twentieth- and early-twenty-first century science has drawn attention between the predictability and precision of our solar system with its relatively small number of planets and moons and the atmosphere, to employ Palmer's description, as 'a turbulent fluid with literally trillions upon trillions of whirls and eddies with all sorts of different sizes'.[11]

This scientific image of the earth's atmosphere is a much more turbulent depiction of the cosmos than we find in many mid-twentieth-century nature writers like W. P. Hodgkinson, for example, who, writing of the Severn valley, says simply that 'the stars have their silences and the thunder has its voice'.[12] But is this, as Smith would say, merely an attempt on Hodgkinson's part, as most of ours, to cope with and contain chaos?[13] Telescopic images of the cosmos offer Clarke, with her profound interest in cosmology which Chapter 2 unveiled, a deeper but also disturbing view of the cosmos as chaos which, despite her counter appreciation of its wonder and beauty, haunts her post-1990s writing. This sense of chaos enters her work not only through her personal and global anxieties around climate change and the gradual, persistent destruction of the environment – important themes in her work as we shall see – but arises from the possibility, as Palmer says in discussion of extreme events, that 'chaos is a property of the planets and the weather, precisely because chaos is a property of the fundamental dynamics of the universe'.[14]

As Smith points out: 'From the time of Newton until the close of the 19th century, most scientists were also meteorologists. Chaos and meteorology are closely linked by the meteorologists' interest in the role uncertainty plays in weather forecasts.'[15] He goes on to maintain that chaos theory has changed the way in which we see the so-called 'real' world, especially in terms of forecasting, questions of climate change and the strength and impact of global warming.[16] In her August journal for 2007, Clarke admits that she is deeply troubled that 'nature, with flood, hurricane and earthquake, would shake us off the planet'.[17] It is the intensity with which the idea is expressed rather than the concept itself that characterises Clarke's writing in the new century. Shortly after she began writing, 'Storm Awst' (1978) introduces the reader to the contradictory cosmology which underpins her work that is consoling one moment – nature filling people with delight – but disturbing the next:

> The rain stings, the whips
> Of the laburnum hedges lash the roof
> Of the cringing cottage. A curious
> Calm, coming from the storm, unites
> Us, as we wonder if the work
> We have done will stand.[18]

The extent to which severe storms, the flipside of the planetary weather systems, can have a devastating psychological impact is broadened, conceived and intensified in 'Storm', published in *Letting in the Rumour* (1989). The cat feels compelled to keep low and out of sight, and the primary sense in the poem is hearing which accentuates the terror of what is coming on-land because it can be heard and felt but not fully seen. Although the poem is developed around sound – 'The hill's a wind-harp. / Our bones are flutes of ice.'[19] – it is a very physical poem, dependent upon deep, bodily consciousness in which, as in 'Storm Awst', the impact of the storm on nature enters the physiology of the listener: 'The heart drums in its small room / and the river rattles its pebbles.'[20]

In an entry in her journal for August 2020, she invests the August storm with even greater anxiety than she did in *Letting in the Rumour*: 'In late August, the *storwm Awst* brought a rage of Atlantic hurricanes, tantrums of wind and rain, one after another, ripping summer to rags.'[21] There is no story here, no poetry as such. It is the recording of a cosmological event that is unexpected in its violence and attack. It is as much about emotions – 'rage' and 'tantrums' – as cosmology. By contrast, the entry in her journal for the previous year placed the storm in a wider context which was in fact more of a narrative: 'This year it comes earlier and wilder than ever. Trees are down, trains are cancelled, power stations out and electricity cut.'[22] Characteristic of much of Clarke's work, the writing begins with sound, sensation and embodied fear, which becomes a rhythm and rhyme, then edges toward story. In the poem 'Storwm Awst', published in *The Silence* (2024), this pattern almost repeats itself, but it is more complex and more deeply cosmological in its perspective. The storm's arrival, out of a period of intense silence and dry heat, becomes a story – suspensefully 'not a leaf moves'[23] but then the downpour comes in 'a sudden rush of wind'.[24] The background of a particularly dry season determines the storm's reception which is itself a story within the storm's story: 'We're glad of it, the sound of earth / drinking after months of heat.'[25] Initially, the suddenness of the storm determines the poem's structure – its arrival is a bridge between the first two verses – but the poem itself, embedded in the 'music' of the earth drinking, is driven by the storm's rhythm and opens up the human senses. Throughout *The Silence* a new kind of emphasis in Clarke's work on the minutiae of language and the subtlety of sound, drilling down into the relationship between carefully positioned letters, is linked to new levels of consciousness of the changing outside world, felt deeply within the self. In 'Storwm Awst', the intimacy between the storm and the smallholding initially enveloped in violence where the rain snarls aggressively in the double 's' launches into a repetitive heavier thumping 's' – 'a hiss of rain strums slate'.[26] But the poem overtly becomes transcendental as the poet inevitably looks upward to find a kind of tranquillity (embodied in the repetition of a different 's' sound) – 'sky floats on stone'.[27]

This ambivalence at the heart of the planetary weather systems is part of the deep experience of weather which D. Parry-Jones encapsulates in his countryside memoir *Welsh Country Characters* (1952), written when Clarke was a child in Cardiff. He remembers the sound of the wind in the trees as 'a delight always, and a lullaby' but the noise of thunder 'decidedly terrifying'.[28] As Nicholas Campion maintains, 'having been constructed, a cosmology achieves a life of its own' and becomes 'an active force'.[29] Clarke and Campion share a view of the sky which the anthropologist Karen Armstrong found among the ancient peoples: 'The endless drama of its thunderbolts, eclipses, storms, sunsets, rainbows and meteors spoke of another endlessly active dimension which had a dynamic life of its own.'[30]

For both Clarke and Armstrong, as for Campion, the sky is not a stage for but *is* the enactment of the active, dynamic life of the cosmos. Our responses to it – which can range from awe, wonder and fear to excitement – position ourselves as inseparable from this compelling reality, not distant from it but an emotional and physical product of it. Dillard's autobiographical writing finds in the cosmos and its changing weather patterns a thrill in movement that, for her, resonates with the possibility of something new in the future. But while this is true of Clarke's work also, throughout her poetry and journals a thread of unease runs like a river, flowing underground for a time then emerging once again to full view. This is an aspect of her writing which critics and reviewers have generally overlooked even though it often determines the variation in her voice and mood.

Clarke's work is based, like the physics emerging from chaos theory, on the discovery even in the simplest systems of how, as Gleick says, 'order arises spontaneously ... order and chaos together'.[31] But throughout her work – and especially prevalent in her twenty-first-century writings – discovering how to cope with external uncertainty and chaos is connected with facing inner doubts, a sense of impending personal disconnection from one's self and insecurities that are sometimes dormant but nevertheless always present.

STABLE AND UNSTABLE SKIES

The transition from stability to instability in the skies might have been a preoccupation of weather watchers from ancient times but it is also a very contemporary obsession, as is borne out in the work of twenty-first-century nature writers such as Daniel Butler who have come to live in Wales. Describing the 'strident' nature of the weather in Wales ('One moment it's summer and the next it's autumn – or at least you have a clear blast of what's to come'[32]), he contrasts the 'calm' which all those in rural Wales look for each day in the Welsh mountains with the 'high winds and lashing rain ... which strip the leaves from the branches overnight'.[33]

The experience of studying the different types of cloud and their movements across the changing skies proved fascinating to those who sought to work out their own weather lore during the Second World War, discussed in Chapter 2, and those who dipped into, and sometimes read avidly, the various mid-century weather guides. Anticyclonic *cumulus* clouds captivated the imagination of professional and amateur meteorologists alike not only for the fair weather they promised but the way they might cover the whole sky, projecting, as the meteorologist Sverre Petterssen says, a reassuring sense of cosmic stability.[34] But it is the contradictory nature of the skies that fascinates him – and disturbs Clarke in, for example, 'Storm Awst' – and the way in which anticyclonic *cumulus* gives way to another form of cloud with its ominous 'towers' and 'protuberances' reaching up into altitudes where temperatures are well below freezing and releasing bursts of heavy rain.[35]

Poets and meteorologists share a sublime sense of awe when it comes to thunderstorms and their genesis as if they have a life, like the cosmos itself, of their own. Petterssen's scientific writing captures the accumulating threat embodied in the formation of thunderclouds:

> In the developing stage the cloud is warmer than the outside air so that the cloud air is accelerated upward ... the updraft increases with the elevation, and the cloud builds rapidly to heights where the temperature is well below freezing ... large amounts of cloud droplets, raindrops, and snowflakes accumulate.[36]

It is this instability within thunder clouds that interests but also disturbs Clarke as if it is an insight, as in 'Storm Awst', into the instability of the cosmos itself where amenable toward the life within it one moment, it can suddenly become inhospitable. Our increased understanding of the science of storms helps us to appreciate the anxiety that they create in us, as in Clarke herself, and the way in which we often perceive storms in our subconscious minds.

In 'Cattle, Hayfield, Storm', published in *A Recipe for Water* (2009), Clarke walks the house, while, all the time, 'buffeting in from the west, a herd of squalls / shove and shoulder, kicking up a shindig'.[37] In a rather disconcerting image – the measure of which most of us have experienced – meteorologists envisage a thunderstorm as 'a cluster of thunderclouds'; formed when the thundercloud reaches maturity, they spread from the mother cloud, in a way that resonates with the development and replenishment of species.[38] Thunderclouds, as Clarke recognises in 'Cattle, Hayfield, Storm', capture the powerful energy possible at the heart of the planetary weather systems, impelled by forces that achieve expression in the gusty and increasingly strong winds and the sudden drops in temperature. The dramatic formation of a storm – even in meteorological writing – draws all our senses together in a succession of images which is vividly captured in Clarke's 'Storm-Snake' from *Ice* (2012): 'a stir of wind like the whispering of wheat'; 'the black sky warm'; 'a sudden growl of warning in the stones'; 'serpents of electricity'; and 'the sound of weighty matter heaved across / the floor of heaven'.[39]

Thus, despite the wonder and beauty which Clarke finds in nature, her work examines the cosmos, and her internalisation of it, as an energetic and creative presence always bordering on destruction as much as celestial order. In summarising the cosmos in her essay 'Something Understood', she sees it in terms of 'the sun, the moon, the extreme weathers of storm, thunder, flood, hurricane, earthquake, darkness and light'.[40] While this way of looking at the cosmos has its origins in her poetry of the 1970s, the intensity with which it enters her post-1990s writing owes much to living in a rural, and somewhat remote, part of Wales. Not coincidentally, Butler, attuning himself to a new life in the remote Cambrian mountains, is entranced by the 'strident' nature of the Welsh weather and the different ways in which one feels the cosmos in one's physical being.[41]

Of the value of cosmic thinking, the Icelandic writer and climate activist Andri Snær Magnason has no doubt: 'If it weren't for weather systems and volcanic activity or the Moon that guides the tides, the Earth would be dead, or at best a stinking ball of algae.'[42] This mode of thought has roots that can be traced to the middle of the twentieth century when the emerging scientific approach to weather and climate influenced many of Clarke's generation. Some of the mid-twentieth-century introductory books on the weather intended for a popular but educated readership proved to be best sellers very quickly. Reginald Lester's *The Observer's Book of Weather* (1955) brought some advanced meteorological thinking to a wider audience at that time and, through its revised edition almost ten years later, helped shape the way in which those of Clarke's generation thought about weather, climate and the sky.[43]

Works, such as Lester's book, and wartime observations of how nature responded to different weather systems brought a cosmic understanding to planetary science in the 1950s, re-introducing, for example, the planetary concept of 'phenology'. Phenology, a study of the sensitivity of plants to 'coming weather changes', began in 1917, and, as Lester says, after the Second World War, became 'a very important side of meteorology'.[44] Its influence on Clarke is evident even in her later work, as in her observation, in 'Flowers of the Mountain' (2017), as to how 'the Snowdon lily / trembles in genuflection to the wind'.[45] But it is not that Clarke is simply recalling the biology that was in the air, as it were, in the mid-twentieth century. Suggesting perhaps that science like history repeats itself, one of the most striking features of twenty-first-century nature writing is the way in which the relationship between plants and the cosmos is once again understood biochemically. Butler describes how he has found 'some of the most striking colours, the reds, come from the reaction of sunlight on the increased sugar levels inside the plant'.[46] But Clarke takes a broader view of the symbiotic relationship between plants and the cosmos, including temperature and the interplay of light and dark. In 'Chawton' (2017) published in the same volume as 'Flowers of the Mountain', she observes how 'In the garden, flowers open their throats / to the rummage of bees / till dusk darkens.'[47] And the responsiveness of her greenhouse lilies to heat and humidity inspires one of her most dramatic plant images which picks up the zoological theme of the collection: 'The lilies yawn like leopards / caged all day in the hot house.'[48]

But perhaps most significant of all, as far as anticipating Clarke's work on nature and cosmology is concerned, mid- and late-twentieth-century popular guides to weather brought together, as does Lester's *The Observer's Book of Weather* in the mid-1950s, 'plant observation ... records of insects ... the habits of birds ... [and] data in relation to weather conditions'.[49] Such books combined, as throughout Clarke's work, interest in the science of the cosmos with a deeply felt sense of awe to be found in the skies. As Lester asks, 'Who can fail to be thrilled by the magnificent pageantry of the clouds, or the wonderful colourings of sunsets and other sky phenomena?'[50]

However, as Clarke has pursued her interests in cosmology and the weather into the twenty-first century, like many others, she has become very conscious of extremes of weather, as she observes in her journal: 'This year, October rides the Atlantic on the diminishing power of a series of hurricanes born in the Americas, storms bearing black clouds of torrential rain to dump as soon as it reaches land.'[51] But, by the second decade of the new century, too, Welsh publications, such as Iestyn Hughes's *Tywydd Mawr* (2016), were arguing that in Wales the experience of extremes of weather was not unusual. In his introduction to *Tywydd Mawr*, Hywel Griffiths observes:

> Yn y blynyddoedd diwethaf mae nifer o enghreifftiau o dywydd eithafol, yn enwedig stormydd a llifogydd, wedi taro Cymru. Yn aml iawn mae'r rhain yn ein synnu, ac fe'u gelwir yn ddigwyddiadau unigryw a digyffelyb yn y wasg. Fodd bynnag, mae llifogyddau mwy wedi digwydd yn y gorffennol, a hynny'n amlach nag y maent yn digwydd heddiw.

> (In recent years we in Wales have experienced a number of examples of extreme weather, including storms and floods. These often shock us, and the press call them unique and unprecedented. However, larger floods have happened in the past, and they have happened more frequently than they do today).[52]

Hywel Griffiths draws attention to an aspect of the way in which extreme weather has acquired a particular significance in Welsh history and culture that Clarke, too, appreciates and is keen to articulate. Griffiths points out that the incidences of extreme weather have become 'trysorfa o wybodaeth, atgofion, darluniau, llên gwerin a gwyddoniaeth am y tywydd a'r hinsawdd' (a treasure trove of information, memories, images, folklore and science related to weather and climate).[53] Given Clarke's passion for images, myth, folklore and science, it is easy to see how her work not only resonates with the approach to weather and climate in the twenty-first century to which Griffiths draws attention but is embedded in it.

In this regard, Clarke's writings pursue the way in which extremes of weather in Welsh history and culture are linked to specific places – as in 'Cantre'r Gwaelod'. As Griffiths says, ''Mae gan lawr o'r rhain gyswllt cryf gyda lleoedd ac mae eu henwau wedi magu arwyddocâd yn ein meddylfryd torfol cenedlaethol – Cwm Tryweryn, Cwm Elan, Cwmreglwys, Aber-fan, Dolgarrog, a bellach Aberystwyth.' (Many of these [examples of extreme weather] have strong links to places whose names have developed significance in our collective national consciousness – Tryweryn, Cwm Elan, Cwmreglwys, Aber-fan,

Dolgarrog, and now Aberystwyth.)⁵⁴ Thus, Clarke's embedding extremes of weather and climate in Wales in a mesh of historical memories becomes a means to a deeper understanding of the significance of the 'meddylfryd torfol cenedlaethol' (collective national consciousness) to Welsh identity. But in Clarke's work it becomes part not only of a collective consciousness – as important as recognition of that is – but a collective unconscious, which Griffiths does not mention, that runs throughout her work and is experienced at the collective (national, community, neighbourhood and family) as well as at an individual level.

CANTRE'R GWAELOD AND SPECTACULAR EVENTS

Clarke's work often turns, as do those on Welsh weather generally, to spectacular events. This way of thinking about 'tywydd mawr' (extreme weather) encourages her to write about examples that have become part of Welsh history and stories about the role of the environment in human history behind, for example, Cantre'r Gwaelod, 'The Drowned Hundred', which was written in response to a proposal from *The Guardian* to publish poems about climate change, and the ancient drowned forest on a beach in Ceredigion, 'land overwhelmed by the rising sea'.⁵⁵ Her poem 'Cantre'r Gwaelod' begins in a past which is made by cosmic energies and extremes of weather and invokes ghostly echoes of the biblical flood in Genesis:

> The morning after, the beach at Borth
> is a graveyard, a blackened forest
> thundered out of the sand by the storm,
> drowned by the sea six hundred years ago
> ...
> Relics of stilted walkways tell their story:
> how they walked over water between trees
> longing for a land when the sea-god stole it,
> how they fled, shouldering children,
> with every creature that could crawl, run, fly,
> till time turned truth to myth.⁵⁶

Myth has always been important to Clarke. She says herself: 'My first bookcase was full of folk and fairy tale and the mythologies of several cultures, and my head full not only of Enid Blyton but also of the Mabinogion.'⁵⁷ Her father not only introduced her to Celtic myth and mythologies, as noted in the Introduction, but in his retelling of them, as Clarke says in her own words, 'offered me a place in the myth, and gave myth and naming a place in my imagination'.⁵⁸ Armstrong identifies two aspects of myth – 'the expression of a universal desire for transcendence and liberation from the constraints of the human condition' and the quest for 'a new level of spiritual attainment'⁵⁹ – which conflate the political and the 'spiritual' dimensions of myth in Clarke's poetry. Clarke's own experience of myth taught her that 'the true geography of myth lies in the mind'.⁶⁰ But as Armstrong points out, mythology is an art form and, like 'any powerful work of art invades our being and changes it forever'.⁶¹ She points out that 'a mythical narrative is designed to push us beyond the safe certainties of the familiar world into the unknown'.⁶²

Much of what Armstrong insightfully says about myth comes to the fore in Clarke's 'Cantre'r Gwaelod'. The poem, and the commentary which accompanies it in *Roots Home*, exemplifies how Clarke interlinks mythology, protest and perspectives on the cosmos. Providing an opportunity for Clarke to perceive myth as constituted of mythology, history and archaeology, 'Cantre'r Gwaelod' is a story that is more than simply narrative. Having haunted Welsh culture and the human mind since ancient times, it has entered Welsh consciousness. Not surprisingly, the entry in Clarke's journal on 'The Drowned Forest', November 2018, begins: 'While trees are sleeping, I turn my mind to the haunted woodlands ... the ghostly upheaval of an ancient drowned forest on a beach in Ceredigion.'⁶³

In her journal, Clarke's thinking about 'Cantre'r Gwaelod', which demonstrates myth's capacity to push us beyond safe states, merges with her interest in cosmology, the unpredictability of the universe and, especially, the extent to which the cosmos is amenable to life (discussed in Chapter 2): 'In the early 2000s, during a particularly violent Atlantic storm ... and other storms in subsequent years, ever more frequent due to the increasing results of global warming, huge tide-surges sucked and loosened tons of sand, washing it from the shore.'⁶⁴ Myth for Clarke is an art form that is embellished by archaeological discovery, and is a fulcrum for stories that tell us that how it was in a past cosmology is relevant to our present way of thinking. As she says, all mythologies 'have arisen from human accounts of real events as they were understood ... by an event's first witnesses'; myth's 'function is a way of human messaging' and 'the traditions of storytelling are a framework for words and images to convey what people experienced, believed and saw in their lifetime'.[65] Her thinking about the drowned forest unfolds through, and revolves around, three images: the scattered tree stumps as the blackened remains of a great forest; walkways constructed by a community of people to pass over waterlogged land; and huge tide-sucking storm surges. The content in these images – tree stumps, storms and walkways – do not exist on their own terms but within a larger cosmological structure on which we and other living and non-living forms depend.

As observed in Chapter 2, looking back on the past through archaeology is rather like looking down on Earth from a spacecraft; it makes us appreciate the fragility and preciousness of our planet and of the living and non-living forms upon it. The vivid account of the storms and tides that unveiled more of the drowned forest and the picture of an ancient community using walkways to cope with the rising waters are reflections of our planet and ourselves in the twenty-first century as likely to lose our homelands to the rising sea. Clarke's 'Cantre'r Gwaelod' begins: 'We must use poetry to protest.'[66] But she also sees myth as an art of protest, a case which once again Armstrong expresses eloquently: 'crucially, we need good myths that help us to venerate the earth as sacred once again, because unless there is a spiritual revolution that challenges the destructiveness of our technological genius, we will not save the planet.'[67]

'Cantre'r Gwaelod' uses ancient ways of looking at the cosmos – the Earth as flat – to make the passage of time more realisable and to suggest that every age has its own cosmological perspective that defines it. The ancient peoples that are invoked through the drowned forest employ mythology to make sense of the cosmos and the principal events that occur within it. Thus, the rising sea levels are not understood in terms of climate change but land being stole by the 'sea-god'.[68] The examples of the effects of climate change in our age – the seas rising because of meltwater, a bungalow lost in a cliff fall, a 'monstrous tide' ripping up a coastal rail track, a thousand-year-old oak felled and a seaside promenade almost swept away – are all local stories which have acquired a folklorist and mythical quality.[69] Like the drowned forest, they combine the human capacity to mythologise and turn real events into story in ways that invest the destructive potential of cosmic energy with awe and emblematise the human exceptionalism which has failed to treat the planet with sufficient respect.

'Cantre'r Gwaelod' builds up a catalogue of loss in which individual elements in themselves – the lovesick salmon, mating hares in the March wind, the way birds such as red kites use the thermal currents, bees 'mooning for honey' and butterflies swarming – encapsulate a disappearing natural world with all its beauty and wonder. Each is invoked as related elements within a wider, overarching 'chant' of loss which almost becomes more important than the individual examples within it. I say 'almost' because the accumulating sense of loss – 'Grieve for lost wilderness'[70] the poem insists – becomes all the more profound and psychologically destabilising because of the deep, loving sense of connectivity in each of the examples cited. The historical and archaeological voice with which 'Cantre'r Gwaelod' opens develops into, and culminates in, a voice of protest at 'the balance of things undone by money, / the indifferent hunger of the sea'.[71]

How far the petrified forest has entered into the Welsh imagination, and acquired different perspectives at different times, is the subject of a poem by one of Clarke's younger contemporaries, Samantha Wynne-Rhydderch, in which the drowned forest becomes 'the floating forest':

> Sometimes we call it the petrified forest,
> As if the forest itself is terrified
> of the situation in which it finds itself,
> and cannot move from the seabed,
> or as if we are terrified that this
> is what our Land will turn into
> taking us with it.[72]

But, as in Clarke's poem, the forest is an omen pointing to the future. Both are writing about, and experiencing, extremes of weather at a time when it is a key theme in environmental writing and climate historians are focusing on the often-overlooked importance of the weather and climate disasters in the history of Wales. In 'Cantre'r Gwaelod', Clarke turns, as suddenly and dramatically as the Borth storm, to the future which has already elbowed itself into the present. As the environmental writer Erica Gies observes, the toll of this kind of devastation 'on our mental and emotional health is difficult to fathom, especially because the dominant culture glosses over it, a form of gaslighting'.[73] The emotional impact of the extremes of weather on us is the subject of the next section.

EXTREME WEATHER AND HUMAN EMOTION

The environmentalist Timothy Morton includes extremes of weather in the phenomena for which he coined the term 'hyperobjects' that are 'massively distributed in time and space relative to humans'.[74] According to Morton, they are '*viscous* which means that they "stick" to beings that are involved with them', but they are 'nonlocal' and 'involve profoundly different temporalities than the human scale ones we are used to'.[75] The viscosity with which extremes of weather and climate have impacted on Clarke's writing and psyche exemplifies Morton's point that hyperobjects are 'changing human art and experience'.[76] In her work, as in Hughes's *Tywydd Mawr*, extremes of weather are changing, to adopt Morton's words, 'the possibility of transcendental leaps "outside" physical reality'.[77]

The dark undercurrent in Clarke's poetry which stems from the viscosity which Morton describes propels it into what he labels 'the Age of Asymmetry'[78] – an epoch characterised by our enmeshed coexistence with hyperobjects.[79] For Clarke, as for Morton, propulsion into this Age of Asymmetry is a psychic as well as a physical phenomenon. As Morton says: 'Knowledge is no longer able to achieve escape velocity from Earth, or more precisely ... the surging "towering" reality of things.'[80] And 'knowing more about hyperobjects is knowing more about how we are hopelessly fastened to them.'[81] At the time of completing this book, the BBC Scotland internet news carried a story of a climate change activist giving up her PhD on melting ice caps and rising sea levels – themes which, as I discuss, Clarke addresses in her poetry. Realising that the physics behind climate change had not changed in her lifetime nor was likely to, propelled her into what is now becoming known as 'eco-anxiety', a condition that presents itself, as in Clarke's poetry and journals, 'as a chronic sense of hopelessness and fear of environmental doom'.[82] The article exemplifies, as Clarke's writings, the growing recognition that 'eco-anxiety', sometimes even referred to as 'eco-grief', affects mental and physical health.[83]

An aspect of climate change that runs as a dark undercurrent throughout Clarke's poetry is what Smith calls 'exponential growth', how 'a small uncertainty will grow exponentially fast in a chaotic system'.[84] Her post-1990 poems regularly return to how uncertainty in the weather and the impact of global warming will, as Smith says, 'surpass any linear growth'.[85] This is evident, for example, throughout

Clarke's *A Recipe for Water* (2009) but especially in two of the collection's most disturbing poems: 'The Rising Tide' and 'Cattle, Hayfield, Storm'. Each of these poems underscores the distinction between climate change modelling and weather forecasting in that the former, as Smith points out, 'often contains a "what if" component'.[86] 'The Rising Tide' ponders the consequences of rising sea levels in Cardiff that are perceived as evident already in the increased water activity beneath the city and within the graves in its cemeteries: 'The city knows it in its bones, / in the skulls of the dead.'[87] The opening line of 'The Rising Tide' refers to the physical city and to the bones of its dead. But it is ambiguous and may also be read as meaning the inhabitants sensing – feeling in their bones as the colloquialism goes – the trauma of climate change. They – like the city as a physical entity – are said to listen to their 'own heart murmur' and the 'pulse of water' in their arteries – a reminder that the human body consists of 80 per cent water. Both the city as a whole and individuals within it feel the anxiety and pressure of living with the insecurity facing themselves and life around them. The account of physical changes – 'Salts bloom on basement walls. / House-walls crack in summer drought, / the heave of winter rain'[88] – reflect the extent to which human settlement, even with its most sophisticated engineering, is susceptible to cosmic change but also suggests that it may soon be submerged – as in the imagery of everyday objects beneath river silt and the weight of the sea with which the poem opens. Gies observes:

> Insecurity around the behaviour and availability of water is destabilizing. It is natural to feel anxiety, depression, despair, anger, grief in the face of these losses, bleak-looking future, and the prevailing human systems that seem unwilling to change, even though the need for transformation is obvious.[89]

It almost goes without saying that the submergence of human communities beneath water has a special resonance in Welsh history and culture. In 1965, Tryweryn valley near Bala was drowned in order to provide a new reservoir to improve the water supply to Liverpool despite the fact that it included the village of Capel Celyn, one of the last monoglot Welsh communities (a subject returned to in Chapter 4). The catalogue of the evidence of the rising water-table in the buildings in 'The Rising Tide' betray not only physical and environmental changes but their psychological impact and the extent to which we are mentally unprepared for what is to come: 'the streets will become a delta, / terraces afloat, reflective'.[90]

The background to 'Cattle, Hayfield, Storm' is climate change bringing about not only more violent storms across some parts of the globe but longer, hotter periods of drought in others. The theme of the poem is the psychological impact of the environmental disruption and destruction brought about by climate change and the industrial processes and pollution that have caused it. At the heart of the psychological, as well as physical, disturbance underpinning this poem is the atomisation, as suggested by the three-word title, of environmental elements which were once part of a more coherent natural order. Just as 'The Rising Tide' developed the concept in 'Severn' of the river turning, 'Cattle, Hayfield, Storm' returns to, and examines further, the psychological as well as the physical impact of storms which Clarke raised in her earlier poem, 'Storm Awst' (1978). The cattle outside become increasingly disturbed, galloping ahead of the incoming storm and seeking refuge in the hedge. The way in which the rain-clouds are compared with the cattle – 'a herd of squalls / shove and shoulder' – betrays how the climactic disturbance enters all parts of nature – trees, animals and even the mountains appear to brace themselves for the 'stampede of rain-storms'.[91] But this is not simply a poem about change in the weather, however extreme, and not even solely about what is happening in a relatively small portion of the planet. It encapsulates the uncontrollable volatility of the cosmos; the poem concludes disturbingly with an image of the daylight moon, shutting 'its one mad eye'[92] as the storm rolls in. The image implicitly conflates the mythology around the lunar influence on tides, waves and winds; the volatility and violence of the cosmos which exists alongside, and simultaneously beyond, periods of benevolent calm; and the awe, fear and insecurity which the cosmos inspires. The poem appears to be a plea that the planetary systems will return to a more benevolent state at some point in the future. In fact, this influences the way in which Clarke writes about the eclipse of the moon in her journal where it becomes an expression of one of her deepest fears: 'In eclipse it was just stone. No longer goddess, but a sad stone, looking close and ordinary enough to pluck from the sky, the more moving for being just a pebble … That's our shadow, Earth's shadow that has put out its light.'[93]

Clarke's poetry is permeated with examples of weather and climate change that encourage us to re-think the weather systems of which Magnason speaks, and receive them with a new attentiveness and a newfound sense of awe. As Sophie Laniel-Musitelli says, Clarke's post-1990 poetry 'inspired by climate science, rearticulates the local and the global, inscribing Wales within the broader challenges the Anthropocene poses to poetry'[94] – the era in which humans are primarily responsible for climate, environmental and global changes. Morton maintains: 'When you feel raindrops, you are experiencing climate, in some sense. In particular you are experiencing the climate change known as global warming. But you are never directly experiencing global warming as such … it's massively distributed in time and space.'[95] But while Clarke would seem to accept that hyperobjects, as Morton says, 'force us to acknowledge the immanence of thinking to the physical', she does not believe that hyperobjects mean that we are not '"embedded" in a "lifeworld"'.[96] 'Cattle, Hayfield, Storm' and 'Storm Awst', for example, move from their principal subject, the storm, through widening circles to how non-humans, through instinct and bodily knowledge, are able to read the weather as part of their 'lifeworld' more effectively than humans. In 'Storm Awst', Clarke documents 'the gulls coming in white, / Lapwings gathering, the sheep too / Calling all night'[97] and in 'Cattle, Hayfield, Storm', she captures not only the animals' heaviness but their rootedness in their environment: 'cattle galumphing away ahead of the rumpus / to hunker in hedge and ditch'.[98]

As Clarke's work has developed over more than half a century, its exploration of the links between the local and the non-local have become deeper. The violence associated with August storms is a recurring theme in her journal even in the latter part of the second decade of the twenty-first century. In an entry on 8 August 2019, Clarke is continually thinking about weather systems and the events associated with them as linked to an immediate environment but also to a repetitive pattern of planetary events. At one level, the August storm is part of the locale of west Wales – it 'will come, because it always does'[99] – but the systems moving over the planet are constantly changing, emblematising the impact of climate change. In the following year, as we have seen, Clarke laments despairingly how, in late August, an August storm 'brought a rage of Atlantic hurricanes, tantrums of wind and rain, one after another, ripping summer to rags'.[100] The final image here – 'ripping summer to rags' – is a powerful rendition of how her understanding of the storm has deepened as the storms themselves. But the journal also reveals her widening appreciation of the weather at Blaen Cwrt as part of a global system. Two years earlier, in October 2018, she recorded: 'This October there is no ice ... only unseasonably warm days and nights, wild Atlantic winds, hurling torrential rain, the rags and remnants of transatlantic hurricanes.'[101] The language seems to strain to capture fully the impact of the extreme weather which is ripping apart not only the seasons but belief in the wider amenability of the cosmos to life.

Such interest in examples of extreme weather can be easily traced back through the Welsh press to the 1930s and 1920s and beyond. At one level, it is part of what Iestyn Hughes describes in *Tywydd Mawr* as 'a peculiar delight in storm watching'.[102] As he points out, photographs from the 1930s record the fascination that waves breaking over the promenade had for many residents and visitors to Aberystwyth. When such pictures are examined closely, they show people of various ages – most of them in long protective coats – drawn to watch waves crashing higher than the university hall of residence at the end of the promenade.[103] The observers appear to be choosing what they believe are safe positions where they can enjoy being shocked and made apprehensive – no doubt enjoying being nervous and scared. These photographs are juxtaposed with others, one from 1938 which depicts the damage to cottages and the pier by storm waves and several photographs of the impact of the 2013 storm on Aberystwyth's front.[104] While some of the individual photographs examine the conflicting psychological forces that underpin that 'peculiar delight' in storm watching of which Hughes speaks, viewed in relation to each other, Hughes's Aberystwyth photographs reach into the awe and ambivalence of the cosmos itself.

Stuart Clark observes that in recent years, 'a number of studies have found that the emotion of awe ... can have a transformative effect on our lives. It makes people feel more altruistic, less stressed, less time-pressured and less materialistic'.[105] This is a recurring motif in Gillian Clarke's work where animals and birds are seen in ways that humble the human observer. In 'Tawny Owl', one of the new poems that she included in *Selected Poems* (1985), the 'Plain song of owl / moonlight' marking the 'stations of the dark'[106] fills the poet with a sense of the sublime, articulated in imagery that has a biblical connotation – 'tabernacle', 'stations of the dark' and 'a flame that floats on oil'[107] – that imbues the bird with a priestly quality possessed of knowledge and awareness that transcends the everyday but is also embodied in it. Through her song, presence and nearness to the poet, the owl brings a sense of quiet and calm, 'the wash / behind the wave'.[108]

Smith concludes that 'prophecy is difficult, it is never clear which context science will adopt next, but the fact that chaos has changed the goal posts may well be its most enduring impact on science'.[109] One of Clarke's poems in which this is especially evident is 'Glacier' from *A Recipe for Water* (2009). One of her most emphatic poems on climate change, it seems a very contemporary poem, but it reclaims a much older mode of writing. Fascination with glaciers is something that her work shares with the geologically inspired nature writing that emerged in the Victorian period. Clarke's work shares with this writing an interest in water flowing ominously underground and/or moving out of human sight. For example, the Victorian poet John Lubbock describes how 'below the *névé* lies a glacier, on, in, and under which the water runs in a thousand little streams, eventually emerging at the end ... encumbered and concealed by earth and stone'.[110] In the network of streams, outside human visibility, and the encumbered earth beneath the movement of the ice, there is a sense of power and a destructive energy which might be overlooked. In 'Glacier', Clarke is similarly not so much inspired by the vast majesty of the Greenland glacier as its slow, inevitable movement – 'sliding nine miles a year towards the sea'.[111]

Clarke's work, and 'Glacier' particularly, shares with the geologically inspired nature writers of the nineteenth century a sense of a destructive kind of cosmic energy. This is explicit in the way in which she, like Lubbock, depicts the erosive waters and ice as involved in a kind of conflict with the solid rocks, albeit themselves once molten liquid:

> Then arises a struggle between rock and river, but the river is always victorious in the end; even if damned back for a while, it concentrates its forces, rises up the rampart of rock, rushes over triumphantly, resumes its original course, and gradually carries the enemy away.[112]

But, as a Welsh poet, Clarke cannot help but link the movement of glaciers for which humans are ultimately responsible with the human-made slag heaps of her south Wales childhood and with the movement of one slag heap in particular, in Aberfan on 21 October 1965, 'loosened by a slip / of rain-swollen mountain streams'.[113] In 'Glacier' she recalls how that slag heap moved relentlessly forward until it submerged a junior school and a row of houses. In her linking of the two phenomena, Clarke displays the awesome realisation of the power in the mesh of streams beneath them. The slag heap's disturbingly relentless descent toward the school is carefully captured in an almost cinematic presentation with a first-hand witness-like account of the noise which announced it beginning to slide.

The hyperbolic attack on science for its 'tricks and alchemies'[114] and the unloosening structures of Clarke's poem itself as it proceeds, mirroring the movement of the glacier and slag heap, locates the two disasters firmly in the Anthropocene epoch. The comparison of the melting glacier with the movement of the coal tip caused by rain-swollen mountain streams gives the prospect of the horror of climate change a devastating reality as a consequence of industrialisation and a lack of respect for the environment and the wider natural and cosmic order.[115] The indifference toward the animal life of Greenland – the polar bear and the arctic fox – mirrors that shown the families and homes of the south Wales mining communities by the National Coal Board. The politics around each of these events – the melting of the ice caps and the Aberfan disaster – concerns those who act for themselves at the expense of others and fail to appreciate the interrelationship of life and the environment. Thus, 'Glacier' is intended not only as a wake-up call to how we are destroying the planet – emphasised in the way in which the glacier and the coal tip are described in cosmic and apocalyptic terms – but a call to science to devote itself to find a means of reversing what is happening.

In choosing to mention the polar bear and the Arctic fox in the course of 'Glacier', Clarke pointedly selects two of the most iconic victims of climate change. Between them, they signify the extent of habitats threatened by sea ice loss extending across the Arctic regions of Canada, Greenland/Denmark, Norway, Russia and the United States.[116] Polar bears rely on sea ice as a platform from which to hunt seals, while the Arctic fox faces numerous threats from the loss of the tundra and the depletion of animals and birds on which they feed.[117] But in recognising the psychological impact of such events, 'Glacier' is a link poem between *A Recipe for Water* (2009) and *Ice* published three years later which explores the psychological impact of snow and icebound landscapes, as discussed in the next section.

SNOWSCAPE

Just as 'Making the Beds for the Dead' (2004) – discussed in Chapter 1 – examines the individual and collective consequences of the foot-and-mouth outbreak in north Wales in 2001, *Ice* (2012) turns to the snowbound winters of 2009 and 2010 which left 'motorways muffled in silence, lorries stranded / like dead birds, airports closed, trains trackless'.[118] The familiar landscape disappeared beneath what Clarke calls in 'Ice Music', 'the deepening geography of snow'.[119] Although several of the poems in *Ice* address how the unexpectedly heavy snowfalls disrupted, and even brought an end to, everyday life, the main focus in the volume is on their psychological impact – the mental and bodily change that took place, with many people experiencing for the first time the emotion of awe – an intense emotional elevation – in looking out on the vast expanse of snow and ice.

The severe snowfalls bring about what Clarke describes in 'White Nights', echoing that brought about by the suspension of flights across Europe in 2010 following the eruption of the Icelandic volcano at Eyjafjallajökull (discussed in Chapter 2), as a particular silence 'like the world gone deaf'[120]. The volume *Ice*, as in the poems 'Ice Music' and 'Freeze 1947', explores the psychological change this causes in people. As the volume progresses, the emphasis in the poems shift from a primary focus on sight to hearing or rather a loss of what we are used to hearing as when, as in 'Freeze 1947', the sea was 'struck dumb' and even 'birds held their tongues'.[121] Anticipating Clarke's later volume about silence more generally, *The Silence* (2024) (introduced in Chapter 2), Clarke's poems about ice are a reflection on silence – in this volume, as part of the wider psychological impact of the snowscape, of the 'forever's frozen air' and waking to a 'garden that hasn't stirred'.[122] The power in this ostensibly simple image of a frozen garden lies in the disappearance of the emotional bonds between plants and ourselves which gardens provide. As the environmental writer Samantha Walton, contemplating the spiritual significance of gardens, says: 'But with plants, ecological processes become our friends and familias, tangible and reminding us of the wider world of which we are a part.'[123]

As we turn from poem to poem in *Ice*, individual texts work together to turn the snowscape into as much an internalised as an external phenomenon. For example, 'Ice Music' begins with the poet looking down on the frozen river Ely in Cardiff which enters the poet's psyche in a gothic-like image – 'I show you the silver bones of the river / afloat on black water'[124] – which invokes the skeletons of dead fish within and beneath the ice and suggests, as rivers do in

Clarke's work, the darkness of the collective unconsciousness of the Anthropocene. But in the poem's concluding lines, where the primary sense is hearing, the stillness of the snowscape is supplanted by what can be heard in the new quiet – the expanding ice expressing itself in sounds – its 'moan' and 'cry' – associated with pain and loss.[125]

The snowscape poems allude to the epoch in which, as the geologist Richard Fortey says, 'a great Ice Age, centred on the South Pole ... spread its refrigeration almost completely around the world'[126] but also return us, as in 'White Nights', to the experience of winter which Clarke imagines her more immediate ancestors, like Marged, endured. But within their various and shifting timescales, the poems reverberate with each other to highlight and probe what Clarke in 'Snow' calls 'snow's sensational'.[127] In unveiling this concept, the sensory awareness in these poems shifts not only from sight to hearing but, as in 'Snow', even to taste: the snow-bound world, in which the impression of whiteness and blackness is magnified, 'tastes / of ice and fire'.[128] The poem is structured so as to take the reader into new sensory experiences which the 'snow sensational' brings: 'Listen! / Ice is whispering. Night darkens, / the mercury falls in the glass, glistening.'[129]

The expression 'snow sensational' invokes sublimity – as described by Robert Clewis in Chapter 2 – meaning the intense feelings, and the sense of emotional elevation, experienced before events and objects that are awe-inspiring. But in her response to the presence of ice or snow on such a vast and disruptive scale, Clarke suggests that the sublime is a complex confusion of satisfying and discomforting elements. 'In the Bleak Midwinter' opens with an image of winter trees standing like skeletons but envisages the spring when, like humans who mirror trees, they will become reacquainted with 'how to weep, bleed, bud, grow rings'.[130] In this mesh of discombobulating elements, 'In the Bleak Midwinter', which almost too obviously invokes a specific carol, encapsulates the way in which carols, as Clarke highlights in an accompanying poem in *Ice* 'Carols of the Birds', tell 'of pain and blood, / the troubles of a restless world'.[131] This rendering of carols is a summary of how Clarke perceives the Anthropocene.

But *Ice* amounts to more than simply a critique of the Anthropocene or an examination of how it has brought about climate change and disturbingly extreme weather systems. Through unveiling her concept of 'snow sensational', Clarke invokes an intense affective (or sensory) element which determines the aesthetics of *Ice* as a whole, giving its poems a distinctive emotional dimension. 'In the Bleak Midwinter', like much of the volume *Ice*, develops one of the major questions in the philosophy of the sublime, which Clarke first raised in her earlier poem 'Storm Awst': the relation between the observer and the object. As Clewis says, the sublime can refer to a person's emotions but it can also be applied to what elicits those responses, such as glaciers, waterfalls, raging storms, starry skies and mountain ranges – all of which are recurring subjects in Clarke's poetry. The philosophical conundrum which Clewis identifies is encapsulated nowhere in Clarke's work more effectively than in the closing lines of 'In the Bleak Midwinter'. While the winter trees are said in a stunning pithy phrase to be 'dreaming green', the ice, in an equally stirring image, 'unfurls its foliage / on gutter, gate and hedge, / ghost-beauty cold as snow'.[132] Within the aesthetic of the sublime that unfolds in 'In the Bleak Midwinter', and in her work of and from the 1990s, Clarke moves beyond the extent to which 'Storm Awst' engages with the sublime, not only examining the relation between the participant observer and the awe-inspiring event or object but the distinction itself between 'wonder' and 'sublimity'. This deepens the profundity of many of the poems in *Ice*, especially those concerned with winterscapes – such as 'Freeze 1947', 'Freeze 2010' and 'The Dead After the Thaw' – which place pleasure and displeasure, as do many psychologists as Clewis points out, on a spectrum.[133] The aesthetic experience with which *Ice* provides the reader is mixed and contradictory providing exhilaration, enjoyment and satisfaction in nature and the cosmos but also disquiet, discomfort and pain.

Walton emphasises that the attraction of the sublime has been situated in a 'blend of horror and safety'.[134] As she says, as for those in the pictures who view the dangerously stormy seas at Aberystwyth in Iestyn Hughes's *Tywydd Mawr*, if a threat comes close enough it can work what she calls 'a strange magic in the mind' turning 'shocking sensation into deep reverence' in which awe becomes 'overpowering' and 'addictive'.[135] The security of home is invoked repeatedly throughout *Ice*: for example, in 'White Nights' in 'the deep drift of the duvet' and in wartime bedrooms. But Clewis points out that the 'reality' of the safe position is always dependent upon the person experiencing it.[136] In this regard, *Ice* probes how the interrelationship between awe and fear invoked by the sublime is different from the experience of what Clewis calls 'plain, uncontrollable fear'.[137] This is achieved in 'Freeze 1947', one of the poems in which the reader might feel very intensely the pull of the wild, through the use of allusion to magic, myth and fantasy in the transformation of the natural world to a frozen garden, trees to stone statues and rugs made from polar bear skins coming back to life.

READING THE ICE CRYSTAL

The deepening psychology of the sublime in *Ice* reverberates with a different kind of cosmology – the ways in which we perceive and try to understand the cosmos – from that which informs much of Clarke's work of the 1970s and 1980s. At one point, Clarke links the expansion of ice to movement within the earth's crust envisaging 'a timpini of plates colliding'.[138] The reference to expanding ice, within the context of contemporary scientific thinking about the cosmos, alludes once again to the fine balance on which the Earth exists in the Anthropocene. This is encapsulated in *Ice* in the recurring images of crystallisation. As Gleick observes, snowflakes in new science are seen as 'products of imbalance to the flow of energy' – invoking the formative energy in matter and in the wider cosmos – and as water crystallises it is seen as forming 'a growing tip with a boundary that becomes unstable and sends off side-branches'.[139] Gleick's account of the metamorphosis that creates the snowflake – or ice crystal – and which then brings about a series of transformations within it returns us to the discussion as to how chaos and order within even simple systems give rise to randomness and irregularity but also complexity. In respect of balance and imbalance, the cosmologist Neville Brown reminds us that even if the universe were to 'expand slightly faster than it is doing it would be destined to disperse continuously' but if it were to expand more slowly, it would collapse in upon itself.[140] But *Ice* links this concept of fine balance in the cosmos to what the writer on mythology Jules Cashford calls 'the essential paradox' in which the mind is led 'beyond the frame of the senses' to 'the cycle, the whole' that is 'invisible, yet contains the visible phases'.[141]

In addressing the psychological impact of severe snow storms and the way they transform geography, nature, human and non-human life, *Ice* takes the reader, to use Cashford's words, 'beyond the frame of the senses' to something that is elusive and only partially visible. In her journal in 2019, Clarke tries to recall her earliest memories of the polar bear rug – the subject of the opening poem of *Ice*. These memories lie at the boundary between the pre-symbolic in cognitive development when children begin to use symbols for actions, objects and ideas and become imaginatively creative, and the symbolic when symbols are invested in meaning. However, Clarke is not writing simply about memory but what has remained teasingly outside recollection. Much in this memory of the rug revolves around pre-cognitive senses, needs and instincts: 'I rode the Arctic wastes and frozen seas of Barry on his scratchy pelt. I lay close to his head and fed him with pieces of rusk, which my mother later had to "hoover" from his wide-open jaws.'[142] This creation of the rug as an imaginary in which she was cradled as a child – 'I'm dreaming on the white bear's shoulder, / paddling the slow hours, my fingers in his fur'[143] – suggests a child's 'unreal' cosmology in which adults as parents are complicit. In 'Polar', as throughout the volume *Ice*, Clarke, as the grown-up child, is seeking to reclaim the formative energy in matter and in the wider cosmos of which Gleick writes, with 'a boundary that becomes unstable and sends off side-branches'[144]: 'But I want him alive. / I want him fierce.'[145]

The epoch in which Clarke envisages the polar bear in 'Polar' as alive and dangerous is pre-Anthropocene and provides her with an opportunity to reflect on the cosmology which has enabled human kind in the Anthropocene to see themselves, as the historian Dipesh Chakrabarty says, as possessing 'specialness' and 'centrality'[146]: 'and they had not shot the bear, / had not loosed the ice, / had not, had not ...'.[147] This sense of 'had not' is a wish to return to 'when the map of the earth was something we knew by heart',[148] when meaning was known through psychogeography and not simply physical geography. Thaw in this volume of poems, like the killing of the bear and its transformation into a rug, reveals one of the hidden and most disturbing features of human behaviour.

'Freeze 1947', which opens like a fairy story – 'Long ago in the first white world'[149] – as already pointed out, employs myths and fantasy to envisage a world that is 'spellbound' and suspended in time. The first part of the poem depicts this snowscape while the second part focuses on a dead girl discovered in the snow – the 'Babe in the Wood' murder. Invoking the polar bear rug as risen from the dead, Clarke links this poem with 'Polar' through loss of the 'sacredness' of individual life which makes the murder of this girl, like the shooting of the polar bear, possible. Both poems focus on how the transformative energies which bring about order and complexity in ice, snow and the processes of crystallisation, as Gleick says, can also lead to randomness, instability and chaos. This concept is invoked by the dead girl herself who is hidden in both parts of the poem – by the snow and ice which cover her body and then in the way in which the reports of the murder in the newspapers were kept away from the poet when she was a child. As in the case of the polar bear, in her death there is something beyond human comprehension while being a manifestation of the killing, violence and destruction associated with humans in the Anthropocene and separable from the way in which the polar bear intuitively lives and hunts within a wider relationality in nature.

'Freeze 2010', a companion poem to 'Freeze 1947', opens with the kind of bold, matter-of-fact statement that Clarke favoured in her poems in the 1970s and early 1980s: 'A girl found murdered by the road.'[150] It is the voice of the Anthropocene which enters also a further companion poem, 'The Dead after the Thaw', in which the physical and psychological impact of the severe snow and ice is placed in a wider sociopolitical context – echoing the lives and fate of those on the parish in 'Letter from a Far Country' (discussed in Chapter 1) – where it is the poor, the old, the sick and the homeless who are the most vulnerable. The larger context in which Clarke places climate change, and the human responsibility for it, suggesting that it is the less well-off and ill who are most vulnerable to climate change, is a theme that has come to dominate more 'popular' climatological writings. Magnason, for example, resonates with Clarke's work in pointing out:

> To say that we live in a mythological time is not an exaggeration. World leaders meet and *talk about the weather*. It is near-revolutionary that they meet to discuss how they are changing the weather ... But when people lose all they have to floods, droughts and forest fires, they'll turn against the people who created the problems, those very same people.[151]

The poetic voice in *Ice* is appreciative of beauty, order and the sublime (as discussed in Chapter 2), but it becomes increasingly one that is deeply disturbed, preoccupied with changes in the climate and planetary weather systems that are averse to life itself. *Ice* emphasises what the British theologian J. R. Tennant in the 1930s termed the 'anthropic cosmological principle' which has subsequently become a central question, as Brown says, in cosmology: whether the universe is well disposed to life in general.[152] In her journal for the first decade of the new century, Clarke contemplates how, in a media-dominated age, the hostility of the cosmos toward life on Earth is everywhere, affecting her psychologically with fears, as noted in the first part of this chapter, that 'flood, hurricane and earthquake, would shake us off the planet'.[153] The same section of the journal, records a cliff-top walk toward the end of August, 2006, when the sky appears to shed its mask of order and calm and reveal a different face: 'We hasten back along the cliff, driven by the sight of a vast black shower dragging its skirts over the sea from Ireland. Soon we are stung by hailstones and soaked to the skin.'[154] This journal entry suggests that there are two 'emotional' cosmoses in Clarke's writing, the overall argument of this chapter: one cosmos centred on order, beauty and predictability and the other turbulent, presenting uncertainty, and suggesting that chaos may be the fundamental principle within the universe.

The psychological impact of climate change has been succinctly summarised by Gies based on her own experience:

> Trauma triggered by flooding and water scarcity seems to be all around us today. The landscapes where we live are imprinted upon our psyches, freighted with personal and cultural meaning, so when droughts and floods force us to move, we suffer loss. Loss of property and possessions; loss of home and community; loss of beloved landscapes and the distinctive species, weather, sounds, and scents; loss of quality of life. That melancholy I felt as a child, watching stone fruit orchards fall to silicon chips, is a feeling that stalks many of us today.[155]

In the second decade of this new century, the tenor of Clarke's thinking and writing about climate change itself changed. She comes to think of herself, with wider political issues such as Brexit and war in mind, as living in 'broken times', a depressive thought that begins with the observation that 'the seasons are changing' but is linked uncompromisingly to the inescapable 'fact that we are to blame'.[156] During the heatwave following a bitterly cold spell of weather in the last week of February 2019, she admits: 'The unseasonal weather makes me uneasy. I am anxious for the spring foliage, for the pulse of new growth setting buds on the move too soon' and that she 'would be happier to wait for a real and timely spring, an April of opening buds …'.[157] Her journal entries in 2019 suggest that she is having difficulty controlling the extent of her stress and worry over the state of the world: 'Our world is wounded. Australia is burning, Indonesia is flooded. The polar glaciers are melting. Oceans are choked with plastic.'[158] The rhythm of this writing – threatening to rip sentence structure apart we might feel – resonates with the way in which the destabilised planetary systems appear to assume disastrous lives of their own.

At times, Clarke admits that 'like so many others I felt a helpless sorrow at the state of things'.[159] But on other occasions, plain-spoken anger sweeps mealy-mouthed politics aside as responsibility for the destruction of the planet is uncompromisingly apportioned: 'The world is burning, drowning, starving, yet the rich are sated with money.'[160] Clarke's journal, like her poetry, does not simply vacillate between despair and optimism over the state of things. It is a search for solutions, how to keep despair at bay and how to cope with what is happening in the world. How to cope and how to clear her mind of this constant anxiety drive much of her recent writing. As she notes, revealingly, in her journal in 2018: 'Usually a good sleeper in these restless times I wake from a vivid dream several times a night, my head full of words, flocks and paragraphs, rhythms and rhymes and images …'.[161] The turn in Clarke's work toward an increasingly complex and disturbing climatology and cosmology gives it a distinctive contemporary edge and relevance. But it also points toward other scientific concerns including the nature of cosmogenesis itself – the subject of the next chapter.

4

SOUND, WATER, BLACKNESS AND COSMOGENESIS

Gillian Clarke's interconnected interests in cosmology, climatology and nature have developed throughout her career as a writer as a consequence of her intuitive convictions, her changing sense of herself as a poet and the impact of contemporary scientific and environmental perspectives. Although the concept of 'cosmogenesis' first enters her work in the 1970s and 1980s, it has acquired, like her interest in cosmology generally (discussed in Chapter 2), a greater emphasis in her post-1990 poetry and journals.

In his recent publication, *Cosmogenesis: An Unveiling of the Expanding Universe* (2022), the cosmologist Brian Swimme defines cosmogenesis in one, unsurprisingly, rather long sentence:

> The universe began fourteen billion years ago with the emergence of elementary particles in the form of primordial plasma, which quickly morphed into atoms of hydrogen, helium, and lithium; a hundred million years later, galaxies began to appear, and in one of these, the Milky Way, minerals arranged themselves into living cells that constructed advanced life, including evergreen trees, coral reefs, and the vertebrae nervous systems that humans used to discover this entire sequence of universe development.[1]

Like Clarke herself but more explicitly, Swimme acknowledges that it is the central theories of contemporary science – 'quantum mechanics, the second law of thermodynamics, the general theory of relativity, plate tectonics, natural selection, encephalization' – that 'have enabled us to discover our cosmic genesis'.[2] But Swimme's understanding of cosmogenesis provides an especially useful introduction to Clarke's poetry because, like Clarke, he thinks of himself as 'much a development of the universe as were stars and galaxies' and believes that 'the stories of the Earth and universe' must 'include the story of the storyteller'.[3] Clarke's writings about cosmogenesis, like Swimme's work, overlap a personal search for meaning with the science of cosmology in that her poetry, and certainly much of her work of the last few decades, is 'woven around the major features of the expanding universe'.[4]

Swimme points out: 'Not one of the ten thousand previous generations of humans knew the cosmic sequence of transformations that brought us forth.'[5] In the shadow of such an awesome observation, Clarke's long-standing interest in cosmology, the environment, earth sciences and climate (and their part in the development of human consciousness and community) have frequently led to engagements with cosmogenesis and natural phenomena that challenge the limits of the human senses and consciousness. Selecting three phenomena that dominate Clarke's work in the late twentieth and twenty-first centuries – sound, water and blackness – this chapter argues that while her work always retains its immediacy, sensuousness and proximity to the natural world, from the 1990s onwards, it displays a deeper interest in planetary origins and cosmogenesis.

Clarke's poem 'The City' (1998), published in *Five Fields* alongside the poem sequence 'Concerto' discussed in Chapter 2, is, like that poem, the product of her residency at the Bridgewater Hall, Manchester in 1997. One of her most ambitious poems since 'Letter from a Far Country (1982), 'The City', like 'Concerto', is constructed around musical and not simply literary narrative. Each passage has its own rhythms and its own dominant notes and in each the content is never more than the extension of the music.

In 'The City', as in 'Concerto', Clarke is not so much experimenting with music as practising working with music. The reader experiences a kind of sympoiesis – a collective or intersubjective creativity – which seems to be what is driving the poem as much as the cosmos itself. The poem's tightly coordinated themes flow together to suggest an elusive story of musical and cosmic change encapsulated in the poem's notes, refrains and echoes. Its sections entitled 'The Music Hall' and 'Voicing the Organ', especially, focus on how the waves propagated by sound as a vibration are transmitted through gas, liquid or a solid medium and how these have had a key part in cosmic creation.

In accord with this emphasis, the poem juxtaposes two versions of the sublime, one probing the origins of water – 'the beginning / trickling, the beginning of streams, rivers'[6] – and the other highlighting the boundless energy generated by geological movements – 'thundering torrents and the wind roaring over the ice'.[7] The language in each case is different, invested with varying force and energy like the water itself. Music emanating from the vast organ at the Bridgewater Hall transcends its origins but appears to capture the sound waves of the cosmos itself. Marvelling at this phenomenon, Clarke ponders how something that appears to have been hidden in the organ's complex structure, perceived 'like the puzzle of bones of a whale',[8] now stands more fully revealed and she is filled with awe at how such 'tons of machine' can be 'taught to whisper like teaching a glacier to thaw'.[9] Despite its sheer size and the astonishingly capacious notes of which it is capable, the organ has the capacity also, like the cosmos itself, to stir us with quiet, subtle sounds, reflected in the image of the organist listening, 'head cocked as the thrush on the lawn',[10] which recalls the poem's opening birdsong. Through the organ and its auditory structure, the poem participates in creativity and emotion that reaches beyond the limits of human consciousness and hearing.

The way in which 'The City' links cosmogenesis with the vibrations of sound waves reflects a theory of physics that became prominent in the 1960s and 1970s. Although it became discredited in some scientific quarters, its notion that reality is made up of infinitesimal vibrating strings which twist and fold to produce varying effects left an imprint on physics, mathematics, Earth sciences, cosmology and cosmogenesis. In Clarke's work, the, albeit distant, influence of 'string theory' is evident in the possibility, as the physicist Brian Greene suggests, that there is an 'explanatory framework' that is capable of encompassing all forces and all matter and, in which – as in the poem itself – 'everything at its most microscopic level consists of combinations of vibrating strands'.[11] This is an important part of the process by which the chaos of noise is transformed, throughout the poem, miraculously into 'music'. Much of the poem, especially in its employment of lists, consists of patterns of sound which are in essence vibrating waves. Appearing to invoke, consciously or unconsciously, the physics of the 1960s and 1970s, these waves consist of 'particles' – words – whose force and energy are determined by an overall 'oscillatory pattern'.[12] In this regard, cosmogenesis is never far away from Clarke's thinking:

> For the first time after the ice, the high notes,
> first drops out of silence, then the beginning
> of trickling, the beginning of streams, rivers,
> then thundering torrents, and the wind roaring over the ice.
> And with the thaw the pain must begin,
> the cry of an earth that's alive again.[13]

In 'The City', Clarke sees musical instruments producing vibrations in frequencies that our ears receive as musical notes and harmonies, as analogous to the way in which in nature and the cosmos, to use Greene's words, 'everything, all matter and all forces, is unified under the same rubric of microscopic string oscillations – the "notes" that strings can play'.[14] But the expansion and contraction of the sound of the organ brings to mind also the physics of the Big Bang which Swimme describes:

> As this sphere moves forward in time, it evolves under the action of expansion and contraction. That is, as the sphere continues to expand, particular subsets are pulled together via the attraction of gravity. This dual action of expansion and attraction set in motion the creativity that has given rise to every existing entity in the universe.[15]

In this regard, 'The City' is an important poem in Clarke's oeuvre because it conceives of the order within nature and the cosmos as not so much a collection of chaotic things and experiences – which a cursory reading of the poem might suggest – but a manifestation of 'patterns of vibration' by which fundamental parts like particles of sound 'interact and influence one another'.[16]

SOUND, WATER AND THE SUBLIME

The way in which Clarke conceives of sound and its patterning in 'The City', reflecting twentieth-century scientific theory that all matter is unified within a 'singular framework' and consists of particles whose force and charge is determined by that framework, informs her post-1990 work concerned with the flow of water as well as sound. The geo-environmental turn in Clarke's writings after 1990 (discussed in Chapter 5) coincided with an anthology of river poems published in association with the London-based charity Common Ground.[17] Although published in England, the anthology has a strong representation of poems by Welsh writers including two poems by Clarke herself, 'St Winefride's Well (1997) and 'Valley' (1998). Rivers, streams and waterfalls in many of these poems, as in Clarke's poetry generally, are emblematic of the interest among writers and artists in the flow of things in and between the material and natural worlds.

The titular poem in the sequence 'A Recipe for Water' (2009) reminds us of the different minerals involved in the composition of water: '*Calcium, Magnesium, Potassium, Sodium, / Chloride, Sulphate, Nitrate, Iron*'.[18] But, as Sophie Laniel-Musitelli points out, water is then developed in the poem 'as the primordial condition of the apparition of life, circulating freely between the organic and the inorganic'.[19] 'A Recipe for Water' opens with water envisaged 'as the primordial condition of life', flowing in dark underground caverns which are themselves emblematic of the framework which contemporary physics still suggests encompasses all matter. The poem takes pleasure in the music of water's flow, suggesting that water is composed of particles that derive their force and charge, like music, from their singular framework, and delights in the deep luscious rhythms as part of a larger natural order.

Re-establishing the sense of the sublime in water, which modernity seems to be gradually losing, 'A Recipe for Water' unveils the deep connections between the first Welsh syllables children learn to speak, the names of rivers and the sound of flowing water: '*Wysg, Usk. Esk. Wye.*'[20] The awe in a child's early experience of words for rivers is juxtaposed with the sensuous pleasure to be found in water itself, conveyed mostly in the kind of simple, active words – 'suck', 'lap', 'spill', 'drops' – which children first learn and in patterns that reverberate within the singular frame of the experience, epitomised in the image of a 'cup of two hands':

> the suck and lap as a small pool ripples
> in the cup of two hands,
> an ecstasy of spill, on skin, hair, mouth,
> drops beading the dust.[21]

This appreciation of the sensory pleasure – the 'ecstasy' – in water provides new insights into how the experience of water in drinking and washing – 'head back, eyes closed, mouth open'[22] – gave rise, Clarke suggests, to the first words for water across many languages and how these words often sought to capture its taste and feel. But her choice of an image of 'the cup of two hands' is scientifically interesting. As Swimme says, 'if you cup your hands together as if getting water from a stream, approximately seven thousand photons of light from the dawn of time pass through the space between the palms of your hands each instant.'[23] The child, to use Swimme's words, 'is in *physical contact* with the very origin of the universe'.[24]

In examining the physical sensation of rain and water in the body itself, and not simply on the surface of the skin, 'A Recipe for Water' deepens our appreciation of the cosmos as an 'embodied' phenomenon and the way in which rain and water acquire different properties in different environments and seasons. The suggestion in 'A Recipe for Water' that the dry spell is about to end is felt through the senses – frost slipping, ice loosening, a breeze in the air and a hint of rain. It causes Clarke to reflect (as noted in Chapter 2) that some ancient peoples were more advanced than many of us today in their intuitive, cosmic awareness: 'No wonder they felt the need to appease the gods. We know, and they knew, that if we hurt the planet, we die.'[25] This need, translated into our early-twenty-first-century situation, inspires one of her most disturbing images relating to climate change: 'all the world's spare water stacked miles deep / in the waking ice of the glacier'.[26] This resonates with an important point that the environmental writer Andri Magnason makes, 'if we could perceive in granular detail what the words 'global warming contain, they should be like the threat in the fairy tale, we should feel terror'.[27]

THE SEVERN

'Severn', another poem sequence in *A Recipe for Water*, reclaims a sense of wonder at the different stages of a river's life, capturing its gentle sublimity at quiet moments but also the power into which it eventually builds. The inspiration behind Clarke's writing is increasingly diverse in the 1990s and subsequent decades and 'Severn' is no exception. The opening poem of the sequence, 'A Barge on the Severn', is based on a painting by Colin Jones depicting the river losing itself and its name to the sea in its estuary. By contrast, the second poem, 'Source' – as the title suggests – is based on a journey to the origins of the river which provides Clarke with a much quieter experience. The pleasure that she finds in the mountains is not in the vastness of space which many eighteenth- and nineteenth-century writers celebrated. Standing at the source of the Severn, Clarke feels what the environmentalist Samantha Walton usefully describes as coming from 'the slipping of boundaries between the self and the place, and the escape (even if it is momentary) from social being'.[28]

In this experience of the 'slipping of boundaries' at a point of origin – of cosmogenesis – Clarke becomes aware of pulsating vibrations in the waters and the sound they make in running through, and from, their underground channels and how each vibration carries a force that is determined by the different gradients over which the headwaters move. At the source of the Severn, Clarke carefully chooses words to convey the bodily experience of walking through bogland – 'plodding', 'squelch' and the 'muscle of pooling water' – and the feel of the vibrations generated by the energy of water under pressure – 'hurtling', 'shove its way', 'fluent under bridges'.[29] However, these words are not presented as single sounds and vibrations but as patterns that interact with each other, suggesting something of the deep time in which the river originated. Drawing on the experience of childbirth, as Clarke often does in her work, the underground location of the river's waters are felt as a 'pulsating placenta' and come 'gurgling' out of the earth as if it were a womb.[30]

The different ways in which rivers like the Severn are experienced in its different stages enhances their mythologisation and places the presence of water deities in many cultures and religions in a wider context. This is the subject of the third poem in the Severn sequence, 'Sabrina'. While the opening poem of the sequence, 'A Barge on the Severn', is concerned with the history of the river, the focus of 'Sabrina' is on mythology which the poem perceives as coming before so-called 'real' history. At one level, stories of river and water deities are attempts to explain in relation to water the origins of landscape, the cosmos and the phenomena of birth and death. But they also exemplify the potential of art to heal, transform and clarify life journeys. Walton points out that it is almost impossible to find a culture or religion without its own water deity, 'a health-bringing spirit of the spring, river or coast'.[31] In many cosmologies and faiths, as Walton says, water is a 'primal metaphor of cleansing, nourishment and renewal' and running water is regarded as sacred.[32]

But Clarke's poem takes an innovative approach to myths of water deities by focusing on the sensory experience of water, the changing nature of rivers and the physical energy generated by and encapsulated in currents: 'In the sway of the currents the white limbs / Of a girl caught in a shoal of silvers / Turning and turning in the turbulence.'[33] In order to capture the pulsations as effectively as possible in her oscillatory patterns of sound, to get as close as she can to the river's energy, Clarke strips her writing to only one or two words before lifting, like the sound of the river itself, into a longer phrase: 'Among migrating salmon, sewin, elvers, / Lampreys, eels taking their ancient water-roads.'[34] While the narrative of the drowned daughter of a faithless man is but a story, the myths about water deities are integrated with the sound and vibration of the river currents and add to the sublimity and sense of mystery around them.

King and Clifford remind us that 'the variegation found in a single river valley and the differences among catchments are part of the workings of nature, time and geology'.[35] Clarke's fourth poem in 'A Recipe for Water', 'Ice', recalls a way of thinking that informs 'The Stone Poems' (in *Making the Beds for the Dead*, 2004) (discussed in Chapter 5) with an emphasis not on seasonal time or cosmological cycles but geological æons – the daughter in 'Sabrina' is said to have drowned between the Ice Age and the Stone Age. The river in the 'Severn' sequence acquires an awe that is rooted not only in the different phases of its course, but, anticipating *Ice* (2012), discussed in Chapter 3, in its pre-history including the freezing of its estuary during an ice age and the later slow thaw that enabled the movement of the melting glaciers. In this regard, it is especially ironic that millions of years later *Homo sapiens*, who flourished following the thawing of the ice age as a result of warmer temperatures, evolved to become responsible for a planet in which the Arctic is melting, threatening catastrophic – if not apocalyptic – environmental damage and climate change (as discussed in Chapter 3).

As one of the most powerful poems in 'Severn', 'Ice' arises from Clarke's interest in the influence of the river's course on human settlement and development – it 'let loose / the coal, iron, limestone, clay, / that would change the world'[36] – which reflects the 'human turn' in geology in her work and the geological agency which humans acquired in the industrial revolution (discussed further in Chapter 5). But the following poem, 'The Tide', takes a different perspective on human settlement along the Severn emphasising the sheer variety of detritus from human activity and settlement left behind by the low tides. Sound patterns, assonance, consonance and rhythm are exploited not simply to convey the diversity or even the poet's wonder, bordering on despair, at what is made visible but a sense of spent-energy: 'you couldn't tell sea from pools, pebbles, mudflats, / wet acres of seaweed, shells, old rope, bird-bones, / fishing lines hooked in the silt, worm-casts, stones.'³⁷ While at the level of creative composition there is vitality in the interaction between sounds, the force and charge in the individual objects have expired and, redolent of Greene's conception of a singular frame in which all things are held together, the discarded fishing lines are analogous now to the loss of a once cohesive energy at a planetary level. The references to rope and fishing lines suggest the importance of the sea in supporting human settlement but also the way in which affiliated human development has become part of human domination and destruction of the environment in the Anthropocene. Evolving into a kind of elegy for coastal life, the poem erodes the distance between objects and observer, emphasising the mesh in which living and non-living forms exist together. Questioning the amenability of the greater cosmos to life, the poem casts doubt on the supportive relationship between geology, the sea and life.

At one level, Clarke's account of the driving energy of the Severn recalls a theme in Victorian writing exemplified by John Lubbock's *The Beauties of Nature and the Wonders of the World We Live In* (1897):

> A patch of bright green, mottling the brown healthy slope, shows where the water comes to the surface, a treacherous covering of verdure often concealing a deep pool beneath. From this source the rivulet trickles along the grass and heath, which it soon cuts through, reaching the black, peaty layer below .... Excavating its channel in the peat, it comes down to the soil, often a stony earth .... Deepening and widening the channel as it gathers force with the increasing slope, the water digs into the coating of drift or loose decomposed rock that covers the hillside. In favourable localities a narrow precipitous gully, twenty or thirty feet deep, may thus be scooped out in the course of a few years.³⁸

But accounts of the journeys made by rivers through different landscapes, their various phases invoking and reflecting different moods and states of being, entered modern Welsh writing during the Second World War in country memoirs and works such as Robert Gibbings's *Coming Down the Wye* (1942). Gibbings's narrative anticipates late-twentieth-century scientific thinking in its focus on the way rivers reflect a deeper 'reality' composed of vibrations and reverberations that twist and turn with different effects: ' At first sight it seems odd that the river flowing quietly over the plain at Ross should cut its way into the hills ... continue a torturous course ... charge back and batter itself among the rocks and cliffs.'³⁹ The awesome, seemingly contradictory, character of the Wye becomes, as the Severn and Taf for Clarke, an image of the cosmos itself, of the emergence of form from formlessness and of the interplay of different forms of energy. As in Clarke's later river poems, there are moments of exhilaration and others when Gibbings falls into sloughs of confusion, anxiety and disbelief: 'I bent over and groped in the shadowed water. Sure enough, and to my surprise, I soon found myself stroking the sides of a fish. It was an uncanny sensation, not unlike a dream in its seeming absurdity.'[40]

It is not unusual to find nature writers reflecting on their ambivalent experience of watery environments for, as Walton observes, streams and rivers may be 'a vital source of life, but their waters are also shifting and slippery substances, equally creative and destructive'.[41] In an incident which is comparable to Clarke's account of being caught in a heavy storm on a clifftop in *At the Source*, the Severn turns against her and her family: 'It surged thundering up the steep sand, carried and cast ashore like detritus / then tried to drag us back on retreating waters.'[42] The comparison of what happens to her with a mythological story of a sea-king stealing an old man's daughter signifies how fundamental are questions around the amenability of the cosmos to life. The sequence of poems about the Severn acknowledges how the legendry Severn Bore, formed when the rising tide moves into the funnel-shaped Bristol Channel and Severn Estuary and forces its way upstream in a series of waves, has been mythologised as a water-dragon and dragons in cosmic symbolism are usually representations of chaos and destruction. However, just as the poet and her family were almost drowned and tossed around by the Severn in 'Tide', the Severn Bore is perceived not only to be a feat of awesome energy – 'a self-powering soliton / heaving upstream'[43] – but as signifying that the cosmos abides by its own rules: the sea charges against the mighty Severn and 'rolls-up country / where no wave should be'.[44]

The suggestion, through Clarke's personal experience of the Severn suddenly turning against her family in 'Tide', that the cosmos may not be entirely amenable to life is developed in this poem in the account of the river's threat to life and human settlement more generally – eroding river banks, destroying bridges and footpaths, taking away cars and sheep, hauling tons of stone, and carrying off surfers. However, the relationship between water, cosmos and human settlement involves more than psychological, religious and emotive factors. Human settlement is not only about the amenability of the environment, or indeed the cosmos, but involves politics. Clarke's work looks at the politics of environmental issues not simply from the perspective of human interests but as part of a wider recognition of the relationality and interconnectedness of all forms of life and non-life on the planet. This is the subject of the next section.

THE PSYCHOPOLITICS OF WATER

In one of her geological essays 'Slate' (2021), Clarke notes how water brings rural communities together but, not surprising given Clarke's interest in cosmology, in a way which sees water as part of a wider cosmic 'reality':

> Hand-churning butter is hard work, and there were ten children in the family. Opposite the farm door there was a gap in the wall high above a fast-flowing stream. The churn was placed in the gap, and connected to a waterwheel turned by the current in the river below. Thus every day milk was churned to fresh butter. A few hundred yards downstream the same millstream ground the corn for flour. The power of water is infinite and its uses multiple. It is never exhausted.[45]

The role that water has played in geopolitics – the impact of geography in determining politics and international relations – is a prominent theme in her later writings. In her essay 'Slate', it is a subject on which she is particularly outspoken, insisting that 'the rise and fall of demand, and storage of unused power, are still unsolved problems in the generation and use of electricity'.[46] Thinking of how things are at present, she does not bide her words: 'We must generate for maximum demand, and waste the rest.'[47] Her politics are rooted not only in broader global discussions of water usage and solutions but around the generation of power, a model for which is almost on her doorstep:

> One of Britain's most impressive electricity power stations is at the abandoned Dinorwic slate quarry, its machinery buried deep inside the mountain, Elidir Fawr. Water is stored high above in the Marchlyn reservoir. At times of peak demand, the gates are opened and water is set free to pour down, down through the turbines into Llyn Peris. At night, times of low demand, the water is pumped back up into the reservoir and held until needed. Power withheld.[48]

In the preface to their anthology, King and Clifford neatly encapsulate the issues around the politics of water: 'We are united in our need for water, but are increasingly divided by its scarcity, its profusion – or big ideas for its use.' [49] It goes without saying that these are emotionally charged subjects in Wales. The flooding of rural Welsh valleys in order to provide English cities with water began with the Elan Valley reservoir in 1882, constructed to supply Birmingham with water, and (as observed in Chapter 3) culminated in 1965 with the Welsh-speaking village of Capel Celyn in the Afon Tryweryn valley being flooded to supply Liverpool and the Wirral valley with water. The latter proved a pivotal moment in the development of Welsh nationalism, demonstrating that Wales had no control over the use of its natural resources. The destruction of the Welsh-language and culture which this involved is captured by R. S. Thomas in his poem 'Reservoirs' (1968) in which the drowned communities are manifestations of the wider destruction of the Welsh nation by those who have removed themselves from it.[50]

Drawing attention to the wider issues involved in the control and use of water, King and Clifford argue:

> Through two centuries of industrialisation, we have turned our back on the city river; in only five decades, intensive farming practices have filled the country river with chemicals; engineering has straightened the meanders, rendering the river more, not less, unpredictable. Fashions in fear, and development, have conspired to push running water away from our everyday experience, increasingly reducing streams to ditches and finally to culverts.[51]

This makes Clarke's water poems timely for, as King and Clifford go on to say: 'At the very moment when we need the closeness of water to feed our humanity and imagination, we seem to be denied literal contact, and have lost sight and sound of its magic.'[52] In Clarke's poetry, the notion of a relational universe integrates the psychology and politics of water. For example, as a 'protest' poem, 'Barrage' from the Severn sequence, driven by the repetition of the phrase 'No entry' – which at a strategic point is changed to 'No exit' – vociferously argues that engineering on the Severn to make the environment more amenable to human settlement disrupts and destroys the ecosystem of the river, the life patterns of migrating and homecoming birds, and the natural life cycles of its fish until, having trod where we should never have entered, we find there is no way out for any of us.

The Severn poems encapsulate what we have lost in the awe and sublime that water brings us while demonstrating how this is bound up with politics. This theme is taken further in the third key sequence of poems from *A Recipe for Water*, 'Mumbai', which reclaims our consciousness of the sublimity of water, its characteristics as a life-giving and spiritually enhancing element, and the sensory pleasure which we find in it. Attuned to their Indian context, the poems unsurprisingly examine the politics of water, in terms of access to it, pollution and purity and how they are integrated – contradictorily – with the religious, spiritual and aesthetic cultures of the Indian subcontinent.

The first poem in the sequence, 'Man in a Shower', recalling the 'diary' poems with which Clarke began her career as a writer, is based on catching sight of a man taking a shower under a waterfall. The poem combines the sensual pleasure of natural, clean water with its association in numerous faiths around the world with spiritual cleansing, purity and the bestowing of blessings. But the poem also tries to convey the pleasure and elevation in mood derived from immersion in water which Walton attributes to the stimulation of chemicals in the brain but expands to capture how it involves 'the emptying and flooding of the mind, or the way the senses are closed down, and then brought back to vivid intensity, that acts on the mind like a drug'.[53] This succinct summary of a profound bodily experience provides a useful commentary to Clarke's 'Man in a Shower' in which the cosmic dimension of his experience of 'wild' showering – 'absorbed in sunlight and water'[54] – is integrated with the wonder in the human body and skeleton that are surrendered to the falling water.

The image of the man taking a wild shower signifies the amenability of the cosmos to life but this is suddenly and sharply contrasted with the congested, air-polluting highway and the city of Mumbai itself. The sensory pleasure in nature and water that opens the poem is left behind, not only in the moment but more permanently in modernity. Unlike the cosmos of which the man in the shower becomes more fully aware as he immerses himself in the waterfall, the expanding urban development is not amenable to life or in harmony with the wider cosmos. And the way in which human pollution is making the cosmos in which we live more hostile to life is developed in the second poem in the sequence, 'At the Banganga Tank', where the potential purity and cleansing power of water is undermined by its toxicity and by the scarcity of clean water. As the environmentalist Erica Gies reminds us, climate scientists have warned that 'we have about a decade to dramatically reduce our greenhouse gas emissions to avoid catastrophic changes like the water extremes we have already begun to suffer'.[55]

However, the 'Mumbai' sequence is not simply concerned with the pollution of water, and the extent to which the cosmos is amenable to life, but with the conundrum as to what is it that attracts people to sacred waters even though they are clearly polluted and enables them to find sensuous and spiritual pleasure in using them even for washing. Walton succinctly summarises this profound paradox which, as she says, seems to 'work against environmental messaging': 'In the Ganges in India, Hindus bathe, cast flowers and light *diya* lamps on flowing water that symbolises purity, although it is one of the most polluted river systems on earth.'[56] She suggests, citing the environmental sociologist Sonya Sachdeva, that it may be that participants think that their sacred beliefs offer them immunity to the harmful effects of pollution.[57] There is a psychology, entwined with the perceived nature of sacred space, around the purity of polluted water which intrigues Clarke and which Walton tries to unveil through her own experience of wild swimming in the UK: 'I have no faith to base it on, but my belief in pure and healing waters, untouched nature, a living sacred realm, is stubborn and hard to do without, even though there's a reality to face, and I don't want to get sick.'[58] Both Clarke and Walton recognise that water, to employ Walton's words, 'is often a medium of liberation, an environment in which women grasp toward a sense of freedom and reality'.[59] In this regard, each of their writings can be seen as a commentary on the other's.

'Mumbai' juxtaposes different examples from the city of the politics of water, poison and industrial pollution. As Magnason says of Mumbai: 'Absolute destitution on one side, complete excess on the other.' [60] In the ritual underpinning Clarke's poem 'In the Taj', poor women of presumably lower caste clean handles and taps in the toilets so that they may not taint the hands of privileged guests to whom they hand out towels and soaps. The opulent washrooms in the Taj Mahal Hotel stand in contrast to the laundry area in the Tulsi Pipe Road, described in the next poem 'Laundry', where women, who may well attend to tourists in the Taj Mahal for a pittance, wash their clothes by hand in the open air, mindful to catch every drop of scarce water from the clothes they wring. They are contrasted also with Clarke's ancestors who, too, because of their poverty, would have washed their clothes by hand in rivers and streams but in water that was much cleaner and purer. Their clothes would have been hung from trees or washing lines to dry in fresh Welsh mountain air and they might well have felt, as the poem implies, that the cosmos was indeed amenable to life. But this is not the case in the human-made cosmos of twentieth/twenty-first century Mumbai in which clothes are hung on wires and trees and are immediately dirtied again before they dry by the polluted air of the city, which is comparable to the clothes hanging on washing lines in mid-twentieth-century industrial Wales – about which Clarke quips in 'East Moors' when the Cardiff steel works closed (as noted in Chapter 1), 'now, washing strung / down the narrow gardens will stay clean'.[61]

The poem 'Hands' from the 'Mumbai' sequence implicitly and ironically juxtaposes the ritual of the toilets in the Taj Mahal Hotel, which guards against the pollution of taps by tainted hands, with the poisoned water fed to babies in their powdered milk. The poet provides bottles of spring water – which might well come from springs in the mountains of Wales – for the mothers as an alternative to the polluted water. The politics of water in this poem is a complicated mesh. In many non-European industrialised nations, clean water is a privileged commodity, but spring water in high-income countries is bottled and distributed across the world for those who can afford to buy it. The spread of disease through polluted water in low-income countries poisons the poor who also have no health care. The image of a young girl struck by a speeding car toward the end of the poem encapsulates the indifference and violence shown to the poor by those with money. This is aligned with the indifference toward the environment and climate change displayed by the motors of ferries and jets. The final lines of the 'Post Script' present an image of a 'world torn / like a shot bird'[62] to which Clarke's poems of the twenty-first century especially are addressed.

Within the frame of cosmology, psychopolitics embraces theology, philosophy and nature. Modernity's cosmic disenchantment, as the cosmologist Richard Tarnas says, resulted from a tremendous increase in individual autonomy;[63] the objectification of the external world;[64] the modern mind (in the Copernican revolution) acquiring supreme confidence in itself and the enormous shift that came to a head in the sixteenth and seventeenth centuries that brought about the militant 'desacralization' of the world[65] with humans playing a larger role in the scheme of things.[66] In 'Valley' (1998), included in *Five Fields* – a poem inspired by a stone carver in north Wales working with rocks left by glaciers – Clarke coins the term 'water-memory' in which, in her imagination, she returns to cosmogenesis, the 'million million years of water-work / to make this place' and the rivers 'tumbling boulders for the walls of farms'.[67] In doing so, she embraces a question that has dominated cosmology and cosmogenesis for many decades. To employ Swimme's words, she asks, did 'the early universe [aim] at bringing forth the conditions that would make the emergence of rocky, Earth-like planets inevitable?'[68] As 'Valley' demonstrates, intention for Clarke, within her most cosmological writings, as for Swimme, is bound up with energy that originated 'at the beginning aimed at constructing stars and galaxies'.[69] For both Clarke and Swimme some 'intention lives at the level of matter itself'.[70] Even a cursory reading of Clarke's work suggests that she has a preoccupation with cosmic darkness but this has to be appreciated not simply by an interplay of light and dark in her poetry but by the nature of 'blackness' and the extent to which intent lives in blackness, to which I now turn.

THE COSMOGENESIS OF BLACK

In Clarke's poems of the 1970s and 1980s, deep rivers and aquifers have an intensity of blackness which is often disturbing and, at times, destabilising. The artist and colour theorist Kathryn Simon suggests that black may be disquieting because it 'is not in the rainbow nor is it a prismatic colour, which so defines colour theory' and that it 'reflects no light and emits the lowest frequency on a light spectrum'.[71] Or, she argues, it may be because of 'a very tightly held Western bias' and the 'constellation of resonances [that have] accumulated' around the colour black.[72] But, at another level, Clarke's poetry sees the colour black as part of a performative process and in her work it is not simply a colour but an activity. In order to fully understand this, it is necessary to follow the approach that Simon takes in her thesis, in which 'black' has to be replaced with 'blackness'.

Staying close to blackness in order to allow, in Simon's words, for 'resonance and cadence',[73] Clarke's poetry renders encounters with blackness through a visceral language. For example, the poem 'Journey' published in *The Sundial* (1978) – in which Clarke is a passenger in a car driven by her husband – concludes:

> As you hurl us
> Into the black contracting
> Chasm, I submit like a blind
> And folded baby, being born.[74]

This final image reminds us that, as Simon also notes, 'everything is born in darkness. Gestation and birth begin in the dark'.[75] The anthropologist Karen Armstrong, too, associates underground passages of darkness with birth as well as death. But, in doing so, she explicitly notes what Clarke implies that birth is a separation from integration with, and the protectiveness of, the mother's body: 'Every baby forced through the narrow passage of the birth canal ... has to leave the safety of the womb.'[76]

As Armstrong observes, among ancient peoples the experience of black(ness) was associated with dangerous underground passages which involved a descent 'ever more deeply into the heart of darkness', 'situations in which we come face to face with the unknown' and 'the final rite of passage, which is death'.[77] Clarke's work vacillates between black as a symbol of extinction and nothingness – in 'Snow on the Mountain', she watches a rider's joy 'fall like laughter down a dark / Crack' and, travelling at night in a car in 'Journey', she feels 'we are driving into oblivion. On either side there is nothing'.[78] But in her work as a whole, blackness has a vibrancy and energy from which life emerges. Clarke, like the cosmologist Richard Tarnas, thinks of the night sky, for example, as the dark but 'fertile void of the cosmos out of which all stars and all suns emerge'.[79] Not as 'the black wastes / of space',[80] to invoke a phrase from Clarke's 'God's Eye' (1998). In this regard, Clarke once again takes us to the moment of cosmogenesis when, as Swimme suggests, 'the universe was filled with chaotic interactions, violent collisions and chance events' but, and this is a large 'but', in Clarke's work (as Chapter 3 suggests) 'even so, the universe found its way to construct complex spiral galaxies'.[81]

Simon maintains that 'dark matter' – a hypothetical form of matter in a universe composed of particles that do not absorb, reflect or emit light – 'is not necessarily black, though it is so completely unknown it is called "dark" or "black"' and 'scientists speculate that we may not even have the framework or vocabulary to understand the explanation. It may simply be beyond our current framework of knowledge.'[82] In rural locations where Clarke has spent most of her adult life, we are more aware than ever that darkness, as Simon notes, 'blackens or obliterates the world around us (the colourful world of things, the full spectrum of emotions, etc.)' and that 'it is also the colour of chaos because the darkness makes it hard to see, to discern'.[83] But in the countryside, the blackness or darkness that comes with the transition from day to night also appears to be more 'performative' than has often been acknowledged. For example, the award-wining writer and journalist Rob Cowen draws attention to movement and vibrancy within the blackness around us at night, how 'noises register' in 'footfalls' and 'brushed foliage', and 'things shuffling, gathering, dispersing'.[84] In an extract from her journal for 2007, Clarke describes how:

> Looking prints the mind with an imagined image. One moonlit spring night David [Clarke's husband] shone his torch on the water to look for newts. There was a loud splash, and the torch showed the whole surface of the pond in turmoil and the water cloudy. Something dived in and concealed itself at the deep end, or maybe scarpered in a fright and was off along the bed of the stream too fast for even a glimpse by torchlight.[85]

Clarke's work offers what colour theorists like Simon are arguing for: 'an expanded reading of black beyond the usual determinations and fixed boundaries'.[86] Such a reading of blackness, as in the above extract from Clarke's journal, contrasts what Simon calls an 'absolute, pure or achromatic black' with a 'relative or chromatic black' which exists at the edges of the torch beam in the above extract.[87] Black in this context is synonymous with the 'Other' in Western metaphysics that lies beyond light while Clarke's torch signifies the positive valuation of light in Western thinking as overcoming the negativity of darkness.[88]

Light in Clarke's work, in breaking through black, often takes us back to the origins of the universe and conveys the excitement in being able to feel we are a part of the developing cosmos. As Swimme says, 'It is astonishing ... this light has been travelling toward us for billions of years, and now, for the first time in human history, we can see it as it arrives, freshly, here on Earth.'[89] But the passage that I have been discussing is an example of the complexity in Clarke's approach to blackness. In centring on the torch beam, Clarke suggests, as Simon says of the duality of light and dark, that 'while light makes objects and seeing things in the world possible, we are called upon to remain whole, to live with, in fact to embrace the unknowable, which is the "black"'.[90]

In Clarke's 'Ode to Winter', from *Ice*, the encroaching blackness initially generates a sense of panic – almost something terrifying – which renders the need to hold on to a light somewhat desperate, intensified in the almost Nordic succession of single, hard vowels: 'We hoard light, hunkered in holt and burrow, / in cave, *cwtch*, den, earth, hut, lair.'[91] But in the poem, Clarke juxtaposes the notion of black as synonymous with the 'unknowable' with a heightened awareness that, to use Simon's words, 'within ultimate black there is light'.[92] For both Clarke and Cowen, darkness is, as Simon suggests, 'a nuanced black, not quite black at all but a very, very dark colour or density created by the lack of light'.[93] But there is the hint in their work, of what Simon calls 'another, far deeper, heavier and awesome "pure black"'.[94] This, as elsewhere in Clarke's poetry – for example, in 'Nightride' and 'Journey' – is mostly only experienced, as Simon maintains, 'as an idea'.[95] In 'Nightride', Clarke says as much in the turning point of the poem: 'Rain rhythm, beat of the windscreen wipers, / I push my knee against his in the warmth / And the car thrusts the dark and rain away.'[96]

The 'active', almost 'performative', element in blackness in Clarke's poetry – that in her work it is alive – resonates with Simon's thesis that 'within it light / dark, white / black, day / night, all things exist including the mystery, both negative and positive'.[97] As such, Clarke's writings offer us an example of work in which, as Simon recommends for the advancement of our thinking about black(ness), notions of permanence are replaced 'with the vibrancy of being, in a sensual and alive universe where both light and darkness form the remarkable experience of aliveness'.[98] This notion is particularly appropriate to Clarke's work which, in its contemplation of the energy within blackness or darkness, frequently moves us to an imagined/ spiritual place in which (as Simon stresses) lightness and darkness constitute a sense of something 'alive'. An example of this occurs in her Christmas (but also cosmological) poem 'Hunting the Wren' (2012) in which Clarke cryptically links her cosmological thinking with the presence of a bird: 'Above ... the electric galaxies, / on the tree's topmast / something alive, a dark star, a flutter of flight.'[99] The poem takes the reader into a phenomenological encounter with the experience of darkness or blackness that lies outside the boundaries of representation. But, like Simon's artistic use of the colour black, it 'unfolds and explores the metonymical, poetic movement and the play of this signifier in relation to darkness, emptiness and nothingness'.[100]

The bird's perception of the Christmas tree which the poet has erected in her home and which it can see through the glass, constitutes an interplay of light and shadow, life and non-life forms and the continuity and discontinuity between darkness, light, nothingness and life. In this complex interrelationship, Clarke turns once again to cosmogenesis, or rather the myriad of ways in which it has been perceived and conjured across religions, cultures and the sciences: 'A wren has dreamed of a forest / multiplied in glass, / as tree dreamed bird into being, / its boughs and shadows spread / on a forest floor of snow.'[101] As such, the poem becomes what Simon describes in her account of the vibrancy of darkness, a 'passageway' to where black(ness) is an 'opening onto a call to act in a vibrant world'.[102] This linking of blackness, for both Simon and Clarke, resonates with cosmological thinking about cosmogenesis and 'intent'. As Swimme summarises, 'we need to understand that the universe can intend something even before human consciousness emerges'.[103]

In regard to the vibrancy of black as a colour and the sense of energy within it, the cover design of Clarke's first *Selected Poems* (1985), which is by Clarke herself, is worth a mention. The design depicts a white hare inside a black circular disc which has a narrow white border, outside which there is an even narrower black circle. The picture has some resonance with the symbol in Taoism that represents life in perfect balance. Simon describes the Taoist symbol as 'a circle divided by white appearing in black and black appearing in white, referring to the intertwining of both light and darkness that makes the texture of life. Even the shape between white and black is curved and embryonic.'[104] In Clarke's cover design, the hare's hindquarters and rear legs are slightly smudged with black which subtly blends the whiteness of the hare with the black of the disc on which it is situated, from which it would otherwise appear more distinct.

An outline drawing of a hare to illustrate the cover of *Selected Poems* is an interesting and symbolic choice in itself. As Cowen has pointed out, the hare has leapt into our imagination 'as mythical life-bringer and fertility icon'.[105] Almost invisible for most of the year, the hare is associated with the spring when it appears among the crops and grass of arable fields and, as Cowen observes, in numerous flood myths, is associated with Easter and in Egyptian thought denotes 'to be' and signifies 'persistence made flesh'.[106] At one level, the blackness in Clarke's cover design suggests the nothingness from which life emerges and into which, like day itself, it will finally merge once again.

The whispers of black on the hare's whiteness betray the hold which black has on the hare despite its snowy-white, almost transcendental, purity. Black is the more dominant colour from which the vibrancy of the design seems to emerge. But the two narrow circles at the circumference signify the tension or dialectical relationship between the two colours and what they represent.

Clarke's 'The Hare', a new poem in her *Selected Poems* (1985) is republished beside 'Hare in July' in the later volume *Letting in the Rumour* (1989). The juxtaposition of the two poems suggests that in the 1980s Clarke was beginning to think in terms of linking several poems in sequence by variations on a theme. 'The Hare' offers a contrasting approach to the death of a hare, or rather in this poem the death cries of a hare, to 'Hare in July'. The hare's cries are the central presence in a night that Clarke remembers spending with her friend – the poem is in memoriam to Frances Horovitz (1938–1983). It invokes the restless darkness of the night caught by what Clarke describes as 'ears and eyes soon used to the night': 'The cattle in the field were shadow black. / A cow coughed. Some slept, and some pulled grass. / I could smell blossom from the blackthorn.'[107] But this darkness stands in contradistinction to another kind of blackness from which comes the cry of the hare: '"A hare", we said together, not speaking / of fox or trap that held it in a lock / of terrible darkness.'[108] This ambivalence of the night denotes the two faces of the countryside, one of which is more palatable than the other, as summarised by D. Parry-Jones in his country memoir:

> The country has not only things to see but things to hear as well, and I like nearly all the noises that its rich and varied repertoire can produce. There are exceptions: the squeal of a rabbit followed by a weasel, the sharp, heart-rendering scream of pain which it sends out when caught in a trap, and which one hears in the late night as the rabbits move into the hedges and their warren.[109]

Clarke's poetry encourages us to distinguish between black and blackness or darkness which possess what Simon has called 'qualities of luminosity'.[110] The latter admits the reader into an interplay of signifiers within Clarke's writings in which blackness is associated with a range of different cultural associations and emotions including death, emptiness, nothingness, concealment, shelter, chaos and uncertainty. But blackness in Clarke's work often takes us to cosmogenesis and the kind of black from which form emerged out of formlessness within which there is light, vibrancy and a performative element. While one aspect of her work is drawn toward the black of nothingness, chaos, uncertainty and the obliteration of light, a more important black to her is that which Simon calls 'black light' or 'luminous black'.[111] The 'formless state' out of which the cosmos emerged is historically associated with black, emptiness and nothingness. But for Clarke, and contemporary science, the cosmos did not emerge from this absolute black but one possessing qualities of vibrancy and luminosity that 'do not come from an outside source, but are rather internal and immanent'.[112] This 'turn' is also evident in the approaches to geology in Clarke's work, especially in her post-1990 work – the subject of the next chapter.

5

Geology, Human Development and the Anthropocene

As discussed in Chapters 2 and 3, Clarke's interest in cosmology developed as part of a wider concern in her poetry and published journals with climate change, the environment and the Anthropocene. This environmental and planetary turn in her work is evident also in the new perspective on geology, its links with human development and its associations with the psychology and politics of water in *Five Fields* (1998), *Making the Beds for the Dead* (2004), *A Recipe for Water* (2009), *Ice* (2012) and *Zoology* (2017). In *At the Source*, she admits that her interest in science and nature was ignited by her father:

> I left education largely in ignorance of science, but I know now that the seeds of excitement about the facts of physics, biology, mathematics, were sown on those westward journeys with my father when, between stories, he taught me about electricity, gravity, how radio worked, how he sent messages in Morse code during his years at sea as a wireless engineer, where the weather comes from, what the stars are. An interest in natural phenomena and the living world arises directly from our night watches for otter or badger, listening for curlew, or spotting a kingfisher, hunting for a rabbit or a trout to supplement wartime rations.[1]

But Clarke's childhood interest in science coincided also with the popularisation of geology in books, as in the case of weather (noted in Chapter 3), targeting general enthusiasts and hobbyists. In one of her autobiographical essays, 'The Poetry of Stone: Pentre Ifan', published in 2008, she remembers her own favourite book: 'Igneous, metamorphic, sedimentary rock. How I loved my *Guide to Minerals, Rocks and Fossils*.'[2]

It almost goes without saying that the widespread public interest in science and geology immediately following the Second World War continued into subsequent decades evident, for example, in best sellers such as A. C. Bishop's *Guide to Minerals, Rocks and Fossils* (1974) published in association with the Natural History Museum.[3] But it would be impossible to mention a Welsh child's discovery of geology without acknowledging that many key figures in geology were born, or came to work, in Wales such as Alwyn Williams, Owen Thomas Jones and Douglas Basset who became Director of the National Museum of Wales (1977–1985). About the same time as the publication of Bishop's book on rocks, minerals and fossils, Welsh geologist Thomas Richard Owen (1918–1990) published *Geology Explained in South Wales* (1973) and *The Upper Palaeozoic and Post-Palaeozoic Rocks of Wales* (1974).[4] To a child in mid-twentieth-century Wales, geology would have felt like a Welsh science – many of the æons, the largest unit of geological time, had names that invoked Wales. For example, *Cambrian* and *Pre-Cambrian* derive from the Roman name for what became Wales and *Ordovician* and *Silurian* are the names of ancient peoples who inhabited this geographical area.

The readers of beginners' guides to geology wanted, as I. O. Evans says in his *The Observer's Book of Geology*, 'to recognise the different types of rock and to know something about them'.[5] In Clarke's 'The City', a poem sequence published in *Five Fields* (1998) and discussed in Chapter 4, it is clear that even as an adult she remained inspired, as she was as a child, by the language of this particular science and the thrill of identifying the different rocks, on this occasion on her journey to Manchester: 'Ordovician flags, shale, mudstones, / Silurian shale, grit, greywacke, limestone.'[6] But the poem also demonstrates that Clarke's love of the language of landscape goes beyond geological description. The changing character of the environment and the rocks that constitute it as Manchester is approached is encapsulated in the differences between the language of north Wales and the dialect of north-west England: 'where mountains become fells, and valleys, dales, / *craig* is *bluff*; *afon* and river and stream, / are *beck* and *gill*; a waterfall's a *force*'.[7] Implicit in the words themselves, the landscape has been constructed around moments of physical tension and resistance as 'where Irwell and Medlock meet / under the watershed of gritstone moors / and the limestone peaks of Derbyshire'.[8] The hard

Anglo-Saxon sounds reflect the harshness of many of the outcrops of rock and defamiliarises them in a way which enables Clarke to think of the laying down of different layers as analogous to the acquisition of language and the function of mental processes: 'words laid down on the mind's bedrock'.[9] But also the way in which the environment became increasingly shaped and dominated by humans in the Anthropocene.

Evans maintains that geology inspires 'trains of philosophical reflections and has profoundly modified our religious ideas'.[10] In her journal *At the Source* (2008), Clarke follows suit, pondering how 'Earth took its time with rock. It took ages. Then life began, fidgeting and wriggling for an unimaginably long, slow time, for ages, æons, chrons.'[11] Throughout her post-1990 writing particularly, she is excited and fascinated by one of the themes in geological science which the physicist Dennis W. Sciama succinctly summarises: 'that life is possible only during a relatively short phase of the evolution of the Universe after the galaxies have formed and when the stars are shining in a stable manner.'[12] Her post-1990 work – for example, 'The City' which invokes 'crushed fossils', 'petrified stems' and 'coal-bearing shales'[13] and 'The Stone Poems' in *Making the Beds for the Dead* (2004) which conjures 'sedimentary time laid down and shaped / with the patience of stone' and 'the long upheavals, continents / lapping like plates of a baby's skull'[14] – presents her wonder at the metamorphoses and interactions of organic and inorganic matter which geology unveils.

THE HUMAN TURN IN GEOLOGY

Mid-twentieth-century introductions to geology, like the book which Clarke says she still cherishes, often maintained an interest in rocks which was not linked to human development. It is a thread that has always run through Clarke's passion for geology. Her avid interest in the cosmic energy which brought into being the molten planet Earth – 'Ancient upheavals hurled molten stone from deep in the mantle of the earth'[15] – and the subsequent formation of different types of rock are encapsulated in the rocks at her writing table. In her essay 'The Poetry of Stone', she ponders with wonder, 'three fragments of planet earth: a granite sett ... a small block of purple slate from Penrhyn – five-hundred-million-year-old metamorphic rock ... and a tablet of limestone ... a stilled seethe of primitive life-forms and shell fragments, and what looks like one very small trilobite as real and wide awake as if it lived.'[16]

How geological time is presented, directly or indirectly, in 'The Stone Poems' (2004), can be traced back to the wartime and post-war popular guides to rocks, fossils and minerals with which Clarke was familiar as a child, emphasising different rocks, their distinctive formations and the periods of geological time to which they belong. For example, granite dating from the pre-Cambrian period is seen, as in these books, as providing, in the words of the eminent mid-twentieth-century geologist Albert S. Seward 'the earth's foundation-stones'.[17] Coarse-grained sandstone from the Devonian epoch and coral-based sedimentary rocks formed in the Lower Carboniferous are preserved as part of a process in deep time which, as the title of Clarke's volume suggests, involved 'making the beds for the dead'.

These rocks and the processes which brought them into being are an extension in Clarke's writings of her interest in cosmogenesis and how planet Earth emerged from a state of formlessness (discussed in Chapter 4). But while geology, and astronomy, usually approached the formation of the cosmos and planet Earth as a sequence of scientific mysteries and solutions, Clarke, as in 'The Stone Poems', as Laniel-Musitelli observes, 'connects human temporality and geological times', drawing 'on the scientific imagination to alter the scales of space and time prevalent in her earlier work'.[18] Such links between geology and human history reverberates with a wider transformation in geology which is evident in Richard Fortey's *The Earth: An Intimate History* (2005) which Clarke read and reread as she says in her journal in August 2007.[19] In keeping with the human turn in geology, Fortey maintains that his book is concerned with how and where 'geology and history are interwoven' and with 'the influence of geology on the character of landscape and the character of people'.[20] The historian Dipesh Chakrabarty assumes a more critical perspective within geology's human orientation that also accords with some of Clarke's twenty-first-century perspectives. He maintains that in a reconsideration of how 'the planet moved from one geological period, the last ice age or the Pleistocene, to the more recent and warmer Holocene' within the discipline, human beings became conceived of as not simply a biological but 'a planetary geological agent'.[21]

The classification of geological history and the formation of rocks – normally unveiled in a backward journey through time to cosmogenesis – is approached in a creative way in Clarke's 'The Stone

Poems'. In a more complicated presentation of geological time than mid-twentieth-century would-be geologists found in their popular guides to rocks and minerals, these poems invoke some of the ways in which geology has shaped human consciousness and in turn has been determined by it. In 'Rock', as in the fragments on her writing desk, Clarke tries to envisage 'old' time before the appearance of life and, subsequently, when living and non-living forms emerged from beds of the dead:

> silt on silt,
> microbe, algae, trilobite, brachiopod,
> first jellyfish, first worm,
> leaf-mould, bone on bone.[22]

As noted in Chapter 1, Clarke's poetry of the 1970s and 1980s was rooted in the present and generally utilised the present tense. Not surprisingly, the second poem 'Hay' in 'The Stone Poems' sequence examines the intensity, and preciousness, of the present and of ordinary life when set – or reset – against geological time: 'Speaking of stone on a day like this, / the silence, the heat, the hay-days, / when the slates creak in the sun.'[23] Having introduced 'the subdivisions of geological time / Earth story's chaptered with eras, / paragraphed with epochs, ages, chrons' in 'Rock',[24] with typical subtlety and aplomb, Clarke compares the present as it is envisaged in human terms with an older age when sedimentary rock and slate were first formed. In contrasting how the 'field's dried to a thin song' in the heat with the 'nourishment of rock', the poem invokes that debate which permeates Clarke's work (as noted in Chapter 3) over the extent to which planet Earth – and the cosmos as a whole – is amenable to life.

The pattern of rural life in 'Hay', when set against the linearity of geology, encapsulates an alternative cyclical way of looking at time which in the second stanza of the poem resonates with the movement of the planets, especially the moon. It is not true, as Laniel-Musitelli suggests, in an otherwise very perceptive essay, that there was a time, in the 1970s and 1980s, when Clarke's geography was stuck in 'a static cartography of Wales'.[25] As noted in the discussion of poems from *The Sundial* (1978) and *Letter from a Far Country* (1982) in Chapter 1, Clarke's awareness of landscape, history and time has always revolved around what Laniel-Musitelli also describes as 'a game of shifting scales' and particularly the upheavals of the planet and the cosmos.

Seeking to capture the ambivalent nature of cosmic energy and of the geological processes that brought the Earth into being, Clarke's 'The Stone Poems' slide together, like the continental plates themselves. But thinking back to, and beyond, her childhood *Guide to Minerals, Rocks and Fossils*, Clarke contemplates, in her essay 'The Poetry of Stone' and her poem sequence 'The Stone Poems', how humans not only make use of but live with stone. In her poem of that name, Clarke ponders the way in which granite (created over epochs prior to the emergence of life) has been cut 'to pave a city courtyard or a street' or 'a floor hewn from the batholith'.[26] As Richard Fortey maintains in his volume *The Earth*, which Clarke is undoubtedly remembering, 'the durability of granite is a gift'.[27] In 'Granite (Pre-Cambrian)', ordinary activities such as drying laundry in the warm air of a European village, airing bed linen out-of-doors and drinking wine at a café table at dusk might seem transitory and meaningless against the vast realms of time and space. But, from another perspective, when set against the 700 million years it took to form the granite out of which the village was built, these small units of time seem all the more valuable, a wonder that they happened at all.

Turning for a moment to one of Clarke's earlier 'geological' poems from *Five Fields* (1998) and her interest in the contribution of another type of rock to human history, her geological eye and poetic imagination transforms the way she sees the slate landscape in 'Into the Mountain': 'Light fingers it / with a shimmer like water / on roofscape or slate tip.'[28] The gentleness of light upon the slate – an example of Clarke's characteristic interplay of light and dark – and the quiet movement of an owl reflects the way in which they have slowed the poet's pulse but also suggests that they can only be sensed through an unpressured and calm mind's eye. With the inner quietness derived from sensing the wonder of Earth's organic and inorganic history, and highlighting the inner silence necessary to achieve awareness of it, the poem imagines the lives of Clarke's nain (grandmother), pressured by the domestic chores that had to be done, and her tad-cu (grandfather), an ex-miner disabled and dying from silicosis. Freed momentarily from the kind of pressures they endured in their brief lives, the poet is capable of finding some solace in the wider span of time, deep in the dark and silence of the mountain in which there is a profound vibrancy, energy and premonition of life.

In Clarke's later essay 'Slate' (2008), in which she dwells on the slate's formation 'in a furnace of low heat and pressure', she admits that from a perspective of geological time 'thoughts of those ages' make her 'dizzy, aeons of volcanic activity, the rise and fall of oceans, pressure of sedimentary leftovers, glaciers and their detritus'.[29] But, from another perspective, through the various ways in which slate has provided for and supported human life over the years, the poem 'Slate (Cambrian)', from 'The Stone Poems', conveys her excitement over the part that slate plays, and has played, in contemporary Welsh cultural life. In this regard, slate is linked to a geological epoch 'settled from silts and mudstones',[30] from which it acquires a greater sense of energy. Thus, the pallets of slate delivered to Clarke's smallholding as seemingly mundane building materials acquire associations which only a poet with a profound sense of geology and the life-force in matter (discussed in Chapter 4) might intuitively grasp and perceive in the context of the mesh in which all living and non-living forms are connected.

GEOLOGY AND COSMOLOGY

The two poems about sculpture in 'The Stone Poems' suggest that poets, sculptors and artists intuitively grasp and work with a cosmology inherent in matter. 'Woman Washing her Hair (Devonian)' conflates a sculptor working in one moment of time with the æon from which his rocks – the material which he is reshaping – came. Devonian was an epoch which eventually became aquatic, during which plants with roots and leaves and the first seed-bearing plants formed forests of vegetation and from which an enormous diversity of fish emerged. While Clarke thinks of poetry as constructed in layers, the strata of rocks with which the sculptor is working, like words themselves, carry memories of different times and cosmologies.

The sculpture of a 'sandstone woman, leaning still / over waters that are not quite there',[31] encapsulates all women, linked through their bodily awareness, across æons of time: 'curled, primitive, crouched on the folds / of her thighs'.[32] The description of the corporeality of the sculpture conflates the present (as pre-sent) with earlier human histories, fusing flesh and stone as examples of the life within matter, an intention or consciousness of some kind, as noted in Chapter 4. The modes of seeing and feeling that bring this to human consciousness are embedded, the poem suggests, in the body, that Clarke as a sensual poet reclaims throughout much of her work.

The animal sculpture in 'The Stone Hare (Lower Carboniferous)' in the 'The Stone Poems', like the carving of the woman washing her hair, is similarly important for the memory in the stone out of which it is struck, a memory created in the carboniferous period when animal, especially amphibian, life became established. Clarke finds in the carving not only its carboniferous origins but the entire trajectory of life on earth: 'Woman Washing her Hair' is focused on the sculpture itself within the context of the evolution of living and non-living matter; 'The Stone Hare' takes the reader into the diversity of nature and vegetation in the Lower Carboniferous period which eventually died and were bedded in stratified rocks. Both sculptures retain the living force within the matter from which they came, embracing what Clarke terms 'a premonition of stone'.[33] In other words, she finds the Upper Carboniferous æon, the coal-bearing epoch, anticipated in the Lower Carboniferous period turned to below in a discussion of her poem 'Coal (Upper Carboniferous)'.

In her essay, 'The Poetry of Stone', Clarke mentions that close to her desk is 'a life-size limestone hare, sculpted by Meic Watts, its polished body another moment frozen from the life of an ancient sea, "a premonition of stone" from the Palaeozonic'.[34] 'The Stone Hare', like the essay, looks into the sculpture and the rock from which the hare has been carved and then through to what is beyond them – the 'story of the earth', 'the long trajectories / of starfish, feather-stars, crinoids and crushed shells' – and even beyond that, 'its eye a planet'.[35] But it is also a window to developmental biology in which science, as Laniel-Musitelli observes, explores the changing structures of organisms over time through 'differentiation, pattern formation, morphogenesis and growth'.[36] In talking of a 'premonition' of stone, and by implication a premonition of the formation of life, Clarke's 'The Stone Hare' implies that there is a life force or energy, if not an intention, flowing through the cosmos. As Laniel-Musitelli points out, '"The Stone Hare" explores the formative energy at work within matter, and the common drive towards form in inert matter, living matter, and artistic objects. The stone waiting for the hand of the carver to reveal its form shows that form is latent within matter itself.'[37] Clarke's own cosmological perspective suggested by this poem, and 'Woman Washing her Hair', would seem to be based on her intuition of some kind of continuum in the diversity that constitutes the different geological æons.

However, this cosmological perspective poses questions about the relationship between a 'drive toward form' and the different kinds of irregularity which the new physics has found in the natural world. James Gleick observes that in the new science 'the universe is randomness and dissipation, yes. But randomness with direction can produce surprising complexity.'[38] Clarke's work becomes increasingly preoccupied with examples of complex forms as they emerged within the wider diversity of evolution:

> In its limbs lies the story of the earth,
> the living ocean, then the slow birth
> of limestone from the long trajectories
> of starfish, feather-stars, crinoids and crushed shells
> that fill with calcite, harden, wait for the quarryman,
> the timed explosion and the sculptor's hand.[39]

Clarke's examination of the formative energies of the cosmos in 'The Stone Poems' is focused, as in 'Behind Glass' in the later volume *Zoology* (2017), on those moments when the animate becomes inanimate, preserved in fossils. She observes the sculpture of the hare standing in 'the grass, moonlight's muscle and bone, / the stems of sea lilies slowly turned to stone'.[40] As in 'Woman Washing her Hair', the sculptor works in a space in which the distance between the creator and the object dissolves. In this regard, he does not so much work with but follows rock.

The premonition of the future in the past has long been the inspiration behind studies of geology and, particularly, the prehistory of the cosmos. Thinking of the origins of coal in the tropical swamps of the Upper Carboniferous, Clarke imagines it as having had a premonition of it being worked in the distant future – by human life not yet formed. 'Coal', like the other poems in 'The Stone Poems', turns on more than one timescale, the nineteenth- and twentieth-century mining of coal, focused on whole civilisations dependent on fossil fuels and generations whose lives have been shaped by the industry and the Upper Carboniferous epoch when living carbon-based life forms metamorphosed into coal. Given the connections that Clarke makes in 'Glacier' between the large icebergs of Greenland and the slag-heap that brought disaster to the Aberfan mining village in south Wales (discussed in Chapter 3), it is surprising that this poem is not more explicit about the dangerous nature of mining, and the environmental damage caused by fossil fuels. Clarke is more outspoken on these aspects of mining in her prose writings where she points out that 'the life of a falling miner was soon replaced from the endless queue of the jobless, trying to add to the income of subsistence farming'.[41] In her essay 'Slate', Clarke calls out the dirty business behind mining, bemoaning 'not just slate, but copper, and other metals and minerals were worked from these mountains, left hollow and haunted once the profits were made' and how 'departed profiteers leave nothing behind but ghosts'.[42]

The absence of the damage caused by mining fossil-fuels in 'Coal' enables Clarke to emphasise and pursue the theme of time, in different manifestations, which is a central theme in 'The Stone Poems'. A key poem in this regard is 'Edward Llwyd and the Trilobite (Ordovician)', referring to the Welsh geologist who was responsible for the discovery of the Snowdon Lily and trilobites. Clarke seems fascinated by the fact that he worked under the illusion that Earth, according to biblical history, dated from 4004 BCE despite being confronted by the fossil of the trilobite that suggests a much older sense of time:

> A strike of his hammer broke the heart of limestone
> clean as a conker, and trilobite stared
> with four-hundred and sixty-five-million-year-old eyes
> from a dark age deeper than his fathoming.[43]

As this poem suggests, Clarke, like many amateur and professional geologists, became entranced by the trilobite – the name refers to the three-lobed form of its body – now extinct but reaching its greatest development in the Silurian and Ordovician epochs. It is an example of complex organisms that evolved out of, and alongside, the randomness of evolution. Its nearness to scorpions and spiders suggests that its three-lobed form and eyes betray an intent and some kind of consciousness of life. Seward points out in his wartime introduction to geology that it is their eyes – as Clarke notes in her poem – sometimes made up of as many as 1,500 facets that perhaps most transfix us.[44] When Clarke was working on 'The Stone Poems', Fortey published, to considerable critical acclaim, his *Trilobite! Eyewitness to Evolution* (2001) which, like Clarke's 'Edward Llwyd and the Trilobite', acknowledges Llwyd's discovery three hundred years ago of 'flat-fish' in Llandeilo, pointing out that while Llwyd was wrong in describing the trilobite as a fish, and being unaware of the forces that compressed it, he was certainly right to draw attention to its eyes.[45] As Fortey says, 'So when you see – with your own eyes – the eyes of the trilobite, you recognise a kinship of vision stretching across hundreds of millions of years.'[46] Clarke's poem, like Seward's book, suggests what Fortey more explicitly states: 'The trilobite will always keep a certain distance from us; there will be limits on the intimacy we can attain. What we can guess is that the honeycomb-like trilobite eye may have permitted comprehension of the world in the same fashion as the similar compound eyes of living anthropods.'[47] In other words, the trilobite causes us to rethink the randomness of creation. While appearing anatomically to be some kind of distortion – which led to Llwyd's description of it as a fish – it had actually developed to meet the needs of its time.

'The Stone Poems' sequence is ultimately not about geology per se but different perceptions of time; wonder in the way in which the cosmos as a whole emerged from formlessness; and human life developed from cosmic processes in deep time. They vacillate between understanding and incomprehension, between scientific fact and poetic intuition, and between a strong sense of the present and an ever-present apprehension of 'human' time slipping away into the timelessness of the cosmos which is itself difficult for the human mind to fathom.

The final poem of 'The Stone Poems' sequence takes as its title the Mesozoic epoch which lasted from 252 to 66 million years ago and which saw the larger of the mass extinction events which chart the earth's history, that included the non-avian dinosaurs, and was a period of significant tectonic, climatic and evolutionary activity. The poem also alludes to the older Miocene period, characterised by the expansion of the Arctic ice sheet and global warming. Post-War geology thought of the Miocene, as in Clarke's poem, as a gap in Earth's story located between the Pliocene epoch when the climate became colder and a period when the climate eventually became warmer again.[48] This notion of a gap in the planet's story is reflected in the bipartite structure of this poem and its eventual concern with human development.

While the other poems in the sequence conjure particular premonitions of the future that may be envisaged as coming out of specific geological epochs, Clarke's 'Mesozoic' initially draws attention to the extinction in the past of the dinosaur and the large mammals and the end of the dominant strains of life on the earth. Underpinning the poem is the way in which glacial epochs that have taken place over the last 35 million years or so have fossils that have not been subject to deep burial and metamorphoses and, as James Woodward maintains, provide pictures of 'past ecosystems under glacial and interglacial conditions'.[49] Woodward suggests that 'the ice core records heralded a new era in climate science: the study of abrupt climate change'.[50] He goes on to highlight the new questions that have emerged which helps to place Clarke's poetry more fully in its scientific contexts: 'How did ecosystems and humans respond to these abrupt changes? Were they regional or global phenomena?'[51]

With the phenomenon of abrupt change in mind, 'The Stone Poems' closes with a warning that we must reset the future before it is too late to preserve the planet. In his poem, 'The Dinosaur Park', the poet and environmental writer Robert Minhinnick – a contemporary of Clarke's – conjures from statues of the large reptiles which he encounters in a theme park, the actual creatures that existed and tries to achieve imaginative contact with them as sentient beings:

> I've passed the park a score of times
> But never glimpsed in its entanglement
> These postures struck of combat,
> Rage, the slow acknowledgment of pain.
> And strange to think such creatures shared
> The common factors of our lives,
> Hurt and hunger, fear of death,
> The gradual discovery of betrayal.[52]

But in doing so, Minhinnick's poem, like Clarke's 'Mesozoic', underscores an event of mass extinction: 'Now level with the dinosaurs / The path runs on, there's no way back, / As shadows make their imperceptible surge.'[53] But 'Mesozoic' does not end with this nihilistic sense of what may come and which for many environmentalists and scientists is already happening in the Anthropocene. While the first part of 'Mesozoic' ends with 'ammonite and dinosaur dead',[54] the second part recreates nature and the living world brought about by the warmer temperatures when the ice melted and rivers deposited their rich silt which supported new forms of life. It is impossible not to see the irony in Clarke's poem at this point given that rising temperatures and melting ice sheets in the twenty-first century are the symptoms of apocalyptic climate change and environmental destruction on a planetary scale. Clarke sees the Mesozoic, as did many of the guides to geology in the mid- and late-twentieth century, as an epoch which developed into the Cretaceous period, when plant life emerged that had 'almost a modern look' and included 'flowering plants and such trees as the holly, poplar, and oak'.⁵⁵

The Mesozoic is only tangentially aligned with human development, invoking – rather than addressing – the possibility of the mass extinction of human and, obviously, much non-human and non-living life. Anticipating the worst consequences of climate change and human domination of the environment during the Anthropocene, as discussed in Chapter 3, Chakrabarty argues that humans only became a 'force of geological nature in the geological sense' in the Industrial Revolution and that this is recognised fully only in the second half of the twentieth century.⁵⁶ This contention informs the first part of Clarke's 'The City' (1998), a poem referred to earlier as one of the texts exemplifying Clarke's long-standing interest in geology, as it turns from a journey through geological time to the nineteenth-century industrial revolution. Clarke's poem examines how the power, force and energy embedded in nature and the cosmos change through different geographical periods which are in turn approached not simply as inanimate geological processes but from the way in which they have helped determine the course of human society and have, especially in the Anthropocene, been shaped by it. In the first section of 'The City', we catch glimpses of rural life and also of poverty and deprivation. The sense of awe invoked by the endless thrust and noise of the industrial looms – 'The oscillating beat of the looms' drum / under the singing water of the fells'⁵⁷ – which contrasts with the rhythm of the cottage-based frames becomes the noise of modernity as opposed to the quiet we have to learn in order to hear the birdsong with which the poem opens – a theme to which she returned in remembering the Great Silence of the early 1940s, the grounding of international flights after the eruption of the Icelandic volcano at Eyjafjallajökull and, most recently, the Covid-19 pandemic of 2020, discussed in Chapter 2. The beat of the looms, like the crash of breaking waves and weather fronts, resonates with the chaos and uncertainty of the cosmos as it emerged out of its formless state, while the birdsong reflects the order and beauty of nature into which the cosmos, at least in part, eventually evolved.

AS THE UNIVERSE EXPANDS

Laniel-Musitelli points out that Clarke's renewed interest in science in the twenty-first century – evident in *Making the Beds for the Dead*

(2004), *A Recipe for Water* (2009), *Ice* (2012) and *Zoology* (2017) – 'corresponds to an environmental turn' and that 'attending to the energies of nonhuman bodies and non-living matter is part of Clarke's commitment to environmental poetics'.[58] However, as noted at the opening of this chapter, Clarke's enthusiasm for science dates from her childhood and is a constant presence in her life and work. Moreover, from 1990 onwards, as I have demonstrated, her interest in geology acquired not simply an environmental but an important human turn. Although betraying Clarke's interest in non-human bodies and non-living matter, the section of seven poems about fossils in *Zoology*, written as part of a residency at the Museum of Zoology in Cambridge in 2015, has a profound concern with the development of life as part of the expanding universe, discussed in Chapter 4.

The wonder that Clarke has for the fossil 'archaeopteryx', 150 million years old and, as the geologist Douglas Palmer says, 'one of the most famous fossils known',[59] begins, as her childhood enthusiasm for geology, with the name. The archaeopteryx is known by that name but also by the equally 'magical' German word 'urvogel', meaning 'first bird' or 'original bird'.[60] Such names encourage her, as a poet whose whole life is in language, to conjure the fossil in a moment of origin within the evolution of bird life – 'First bird, / thence every warbler, song thrush, wren'[61] – which is also a point of 'transition between dinosaur and bird'.[62] This point of origin in the poem is based on Thomas Henry Huxley's proposal, following the publication of Charles Darwin's *Origin of Species* (1859), that birds were descendants of dinosaurs. In comparing the archaeopteryx with the compsognathus, a small bipedal dinosaur, he discovered that, apart from their feathers and hands, the skeletons were very similar. Clarke is as equally fixated by finding in this fossil the origin of flight (archaeopteryx is from the ancient Greek for 'feather' or 'wing'), which separates birds from humans. The poem reminds the reader that this was only something which humans achieved through the invention of planes: 'bump-landing, lift-off, touch and go'.[63]

However, there is another awe-inspiring aspect to the fossil in this well-researched poem, how it was 'lost in the limestone of a salt lagoon' in Bavaria[64] but discovered from 1861 onwards along with a huge variety of fossils including dragonflies and fish.[65] For Clarke, the way in which the Archaeopteryx has been so well maintained in the lime-rich muds is itself sublime: 'a mould / from the Jurassic, print, exactitude'.[66] The poem, like Palmer's work, is inspired not just by the fossil itself but how, as a result of 'the right kind of rocks throughout the geological record, it has become possible to open privileged windows on the life of the past that is not normally preserved'.[67] Clarke uses the privileged window, to employ Palmer's metaphor, to revise conventional ways of looking at human and non-human evolution through focusing not only on a narrative of development but on moments of wonder – like cosmologists imagining the moment of cosmogenesis itself. In doing so, her emphasis falls once again on the diversity which the expanding universe has brought about and how this expansion may be seen as mirroring the first epoch of cosmogenesis. Thus, the archaeopteryx is captured at a point in time when dinosaurs began to possess feathers but also when, as Palmer says, 'some small bipedal dinosaurs' began to emerge.[68]

'Ichthyosaur' might be a companion poem to 'Archaeopteryx', but it is focused on a different kind of moment.[69] Again, in making the name alone the title of the poem, Clarke imbues it and the fossil with a sense of wonder. The name, 'ichthyosaurus', is Greek for 'fish lizard', a large giant marine reptile from the late Triassic and early Jurassic periods, and suggests that museums, like zoos and circuses, are interested in displaying animal skeletons and fossils which are rendered 'exotic' on account of their size.[70] Like the bird, fish of this kind achieved knowledge and mastery of a sphere which humans have never attained to the same extent despite their technology. Zoologists stress the streamlined dolphin-like bodies, seal-like paddles, and their powerful fish-like tails.[71] But the moment into which the poet stares is one which breaks down the barrier between human and non-human. As a woman who is a mother with experience of giving birth, Clarke is able to identify with the Ichthyosaurus across time and species:

> Behind glass she dies giving birth.
> Millions of years too late
> it can still move us,
> the dolphin-flip of her spine
>
> and the frozen baby turning its head
> to the world at the last moment
> as all babies do, choked
> as it learned to live.[72]

Although Clarke is studying a fossil, she does not think of it solely as an example of death but a definition of life in terms of intent, captured in the ichthyosaurus's physical features, its capacity to easily flip its body and its baby grasping a few moments of reptilian activity. Clarke compares what she is witnessing in the ichthyosaur fossil to other remembered moments, for example, of a lamb born the wrong way round or strangled by its umbilical cord. An extinct, giant marine reptile, humans and sheep are brought together in a way that transcends conventional natural history and the categorisation of species. The poem offers a fresh perspective on animal studies that is based on the human capacity to empathise with the experiences and sufferings of other animals and species.

The development of humans through the expanding universe is the subject of 'The Company of Bones' – 'Orangutan, Chimpanzee, Gorilla, Man'[73] – but it places human development alongside 'the golden lion tamarin' and 'its beautiful bones' and twenty-six joints in an engineered tail shaped, once again, by its 'intention' as a living being.[74] It makes Clarke think of the intention behind the way in which her own body and skeleton are constructed, 'my own heart working the blood through my wrist'.[75] But the huge variety of different skeletons that emerged through the expansion of planetary life causes her to reflect that only humans have developed the capacity to appreciate the extent of the narrative, incomplete as that is still. However, Clarke's seven poems about fossils stress that this story of developing planetary life, with its frequent twists and turns and end stops and fresh beginnings, is not only about the development of scientific knowledge but an expanding aesthetic awareness encapsulated in a short line from 'The Snowdon Rainbow Beetle' – 'What's beauty for, but to disguise / a beetle as a waterdrop'[76] – and in the beauty of the frozen butterflies in 'Marsh Fritillaries'. The beauty is linked to the notion of intent – the Snowdon beetle 'went its own way'[77] – and the activity that defines life – the butterflies 'hunger, eat, belong, mate, breed and die'[78] – which resonates with the broader nature of human mortality.

Clarke's poetry can be said to be not so much about geology as about *following with* geology. Initially reflecting a science taken largely from popular introductions to the subject, her work – particularly from the 1990s – pursues the human and environmental turns in geology and the natural sciences which Clarke links with a relationship between the human mind and non-living matter, connecting to her interest in cosmogenesis, and to a sense of a continuum in the apparent randomness and diversity of evolution. Throughout her more specifically geological poems, Clarke turns to particular types of rocks and fossils to conjure the expanding story of life and the non-living planet through cyclical moments of wonder. Clarke's geological perspectives displace the privileged position which humans have assumed for themselves in the Anthropocene in relation to other forms of planetary life and replaces conventional ways of thinking with new forms of 'knowing' that are more appropriate to a 'relational' universe. But Clarke's poetry highlights further consequences of human domination of the planet in the Anthropocene through diverse forms of war and conflict – the subject of the next two chapters.

6

War and Peace (Part One)

Clarke's poetry and journals highlight the psychological impact of different types of warfare – the conventional conflict associated with the home front in the Second World War and the diffused warfare of the late twentieth and early twenty-first centuries – the mediatisation of war and the way in which conflict is linked to various cosmological and religious perspectives that have allowed humans, as the historian Dipesh Chakrabarty says, 'a special relationship of mutuality with the earth' reflected in the 'indefinite march of physical aggrandizement' and 'physical power'.[1] This 'mutuality' Chakrabarty defines, in ways that resonate with Milja Kurki's *International Relations in a Relational Universe* discussed in Chapter 2, as being concerned with a number of assumptions: 'the specialness of humans', 'the centrality of humans to the larger scheme of things', and 'the idea that humans have the capacity to have visions of the whole world as totalities, albeit of different kinds'.[2]

The changing nature of war has shaped the content, language and form of Clarke's poetry for over half a century and I start where Clarke began with the Second World War, one of the most important influences upon her childhood. As she remembers, 'Childhood in the 1940s was dominated by a world war which even a child happily evacuated to the loving care of a grandmother, in what still seems like paradise, could not escape.'[3] In fact, she is only one of many writers of her generation who, as the poet Tony Curtis says, 'have been shaped by the World Wars'.[4] Not by chance, her work of the last two decades of the twentieth century coincided with a key anthology of Welsh writing about war[5] and her poems of the first decade of the twenty-first century with a substantial collection of essays on Wales and war.[6] Her reflections on her childhood inevitably became recollections of war and they influenced her thinking about, for example, memory, the nature of 'home', community and historical perspective.

In the published extracts of her journal from June 2019, Clarke reclaims her childhood memories of D-Day. Thinking of that day in her childhood home in Barry, near Cardiff in south Wales, she remembers her mother working endlessly on her Singer sewing machine to make her a birthday dress. At the time, she had a limited sense of the huge historical significance of the day and thought mainly of herself as any other child excited by the prospect of her birthday and a new dress. But, as an adult, she remembers this birthday in a number of ways: as an example of the bond that existed between herself and her mother to which she did not always do justice, as observed in Chapter 1, and for the way in which domestic life and routines were determined by war. A new birthday dress was a significant event in a child's life at this time because it was hard to obtain new materials and children's clothes were usually made, as Clarke recalls, from old clothes.[7] She remembers learning in her wartime childhood to find the extraordinary in the reshaped ordinariness of the everyday.

However, it was to this time also that Clarke's 2019 journal traces the origins of the perpetual unease that haunted her adult life, in, for example, the impact of the blackout – 'Even on a June evening, the room was dark'[8] – and the continuous fear of being bombed. A quotation from Annie Dillard's *Pilgrim at Tinker Creek* (1975), a favourite work of hers mentioned in Chapter 2, seems to summarise a thread that runs throughout her poetry and journals: 'I live in tranquillity and trembling.'[9] It is to this important but also insufficiently discussed aspect of her work that I now turn.

THE PSYCHOLOGICAL IMPACT OF WAR

As Clarke observes, children only partially recognise the wider historical importance of what is occurring around them. Such Clarke realises was the case on D-Day when her father, whom she later acknowledges probably understood the relevance of what was happening that day more than most people at the time from his work at the BBC, sat her on the window-sill of her bedroom and drew back the curtains so they could see wave after wave of bombers roaring toward Europe. Her father opening the curtains is clearly a memory that has remained with her of light dispelling darkness and the beginning of the end of the War. But it was also the beginning of a particular conception of memory threaded throughout her work as a corporeal and cognitive phenomenon. The physical nature of the bond between herself and her father as they sat together on D-Day signifies how she conceives of memory from her childhood onwards. Evident, for example, in the way in which she experiences her three-year-old sister's embarrassment as she is left naked at the edge of the tide when the sea drags down her home-knitted swimsuit and feels in her skin, even years later, the sharpness of the pins that held her birthday dress together as her mother dropped it over her body to check its size.[10] As an adult, she still takes pleasure in her first experiences of snow as a child – 'The plushy sound of it underfoot, the cold on my face'[11] – the sensation of being wrapped by her mother in a warm coat and wellington boots stuffed with socks and of the 'electric charge' she felt throughout her entire body as her father towed her across a frozen lake in a homemade sledge.[12]

These happy childhood memories are characterised by a cosmology which brings children and adults together in a 'mutuality', to use Chakrabarty's word, in which the self-conceived 'specialness' of humans is replaced by a different kind of 'relationality' as discussed in Chapter 2. However, Clarke's reflections on her wartime childhood also bring many difficult memories to mind which involve the way in which humans invest themselves with specialness, centrality in the larger scheme of things and a cosmological perspective that gives rise to indefinite physical aggrandisement and a particular perspective on the natural world. In 2019, she recalls how 'Dead birds lay on the snow, corpses in a war. War! Birds starved to death for lack of bread, as every crumb and crust was saved for the table.'[13] It is clearly a memory that has haunted her. In 'Letter from a Far Country', for example, she muses, 'Before the Welfare State who cared / for sparrows in a hard spring?'[14] and in the later poem, 'The Dead after the Thaw', published seven years before the journal entry, she remembers again: 'Starved birds in the snow of '47, / when no one had bread to spare.'[15]

These images signify how throughout the natural as well as the human world, as Tony Curtis observes, the Second World War 'left a legacy in terms of personal and social loss and advancement: nothing could be the same ...'.[16] This is evident not only in literature – for example, in the work of Brenda Chamberlain, Lynette Roberts, Alun Lewis and Vernon Watkins – but in the art of the time. Ceri

Richards's *Desolate Landscape* (1941), for example, as Curtis says, is 'a maelstrom of dark but organically fertile forms and forces' and his *The Force That Drives the Water Through the Rocks* (1944) is a particularly 'surreal and disturbing piece'.[17] Richards's art, and especially this latter work, was influenced by Dylan Thomas's poem 'The force that through the green fuse drives the flower'. But, while Thomas's poem is a wonderful celebration of creative cosmic energy in nature, Richards's painting, influenced by the blitz on Wales, the destruction of families and communities and stories from the Nazi death camps, grapples with a more violent and destructive energy. *The Force That Drives the Water Through the Rocks* suggests the impossibility of not seeing the cosmos through the lens of war but also the mental unease and darkness with which that generation emerged from war.

As Clarke's retrospective writings reveal, it was the psychological as much as the physical impact of war that affected her. One of the most important Welsh poets writing in English at the time, R. S. Thomas, brought this dimension of the War to the fore. In his autobiography, *Neb*, Thomas recalls when he was a curate at Hanmer (from 1940 until 1942), the German Luftwaffe flying over his church on their way to Liverpool. He observed that what affected him most was the impact of the recurring sound of the bombers' engines and the monotonous repetitiveness of their appearance in the night skies. The memory, like Clarke's childhood recollections, was felt throughout his entire being. When he says that it was not so much the fear that affected him as the despair and hopelessness,[18] he is not so much talking about the Luftwaffe as the kind of mutuality, as defined by Chakrabarty, which they represented and which would inevitably lead, as it does for Thomas and Clarke, to a depressive vision of the relationship between humankind and the world.

In Clarke's account of her experiences of the Second World War, its psychological impact enters, and is shaped by, her child's imagination of legends, giants and shipwrecks that leads to Chakrabarty's distorted and distorting kind of mutuality: 'To a child it was a legendary war, a giant's war of stormy seas, shipwreck, armies that crossed rivers on the body of their commander, bombs that fell from the sky. There was a monstrous enemy leader, and could we but kill him we would all be saved.'[19] Thomas's *The Echoes Return Slow* (1988), published after Clarke had moved to west Wales, must have helped her articulate for herself her childhood experience of the War and the darkness of the accompanying realisation that nothing would be the same again which still haunted her. In Thomas's poem, the image of red skies 'where no sun had ever risen' signifies a perpetual instinctive fear as does the den that has been entered and is no longer safe.[20]

However, the psychology of Clarke's childhood, as she remembers and tries to understand it, involves areas which are outside those of R. S. Thomas's poetry. Her later reflection in *At the Source* examines how her relationship with her parents and the War become entangled: 'Like most children, I found the quarrels of adults painful and bewildering, and what was going on up there and out there was all too raw a re-enactment of the unease in my own parents' marriage, symbolised by their difference over which language they should speak to their daughters.'[21] The impact of her parents' relationship with each other seems to have troubled Clarke all her life. As late as 2018, she remembers in her journal: 'I was troubled and troublesome. My parents' marriage was unhappy, and I knew it.'[22] It is as if, after all these years, Clarke is writing back to her parents and in that plain speaking which, as observed in Chapter 2, is a much over-looked feature of her work. The world out there, as it were, is entangled with the child's inner pain and bewilderment. The 'bomb shelter under the stairs in a house in a south Wales port' is not simply a physical refuge from the bombs but an 'internal' refuge from the turbulence of her parents' relationship with each other and with herself.[23] She contrasts it with her grandmother's home to which she was evacuated where, significantly, she does not talk about safety from the bombers but another kind of sanctuary: 'In my grandmother's house and yard, Welsh and English, birth and death, the real and the imaginary, were all equally natural and elemental and as necessary to each other's definition as the sea is to the land.'[24] The 'real' and the 'imaginary' which Clarke experienced in south Wales as separate from each other were integrated with each other in west Wales and this provided an important, long-standing narrative frame for Clarke's thinking and writing about war even at the close of the twentieth and the beginning of the twenty-first centuries which is the subject of the next section.

WAR AND MEDIATISATION

Clarke's first accomplished poem examining how as a result of the media, in this case radio, we can live simultaneously in more than one 'reality', is 'Siege' published in *Letter from a Far Country* (1982). Clarke herself, admitting that all her poems at this time were true stories, points out that the siege was the Iranian embassy siege of the 1980s which 'came to a violent end witnessed live on radio and television'.[25] In May 1980, a group of six armed men stormed the embassy in London in support of sovereignty for the Zhuzestan Province. They took twenty-six people hostage and, after six days, frustrated by negotiations with the British government, they killed one of them and threw his body out of the embassy. During an ensuing raid by the Special Air Service – Operation Nimrod – all but one of the remaining hostages were rescued and five of the hostage-takers were killed.

In this poem, Clarke says she sought to 'blend three elements: the distant violence, the beauty of my garden, and memories stirred by a box of old photographs'.[26] As she sorts family photographs in the garden in late Spring, the siege to which she listens on the radio is in the background, gathering a momentum which is reflected in and changes the nature of the garden imagery; as in the depiction of the sun as 'fallen', the implicit association of the wren's distant messaging with Morse code, the way in which the birds listen intently and a butterfly moves unsteadily as troops on manoeuvre.[27] As Clarke says herself, 'in such moments of extreme feeling, past and present, faraway and close things, seem to fuse into a single fierce experience'.[28] The poem shifts from a relative harmony with nature in which the human, as in the photographs, is decentred, to destruction and violence implying the kind of physical aggrandisement and power in Chakrabarty's mutuality. In a devastating image of how war in a virtual reality enters and disrupts Clarke's consciousness, the garden suddenly 'burns', fills with barking dogs that might or might not be on the radio and the blossoms in its apple trees (themselves a symbol of paradise) merge with gunsmoke.[29] Through the confusion of these two realities, Clarke turns from fires scorching the grass to a house of 'floors falling, machine guns'.[30]

Not until 'The King of Britain's Daughter' (1993) does Clarke fully confront the way in which during her wartime childhood the relationship between humankind and the world changed for all time. In examining a short poem within this larger work, Katie Gramich finds that it highlights the role of 'the mass news media [in] bringing distant wars uncomfortably into the midst of an ordinary domesticity', skilfully interweaving the mythological story about Branwen with 'how the news of war is first received and understood by a female child in a west Wales kitchen'.[31] But in the poem, the contrasting perspectives which Chakrabarty identifies – the humility of sharing a planetary life and envisaging the world from a human perspective as 'totalities' – are brought into tension. The kitchen with its jar of marigolds, signifying a humbling, relational existence between the human and natural world, is juxtaposed with the radio associated with human ambition to reach out beyond itself to a totalised human world and with the cosmos reflected in the sky and sea.[32] The images of the radio chained to the kitchen window-sill by, significantly, fraying wires and the news falling out of the sky, as would bombs, suggest that the totalised human world is driven by a new kind of human-centred cosmology which, unlike the vast natural cosmos, is brittle and bent on its mutual destruction.

'Gorse', from *The Silence* (2024), integrates nights of storms, with war, radio warnings and tensions within her childhood homes, linking 'sea fizz' with the sound of the adults 'hushing' in rooms.[33] One of the key images in the poem is of Clarke, as a child, lying on a cliff edge listening. Outside, she conjures one reality where there is wreckage, someone crying, a shot and people searching with torches. But at home all this is denied and is 'beyond the black-out curtain' through which she says she 'mustn't even peep'.[34] The black-out curtains and what lies beyond them are both physical and psychological. They hide her from 'something that might float up? Under a scream of gulls, something terrible'[35] which with the mediatisation of different forms of warfare in her adult life is not hidden. 'Gorse' is a disturbing and worrying poem where the emotions associated with individual menacing words are taken up and developed through others as, for example, where 'steep and stony' cliff paths resonate with 'a scream of gulls' and 'a shout in the wind' with the prospect of an undefined fear turning into terror.

In the late twentieth and early twenty-first centuries, a 'quantum leap', as the American sociologist Manfred Steger says, occurred in 'the dramatic creation, expansion, and acceleration of worldwide interdependencies and global exchanges.'[36] Alongside, and as part of these new global dynamics, 'the global cultural flows of our time [became] generated and directed by global media.'[37] As a consequence, the media coverage of war emerged as an increasingly complex phenomenon. The epoch in which Clarke has lived much of her adult life has been characterised by what cultural and political scientists, such as Andrew Hoskins and Ben O'Loughlin, have called the implosion of the twentieth century: 'Once news could be transferred electronically, rather than via printed paper or newsreels on trains and boats, information about war, conflict and catastrophe could traverse distances almost instantaneously.'[38] But Clarke recognises that from the last decades of the twentieth century, the media has not simply reported war but become part of the war itself – a process now termed 'mediatisation' – and we have all, like Clarke, become immersed in what is now called 'diffused warfare' – from the Vietnam War to war over Kosovo and the Gulf and the *event time* of the 1991 Gulf War[39] – a product of a new 'media ecology'.[40]

However, Clarke's work is not an examination of diffused war, or the mediatisation of war, per se as much as the psychological impact of the way in which it and 'everyday life are increasingly embedded in the mediascape'.[41] In her journal for August 2007, Clarke admits: 'My senses are busy with all this while my mind hurts with the private argument and the big troubled world. There is always a war somewhere. Was it always so?'[42] War enters her work from a variety of angles and perspectives but, in addition to the subject of war per se, Clarke's work fluctuates between the joy which she finds in nature and the cosmos and the depression which thinking about war and threats to the planet ushers in: 'The long light of summer, or rain or shine, sets me reflecting upon joy – how it survives and revives us in a world that would make us despair. I reflect too on its opposite, the stone in the heart. Not ecstasy and agony. Just ordinary joy, and everyday downheartedness.'[43] Clarke's poem 'Times Like These', in the CND publication *Glas-Nos: Cerddi Dros Heddwch / Poems for Peace* (1987), begins with the collective depression which affected the 1960s over the prospect of a nuclear war: 'Too heavy-hearted to go walking / in beech-woods. / At night the children's sleep / is racked by dreams. They wake crying of war.'[44] But through the joy of childbirth, parenthood and life lived in contact with nature, the poem acquires a more optimistic note: 'In times like these we should praise trees and babies, / and take the children walking in beech-woods.'[45] In this respect, 'Times Like These' is about peace, like many of her 'war' poems, and resonates with the foreword to the collection by the Chairperson of CND Cymru at the time: 'Peace exists within each and every one of us. Peace is determined by our response to each other.'[46]

Curtis's anthology of Welsh writing about war in English, referred to at the outset of this chapter, includes three poems by Gillian Clarke – 'Oranges' (published in *Letting in the Rumour* (1989)), 'The Night War Broke' (*Making the Beds for the Dead* (2004)) and

'The Field-Mouse' (published in *Five Fields* (1998) and reprinted as 'The Field Mouse' in *Roots Home* (2021)) – in the final, and most contemporary section, entitled 'Post-War, Cold War, New Wars'.[47] War broke out in Iraq in March 2003 – hostilities in the Gulf War had been suspended in 1991 – and the UK and the Gulf are brought together in 'The Night War Broke' through media coverage, the employment of harrier jets which involved the UK in Kosovo, Iraq and Afghanistan, and through the light cast by the moon on both sides of the world. The image of the moon is employed to unite the actual physicality of war in the Middle East with the horror and anxiety felt on the other side of the world in west Wales where it is a virtual conflict but felt throughout the bodies of the observers. The moonlight reveals 'the wide awake in their beds', in the Middle East and elsewhere, 'struck dumb ... with their radios / in the cities the villages the back of beyond'.[48]

In Curtis's anthology, 'The Night War Broke' is almost juxtaposed with 'The Field-Mouse' but separated from it by his own poem 'Crane Flies' (originally published in *War Voices* (1995)). As in 'The Night War Broke', rural Wales in Curtis's poem is juxtaposed with a distant country in which war is raging, in this instance Bosnia. The psychological impact of a war so far away from Ceredigion in which Clarke wrote 'The Field-Mouse' is captured in the way in which 'the air hums with jets',[49] practising with increased frequency and intensity (which resonates with the psychological effect that German bombers flying over north Wales had upon R. S. Thomas in the early 1940s). As Clarke says herself: 'The noise is sometimes a terrifyingly sudden scream, and sometimes a continuous roar, like deep humming.'[50]

But the source of the pain felt by the poet in 'The Field-Mouse', as in 'The Night War Broke', is 'the radio's terrible news'.[51] Like the scream of the jets' engines, it penetrates the outer limits of human hearing, disrupting the peace of the rural environment. As Clarke says in writing about 'The Field-Mouse': 'The rumour of pain, the world's pain, comes from the media, wars and rumours of war.'[52] While both poems stress the psychological impact of the hostilities and the way in which the media is part of the process of the war itself, 'The Field-Mouse' extends the impact of war onto individuals listening, watching and reading about it in the media and to the way in which it changes their outlook on the world and their emotional being. At one level, the hayfield is analogous to the battlefield and the small animals killed in cutting the hay are analogous to the men, women and children slaughtered in Bosnia. But the analogies are not simply literary and cultural conceits, they are manifestations of how the poet's psychology has been affected by the mediatisation of even ostensibly remote wars.

Clarke now remembers, and cannot free from her mind, that the Welsh equivalent of 'cutting the hay' is 'killing the hay' and she cannot look at a dead field mouse without being brought close to the war in Bosnia.[53] 'The Field-Mouse' closes on a nightmare:

> All night I dream the children dance in grass
> their bones brittle as mouse-ribs, the air
> stammering with gunfire, my neighbour turned
> stranger, wounding my land with stones.[54]

Through this dream, the poem invokes a different cosmology from which the poem began. The sense of community, as during the hay harvest in west Wales, arising from the 'peace within each and every one of us' (as the Foreword to *Glas-Nos* says), is overturned. As in post-Second World War Welsh poetry and the work of artists like Ceri Richards, the emphasis on the creativity of the cosmos – encapsulated, as observed earlier in this chapter, in Dylan Thomas's poem 'The force that through the green fuse drives the flower' – shifts to human destruction and the wrecking of the planet.

Intriguingly Curtis's 'Crane Flies' – in which the poet is proud of his son for standing up to his peers who are pulling wings and legs off crane flies – resonates with both of Clarke's poems with which it is juxtaposed. The boys who kill the insects are tantamount to the adults who slaughter people in Bosnia and the poet's son who confronts them is comparable to the children in 'The Field-Mouse' who carry an injured mouse from the 'killing field'. The poet's sensibility is again disrupted by the media transmission of war but, as the media is the television, the psychological impact is even more immediate and horrific: 'All the week the TV has brought us / the phalange massacres in Beirut – / mangled corpses parcelled in sheets.'[55] The televised images strengthen the media's involvement in the process of war. But in both poems, there is a sense that the mediatisation of war is changing, and controlling, the wider cosmology by which we live as the closing lines of Curtis's poem make clear. The crane fly 'beating' in his son's 'cupped hands' is analogous to the creative energy held within the cosmos: 'that sense of life / as a distant, other thing / that would fly if we gave it wing.'[56]

Clarke's 'The Night War Broke' and 'The Field-Mouse', like Curtis's 'Crane Flies', are focused on the psychological pressure exacerbated by media devices, and especially mobile ones, which Hoskins and O'Loughlin have described as 'the embedding of sensing machines in our environment'.[57] In their different ways, the poems emphasise how the resultant 'conditions of connectivity, convergence and immediacy' are transforming all aspects of war and media coverage and 'how images of military conduct are recorded and remediated around the world'.[58] But Clarke's work is not simply based on the fact that this is happening but, as in Curtis's anthology of Welsh war writing, *After the First Death*, our awareness that this is happening. While our sense of ourselves as global beings is increasingly determined by our 'ubiquitous' media ethology,[59] we fail to understand sufficiently the cosmology in which they position us. These poems not only highlight the diffuse nature of warfare, rooted in media technology and media ethology, but the complicated involvement of the media in the changing nature of war. Although the war which Clarke experienced in her childhood instigated an abiding sense of unease and fear, the warfare in Bosnia, the Gulf and Afghanistan which haunted her later life is characteristic of a different type of war which is not so much the result of a politics in which a particular state and its population are deemed under attack but part of a global climate of fear, vulnerability and risk.[60]

WAR AND THE POLITICS OF UNEASE

In the course of her work and life, Clarke seems to have found herself increasingly preoccupied with the mediatisation of the warfare of 'exception', as it has come to be known,[61] in which the boundaries between civilian and military targets are blurred, as in 'Listen', published in *Ice* (2012), which is concerned with the impact of a double-bomb secretly planted in a dusty street in Afghanistan.[62] The poem – beginning with a call to prayer in Samarkand in Uzbekistan thirty years previously – highlights how the 'Big News' processes supposedly key details; in this case, the secretive planting of the bomb, an innocent civilian stepping on it, the soldier's comment that 'it's World War One out here',[63] and the chanting crowd fisting the air at the funeral in response to the media presence. But the poem brings to bear on these events a perspective which Clarke thinks of, to use her own term discussed in Chapter 1, as 'feminine values'. This is evidenced in the poem's key images of a widow crouching in rubble over her son's body, of a shocked mother alone in her room behind a locked door and the despair in the prayers at dusk. The allusions to the First World War and the poppy fields of Flanders invoke a different kind of warfare fought by troops on a battlefield while here there is no boundary between combatant and civilian. The poem adopts, and becomes, a cantata of grief which transfixes the reader as it moves through the different layers and elements as Clarke herself was entranced by the single, pre-modern, authoritative voice with which the poem opens. But while the single voice of the mosque in Samarkand is supplanted by the diverse voices and perspectives that unfold throughout the text, it remains an image of fortitude, resilience and hope which is in the city's DNA as it has survived numerous conquests throughout its history to become a prosperous centre of commerce, education and scholarship.

In her work generally, Clarke's response to war is not simply international nor global but, as in *The King of Britain's Daughter*, planetary and laments the absence in world politics of a planetary or relational voice. In this respect, her work resonates with the way in which opposition to war has become linked to the promotion of ecological issues and green values which can be traced to the wider peace movement in Wales and the Greenham Common campaign which began in September 1981. As Jane Aaron and M. Wynn Thomas maintain, there is barely a Welsh poet of this era who does not have a Greenham Common poem in their oeuvre.[64] Welsh contemporary poets of Clarke who incorporated pacifism and eco-politics into their work – such as Robert Minhinnick in *Life Sentences* (1983); Nigel Jenkins in 'Brawdy', based on an attempt to establish a Greenham Common camp in west Wales and emphasising the eisteddfod prayer as a plea for peace; and the Welsh-language poet Menna Elfyn, joint editor of *Glas-Nos: Cerddi Dros Heddwch* and Chair of PEN Cymru – helped develop a Welsh identity in terms of green politics and peace.[65] However, as the international politics scholar Milja Kurki observes: 'Once one starts to "expect" to hear such a voice because it is ontologically expected by our relational ontology and politically made "possible" to imagine by our critical humanist ethics, the lack of such voices in "international politics" becomes surprising; no, it becomes outrageous!'[66]

In Clarke's poem 'Birthday', published in *Making the Beds for the Dead* (2004), there is the hint of the possibility of such a voice in the people who watch the comet travel 'from the earth's memory' into 'the black Atlantic and the stars'.[67] The blackness has a vibrancy and immanence of light (and life) which, as discussed in Chapter 4, is a motif running throughout Clarke's work and the poem suggests that such insight into the creative energy of the cosmos should inspire a planetary or relational voice in world politics which is indeed what Kurki's volume argues for. Clarke's writings about war, in keeping with her post-1990s writing generally, suggest that without such a cosmology, politics and the planet will always be disconnected. As some parts of the world begin to think in relational terms, as Clarke's and Kurki's work underscore, others in besieged cities can only look into the 'zero' of 'the black mouths of guns'.[68] As the focus falls on the besieged city, the outlook in 'Birthday' is not optimistic: 'Will pity / save them? It'll take a miracle.'[69]

In 'Aftermath', also from *Making the Beds for the Dead*, the moon, a symbol of the relational cosmos in Clarke's earlier poems (as discussed in Chapter 2), exposes 'a shaken world', highlighting the detritus of war left in the desert and the socio-economic, cultural and psychological impact of war, as it 'lights the road for the lost, / the footloose, the fugitive, / the warriors and the wounded'.[70] As one of many poems by Clarke that tries, like Kurki, to unravel what might constitute a relational voice, 'Aftermath' brings together human and non-human life – the moon 'lays linen on the fields, / on beasts asleep on their shadows'.[71] There is something biblical in the way in which the light of the moon – like the star of Bethlehem – brings beasts and footloose humans together. But the sense of a profound connectedness between different forms of life in this line is undone by the image which closes the poem: 'the peeled skull / of a frog, like the husk of a planet'.[72]

Clarke is not a conventional war poet. War enters her work through incremental shifts in her thinking toward what Anthony Burke and others have termed 'planet politics' in which the local, national and global no longer define our only spheres of action.[73] Their manifesto for the future, like Clarke's poetry, stresses the damage that we have inflicted on the planet in seeking to transform it according to our human-centric perspectives and our human needs. For Clarke, as for Burke, there is an urgent need for 'a new kind of responsibility, binding environmental justice and social justice inextricably together'.[74] In her writings, war and the international politics that give rise to war constitute sites of the kind described by Kurki, in which the considerations highlighted by relational ontology are '"washed off" our human horizons, our consciousness'.[75] Both writers look to a future in which, as Kurki says, the state and its human interests are no longer 'wedded into the '"international" structure of human domination'.[76] The integration of the state's involvement in human affairs and the international structure which gives rise to war underpins Clarke's poem 'Tomatoes', from *Making the Beds for the Dead*, based on the Gulf War. The tomato sellers, maintaining a connection with the earth through their agricultural activity, live according to a pre-modern socio-economic structure – their cargo 'not crated, not cradled against a rough ride'[77] – in which they sow their crops on the plains of rivers, nurture the seedlings with dung and irrigate them with water systems from the rivers, as their people have done since ancient times. Through the way in which each ripe fruit is tenderly picked and their hands cup the heads of their babies, the poem suggests that their way of life is attuned to the relational universe. But their simple, and for them fulfilling, life is disrupted by the interests of the state involved in war, emblematised by the checkpoint on the way to the city market in Baghdad. The military regime sees tomato farmers as simply so much collateral damage, as the final image suggests – 'a pyramid of fruit / bumping north / on the Baghdad road, / piled like skulls.'[78] The poem is not advocating another model of democracy, evident through the sympathetic unveiling of the tomato sellers' lives, but calling for respect, as in the Welsh word 'parch' which was fundamental to Welsh pacifism,[79] toward what Kurki calls the 'geostory' of humanity, in order to envisage other potential ways of acting.[80] In this respect, Kurki's work also helps us to appreciate how Clarke sees that 'in the mesh, wars, markets, and global epidemics all involve mediations and negotiations of multiple sets of relations, human and non-human'.[81]

Steger makes the point that 'Lest we are willing to let global problems fester to the point where violence and intolerance appear to be the only realistic ways of confronting our unevenly integrating world, we must link the future course of globalization to a profoundly reformist agenda.'[82] Clarke's 'Tomatoes', 'Aftermath' and 'Birthday' offer the reader what has been called by the political scientist Robyn Eckersley a 'more outward looking hyper-reflexivity'[83] which, as Kurki says, allows us – as in Clarke's poetry – to reflect on the extent to which our 'earthling-ness' connects us with the planet and the cosmos and on the nature of human and non-human interdependence.[84] However, while each of these writers is concerned with the fragility of the planet and the danger of uncritical human dominance over it, Clarke places as much emphasis on how our cosmological orientation, as discussed in Chapter 2, structures our human attitudes to each other and to other life forms.

In 'Mercury', from *A Recipe for Water* (2009), a silver streak left by a jet in the night sky brings to Clarke's mind an event in her childhood. While her parents were asleep or relaxing in other rooms, she found herself searching her father's desk and discovering mercury from a broken barometer hidden in a tobacco tin. As Clarke frequently tries to do in her post-1990s work, she establishes a link (as discussed in Chapter 2) between the sky and human behaviour. Several orders are disrupted in this poem: the night sky by the jet, emotions and peace within the poet's childhood home and the psychology of the child playing with the element in her father's desk drawer. As a planet, Mercury is named after the Roman god responsible for mediation between the gods and humans which conclude or, indeed, prevent war. But the other presence in the poem is the poet's disturbed state of mind, evident in the guilt which she still has as an adult over this childhood event. In discovering the mercury in her father's desk, she realises – in hindsight – that she had been able to 'touch the forbidden' and was only seconds away from experiencing the mythical physical and psychological effect of the element, allegedly able to send people 'as mad as hatters'.[85] These mythical consequences emblematise the psychic unease which she feels over death, war and the destruction of the planet which inhabits her physical as well as mental being – 'It could get under your skin, electricity / running your veins, nerves and bones.'[86] This sense, and fear, of a pending breakdown is set against the stability and order of the family home which by the end of the poem, now linked to mercury, appears somewhat fragile. The final image of the child 'taking / a tiger out of a drawer'[87] encapsulates what is at the heart of the poem, the fragile boundary between the containment and the destructive release of energy in the physical, cosmological and psychological worlds.

It is impossible to read the entries about war in Clarke's journal in *Roots Home* (2021) without noticing the way in which they are linked to a deep sadness which haunts even the most positive and optimistic sections. The entry dated, '19 April Good Friday' (2019), is an example: 'Sorrow in Belfast. A young, gay, woman journalist has been shot, it is assumed by a gunman in the New IRA.'[88] The event is one which once again is mediatised, the media involved in creating the sadness and perpetual unease that emanates from, and is part of the coverage of, this type of war. The 'sorrow' is not only in Belfast, but the wider public that tune in to it. The prose has many of the characteristics of Clarke's plain speaking, intent upon telling it as it is: 'This is what walls do, religious, cultural, racial, verbal. Walls break Britain with prejudice, whispers and lies.'[89] In the published journal, this entry is juxtaposed with a poem which she wrote on the day of the Northern Ireland Good Friday Agreement, 10 April 1998, after helping a ewe to birth her lambs. The journal exemplifies how the plain-speaking voice in Clarke's poems of the 1970s and 1980s, especially those which have a political turn, is something which in the course of her writing career she actively sought to integrate even with her more lyrical work.

'A Difficult Birth' juxtaposes the challenge of bringing the Good Friday Agreement to completion with helping to birth two lambs. The two threads share an initial sense of hopelessness – 'We thought her barren'[90] – which gives way to excitement and optimism, and new last-minute effort, as the birth of the Agreement draws close to that of the lambs: 'and tonight's she's serious, restless and hoofing the straw'.[91] The poem carefully and subtly identifies, and develops from the points where the two themes overlap: anxious waiting for news; the exhausting 'slog'; moments when the Agreement and the birth will not come; and the anxious phone calls summoning further help. But despite the parallels between the two events, the nature of waited 'news' is different in each case. In the Good Friday Agreement, it is part of the process and the drama – the creation of a narrative in which the peace deal is close one minute and far away the next, the breaking of barriers, and the last-minute frustrations. It is an event in which journalists, broadcasters and cultural commentators find a new sense of promise. Its inclusive vision points toward peace but should that fail, further conflict and violence. By contrast, the birth of the lambs is a naturally unfolding process to which the poet and her husband contribute and all involved are part of a wider mesh of relationality which is suggestive of harmony and peace and a more humbled world outlook.

A comparison of the poem with Clarke's commentary in her journal suggests that she saw mediatisation of the Good Friday

Agreement, which was part of the continuous coverage of Northern Ireland politics, as bringing about an important shift in how we approach and formulate politics, in the relationship which we have with the media and with events on which the political identity of Northern Ireland – and our own – is dependent. The birth of the lambs perceived from the poet's connectivity with nature and animal farming is an event which brings about a shift, too, in how we approach the natural world, the relationality of the cosmos and our relationship with non-human life. The conclusion of the poem is based on an interplay of concepts – 'peace' and 'death' – which carry different meanings in each of the contexts. In terms of the birth of the lambs, these notions are primary, real and biological. As far as the Good Friday Agreement is concerned, they are secondary, virtual and socio-political.

The global culture of unease in Clarke's writing enters spheres of life in addition to, but linked with, war which bring nearer an apocalyptic cosmology in which humans are destroying themselves and other forms of life on the planet. By contrast with 'Blue Sky Thinking', from *Ice* (2012) and 'Spring Equinox, 2021' from *The Silence* (2024) (discussed in Chapter 2), some of Clarke's poems in *The Silence* confront the possible origins of the Covid-19 pandemic as a biological agency. In 'The Silence', 'the world belongs to the virus' and 'The crown has passed to a life-form / hatched in the gut of a bat'.[92] This reflects reports at the time – the media claimed that the coronavirus was linked to the Sars-CoV-2 carried by bats – and the poem itself suggests the psychological impact of such coverage and diverse speculation about the origins of the virus.[93] The transition in the poems within the volume *The Silence* not only emphasises the death and destruction caused by the virus but a more despairing perspective on it. 'Today' begins with the uplift of a blue sky but shifts immediately to emphasising those who were taken by the virus who have gone forever, the way in which touching was forbidden and the death of an unnamed thirteen-year-old boy where the poem – 'Who will heal the pain / of those whose arms he slipped'[94] – recalls 'Letter from a Far Country' (1982): 'Before the Welfare State who cared / for sparrows in a hard spring?'[95] In a journal entry for October 2020, the Covid-19 pandemic's 'predatory multiplications' is associated with the ever presence of hunting birds, 'rooks, ravens, crows: corvids'.[96] However, as in her war poems, Clarke highlights the role of the media, perceiving it as involved in dramatising the events which it purports to report: 'the name of a new killer, the name of fear, the word on the air, down radio waves, in the morning *Guardian*'.[97] Clarke locates Covid within the larger web of unease which includes international terrorism and biological warfare:

> The virus is a secret agent undermining our safety, our democracy. Anxiety grows as Covid on its covert way is echoed by talk of Russian and Chinese cyberattacks on our privacy, our security. One seems a metaphor for the other, both real and dangerous.[98]

As in her war poems, the emphasis is not so much on the physical consequences of the disease as the pandemic's psychological impact generated by the new forms of warfare and disease. The intensity of this mesh of anxiety is underlined by the interconnection of Clarke's language, bringing together 'corvid' – a family of perching, predatory birds – 'covid' and 'covert'.

GLOBAL CONFLICT AND THE EVERY DAY

In Clarke's poetry, the experience of terrible loss in the coalfields is analogous to that on the battlefield. The poem 'Six Bells', included in *Ice* (2012), is dedicated to the forty-four miners killed in an underground explosion on 28 June 1960 at the colliery in Six Bells, Abertillery. It is now the site of the artistically acclaimed Guardian memorial to this event dedicated to all mining communities wherever they may be. The focus of the poem is on the involvement of women as wives and mothers, as in 'Listen' based on Afghanistan discussed earlier. The integration of the Six Bells explosion with the home front in the Second World War especially is conveyed subtly through the sound of the siren and the description of the ball of fire. Unlike in the Second World War, when non-combatants on hearing the siren took safety underground, the women gather in the streets but as they did about twenty-years earlier when the all-clear had sounded. The domestic activities with which miners' wives pass time in order to avoid thinking about the ever-present danger in the mines is analogous to the tasks which the women who remained at home – wives, partners, mothers, widows, lovers – undertook to avoid thinking about loved ones overseas and the air raids on their doorstep.[99] But the colliery, like the Second World War especially, turned the homeland into a front line. The explosion at Six Bells had the same kind of devastating impact on those connected with the colliery which some of them would have experienced less than twenty years before in the War – 'a pulse inside the earth like a blow to the heart'.[100]

'Six Bells' is not so much about the 1960 explosion as the peace and community that ordinary people desire, not the devastating explosions in the mines or the slaughter of loved ones on battlefields. Behind the mines and war, there are those who exploit and those who are exploited. The kind of life that the latter would like to live is exemplified in 'Six Bells' in the images of a housewife, as she would have been described in the 1960s, 'holding in her arms the wet weight / of her wedding sheets' and those who look up from 'wringing rainbows onto slate'.[101] In 'Letters from Bosnia' (published in *Five Fields*, 1998), the geographical and cultural distances between Vitos and Llanidloes are mitigated through the shared humanity which the children display in the letters that they write to each other. The misspelling of Wales on the envelope as 'Vales'[102] underlines the distance between the two countries. But there is something delightfully personal about the photographs that are included, of the children pulling faces as children often do when they are photographed. The children's innocence and willingness to share joy and warmth suggests an alternative to the human centricity that Chakrabarty encapsulates in his concept of mutuality. The final image derived from the Bosnian photographs in the last lines of the poem with its reference to the bullet holes left by the war – 'They wave, thumbs up to the future. / Behind them, in the rendered wall of the school / are the bullet holes'[103] – might be said to undermine the promise of the future which the gestures of the children signify but they also make what the children represent all the more necessary and precious.

In Clarke's war poems, the individual and personal – often based on small day-to-day emotions and gestures – are frequently contrasted with the larger, more impersonal forces of war. 'The Listeners', published in *The King of Britain's Daughter* (1993), is one of her most effective poems in this respect. To an extent, the poem is inspired by her father's merchant navy days when, as she says, 'he worked as a ship's wireless officer – the ship's "Sparks" – receiving and sending Morse-coded messages in a circle as wide as long wave would reach across the ocean'.[104] The poem integrates three different interpretations of the 'voices' – the radio room of SS *Hatimura* in 1919,[105] equipment receiving and sending signals into outer space, and two lovers – with the emotion and meaningfulness arising from different voices touching in different contexts and with different expectations.

Through doing so, it emphasises the experience of listening and transmitting, like the children's letters in the later 'Letters from Bosnia', as a hopeful and need-fulfilling process.

However, in each case in 'The Listeners', the signal is sent through a void and is met by a deafening silence. The Pacific Ocean through which the SS *Hatimura* moves is analogous to the vast space through which the radio waves from the ship are 'swimming out forever'.[106] The ship conveys a sense of the loneliness of the planet on which there is more of a need for its life forms to communicate with each other than become involved in conflict and in killing each other, especially as the planet may be the only one to support intelligent life. The poem turns on this disturbing possibility – 'If anyone's out there listening'[107] – that there may be no one or that if there are other intelligent and ordered worlds, their signals will reach us too late for us to answer. The emphasis is not so much on the science of signals and radio waves as the psychology of envisaging not only the world but the cosmos itself as relational. The poem opens with the signal room of SS *Hatimura* which in its mesh of wires is not only analogous to the wider world of electronic communications and wave-based technologies but the way in which each of us is wired emotionally and cognitively. The poem closes with the loop between the ship's wireless officer and someone at home – two voices almost touching: 'I am calling you "from SS *Hatimura*".'[108]

In poems such as 'Six Bells', 'Letters from Bosnia' and 'The Listeners', Clarke confronts and examines what Chakrabarty calls 'the relatively empty but capacious category of "the world" – in its relationship to the human – [which] came to absorb and erase into its vast and vacuous oneness the rich, strange, and intractable diversity of what actuality exists'.[109] In one of her more horrific war poems, 'Oradour-sur-Glane', based on the village in Nazi-occupied France where, in June 1944, about 642 inhabitants were rounded up and murdered by the occupying SS – many burnt alive in their church – Clarke confronts the limits of human aggrandisement and power. But focusing on the way in which, after a new village was built nearby, the ruins of the old were maintained as a memorial and museum, she explores not only the violence of which humans are capable but the way in which the totality of vision, of which Chakrabarty speaks, can create a 'vacuous oneness' that can erase real history. As much as 'Capel Celyn', the village drowned in north Wales to provide Liverpool with water, Oradour-sur-Glane has undergone a process of transformation from real (incomprehensible) event to story and myth. It is the mythologising of the reality which is at the heart of the poem:

> Tomorrow you will visit the village
> that stopped dead
> in its smoking ashes
> the morning after.[110]

The horror of what happened is not gainsaid. But it is almost impossible to articulate. The 'molten bell's tongue / is a dumb lump in its throat' and analogous to the barrier which the poet feels between the present spectacle and the past history which it commemorates.[111] This enables the poem to reclaim the real event – the real horror – against the spectacle that the village has become: 'stopped dead / in its smoking ashes'.[112] Rediscovering and reclaiming the real history and real suffering, as in 'Listening' and 'Six Bells' from a woman's point of view, the real story becomes a voice of protest against the 'spectacularisation' of what happened: 'Don't think of the children burnt in the confessional, / Don't think of the holy child in its mother's arms ... Don't think of the soldiers who raided the cellars.'[113] For Clarke, myth, as protest against the event and how history has turned it into spectacle, is the most active form of story-telling which, as in the second half of the poem, tells it as it was. In doing so, the poem shifts the focus from the victims and the inexplicable slaughter to something equally incomprehensible which has to some extent been overlooked and needs to be spoken of plainly: soldiers waking from dreams of their families, crossing themselves, and setting off for the slaughter.

One of Clarke's most effective poems on the transformation of war into spectacle is 'European Field', published in *Five Fields* (1998). The poem is based on, and dedicated to, an installation by Antony Gormley. The *European Field* was created in 1993 with the help of students and families at Östra Grevie in Sweden. The thousands of figures in this piece were arranged as a forward-facing mass of people, filling a gallery space at Malmö Konsthall. The installation subsequently toured to a number of venues in Europe. War poetry, faced with mass deaths on battlefields, the destruction of towns and villages, the slaughter of large numbers of non-combatants, and deaths in extermination camps, asks, 'Why?'. 'European Field' re-asks this question in an environment that suggests the number who have died in war – in this case 35,000 – are difficult to grasp but the poem makes them at least realisable as individuals through drawing attention to the way in which Gormley presents them, stressing faces, voices and figures. 'European Field' is all the more disturbing, and disturbed, by the contrast between the human-like appearance of the clay and the clinical white of the gallery which helps create the sense of spectacle and the psychological impact which the figures massed together have on the poet. Ultimately, the poem is about the internalisation of the spectacle of so many dead:

> We have paid to see them.
> We did not expect to be stared at,
> or that they would move in to live with us,
> taking root in the field of our minds.[114]

The protest of 'European Field' is written at the boundary between graphic realism – the figures are sculpted in animated poses, standing on tip-toe and with craning necks – and gothic horror; the poem moves from the spectacle in the gallery to the gothic locations of graveyards and battlefields where the wind sounds in the grass. The 35,000 figures in the installation, asking 'Why?', are linked with the graveyard – where grass is reclaiming the graves, the stones and the bones – through the image of them breathing as if they were a field of corn. The gothic context in which the figures are placed in the second half of the poem brings the psychological impact of so many dead to the fore. As the location of the poem shifts to the poet's night-time, the gothic allusions and the animated aspects of the figures which make them appear as the living dead come together to emphasise the terror not so much in the figures themselves as the roots which they are acquiring in the poet's subconscious: 'whispering all night / we are you, you, you'.[115] The poem closes with an image that blurs the boundary between life and death, creation and destruction, past and present, and war and peace. But the intensity with which death and decay are rendered in abject, gothic terms suggests not only the depths of the roots which the installation has put down in the poet's mind but a fear / horror of psychological as well as physical dissolution:

> Thirty-five thousand figures
> crumbling in my head
> to bones and dust and ashes
> under the field of flowering grasses.[116]

In this context, I now turn to another poem in the same volume as 'European Field', 'The City', which I discussed in Chapter 4 in relation to music and cosmogenesis and in Chapter 5 in relation to the Anthropocene, but now approach as a war poem. It is based on the IRA detonation of a 3,300 lb lorry bomb on Corporation Street in the centre of Manchester on 15 June 1996 – the largest bomb detonated in Great Britain since the Second World War, causing £1.3 billion of damage. 'The City', like its companion poem 'Concerto' (discussed in Chapter 2), reflects the way in which a concerto, as the musicologist Reginald O. Morris maintained, was originally conceived as a motet, a vocal musical composition in diverse forms and style.[117] But more significant for 'The City' than Clarke's 'Concerto' is that the concerto's structure, as Morris says thinking so obviously about the decade in which he was writing, could be set against 'our chaotic and discordant age',[118] a point which is especially relevant to the period in which Clarke, too, was writing and to the events that bring 'The City' to its conclusion. The philosopher Tom McLeish, invoking Karl Popper, anticipates the aesthetic and philosophical experience of 'The City', in highlighting that 'A great work of music, like a great scientific theory, is a cosmos imposed upon chaos – in its tensions and harmonies inexhaustible even for its creator.'[119]

While there are moments when 'The City' projects a world of beauty and order – as exemplified in its opening lines, 'the two blue notes of the cuckoo: C and A flat / again and again from oak woods sweet with bluebells'[120] – the focus of the poem as a whole (not surprisingly since the narrative leads to the explosion of the IRA bomb) is on the kind of cosmos which the scientist Brian Greene suggests, 'rather than being the epitome of poetic grace in which everything fits together with inflexible elegance' might be 'a wildly excessive collection of universes with an insatiable appetite for variety'.[121]

Of particular relevance to how 'The City' should be read as a 'war poem' is the way in which its structure is determined by that of a concerto, especially what Morris calls the 'ritornello' form, which consists of essential features that recur with episodes in between.[122] The poem opens with a slow movement that distributes contrasting 'tonalities', which are then developed through a process of repetition and recapitulation, into two quicker parts in which the themes are pursued and brought to a conclusion.[123]

The 'universes' around which 'The City' is composed exemplify the excessiveness and the insatiable appetite of which Greene speaks, which in turn is absorbed into the structure and language of the poem. Indeed, at the roots of this poem are forces and energies which – not unlike human behaviour itself – can lead to the creation of beauty, music, art and wonderful artefacts, but also to what is chaotic, volatile and unpredictable. The poem's movement through different presentations of power and energy, relying heavily upon sound, disrupts and redefines the extent to which we see ourselves as integrated with the planet and the cosmos. In other words, how we conceive of energy is determined by our cosmological perspective(s).

The intensity of sound introduced in the first section of 'The City' with the geological upheavals within deep time, associated with different epochs, gradually merges with Manchester's transformation through its own epochs into an industrial city characterised at different times by 'The oscillating beat of the looms' drum / under the singing water of the fells', the 'great warehouses, / beautiful and boastful as cathedrals' and 'terraced back-to-backs where poverty, / filth and cholera flourished under the smoke'.[124] But the later affluence of post-industrial Manchester's city centre – the scene of the bomb explosion – is reflected in much softer sounds, drawing on assonance and consonance to create a profound sense of security and comfort in the future – although proving ultimately illusory.

The description of Manchester's centre prior to the bomb explosion is composed of lines that are often short, suggesting that people do not have to look far beyond themselves and their deep-centred contentment: 'A girl tries on a dress. / A couple buy a cot in Mothercare. In Smiths people flick through paperbacks.'[125] Everyday life seems determined by, and pressed within, the integration of retail – Mothercare, Smiths, the Carcanet Press – and an historically embedded, cultural landscape – the Cathedral, Corn Exchange and Royal Exchange. The emotional, physical and commercial diversity of the city centre holds together the list by which the poet tries to capture and convey what it means to her: 'An ice cream parlour, a tobacconist, a bistro, / jewellers, boutiques, a Costume Hire Centre, / shops and stalls, offices, Carcanet Press ....'[126]

The last part of the poem returns us to a multiverse which has always been there; the organ takes its inspiration from the instrument's 'thousands of pieces' and the rich diversity of everyday life is rooted in a thesaurus of commercial activity and family engagements.[127] Through nouns connected one with another, like the bricks of the city, the list seems unbreakable. But a short line – so different that it seems accidental – emphatically, and very effectively, undermines this assumption: 'Then the bomb.'[128]

Beneath the sense of order and of intentional development within nature, there is a different reality, as noted in Chapter 3, which physicists like Tim Palmer have described as 'disordered and confused'[129] and a turbulence constituted of 'trillions upon trillions of whirls and eddies with all sorts of different sizes'.[130] In the devastation of the bomb blast, the various parts constituting order are separated from each other and much is returned to the formlessness before form and noise – before music:

> In that moment of frozen time, plate glass
> buckles before it blows. Brickwork bulges
> and is slowly taken apart, Lego-Town
> swept to smithereens by a child's petulance.[131]

The extent of the damage is captured in the nouns that this time derive meaning from the verbs that accompany them – 'plate glass / buckles' and 'brickwork bulges'.[132] The dismemberment of the city centre mirrors the trillions of particles released from within the bomb itself:

> Glass hangs in the air, scarves, tee shirts,
> flowers, newspapers, Kleenex, polythene bags,
> migrating flocks of birds of paradise,
> and real birds, city doves and sparrows
> flung from the centre of violence, torn and bloody
> ...[133]

At one level, the individual details are less important than the sense of things coming apart as the centre disintegrates in waves of energy created by the explosion. The energy in the vowels in each of the lines resonates with the particles cast far and wide in the Big Bang that brought form into being.

New currents of thought invariably enter Clarke's work through startling images and, in this part of the poem, the devastating impact of the bomb is captured in images that disrupt the linearity and self-sufficiency of lists and the thought processes that come with them: 'Lego-Town / swept to smithereens by a child's petulance' and 'city doves and sparrows / flung from the centre of violence, torn and bloody'.[134] The last section of the poem turns to the microparts of the city coming together and rebinding:

Bring out the road-sweepers. Wash the city in rage.
Bring builders and scaffolders, bricklayers, carpenters, shop-fitters;
Bring on the pavement artists and the street players.
Bring the fiddler with coins in his cap, and the lonely saxophonist.[135]

The emphasis is on the verb 'Bring' suggesting the need for collective and purposeful action while also reclaiming the emotive community – epitomised in the street artists, entertainers and musicians – that existed before the explosion. The reintroduction of music – its own multiverse – invokes, once again, string theory, the way in which cosmic forces as Greene maintains (as discussed in Chapter 4) are 'determined by the string's oscillatory pattern'[136] and 'everything, all matter and all forces, is unified under the same rubric of microscopic string oscillations – the "notes" that strings can play'.[137]

In summary, in order to understand Clarke's contribution to war writing, it is useful to turn to Kurki's concept of cosmology, that she shares with Clarke, which emphasises a relational universe that 'doesn't simply "lift" us off the planet and cause us to critique our petty human in-fighting' but '"does" something to our mindsets, our vocabularies, our interests'.[138] Clarke's poetry and journals, through her emphasis on the psychological impact of the mediatisation of war and of linked issues such as disease, climate change and damage to the planet within a wider discombobulating mesh, examine from personal, planetary and cultural perspectives issues which Kurki highlights: 'Being, or becoming, situated in relations is difficult, as we do not quite know where we are, how we are made, and how to "relate to relations"; and yet in these relations it becomes difficult to "ignore" the many relations "we" rely on to process the world.'[139]

In their focus on the psychological impact of different kinds of warfare, Clarke's writings on war and peace confront, and try to understand, the historical significance of human aggrandisement and power. This totalising view of the world which inevitably leads to war – an important element in Chakrabarty's concept of mutuality – should be considered in conjunction with Kurki's view of a relational universe which Clarke had assumed much earlier, especially in her work since the 1990s. These themes are important to Clarke's most ambitious project involving war, her translation and adaptation of the sixth-century, Welsh bard Aneirin's *Y Gododdin*, which is the subject of the next chapter.

7

WAR AND PEACE (PART TWO)

Gillian Clarke's translation and adaptation of *Y Gododdin* – the earliest surviving poem in the Welsh language by the sixth-century bard Aneirin – reflects her interests in emotional communities, cosmology and conflict but also her passion for incorporating Welsh-language poetics into her English-language compositions. Aneirin's poem, in the form of a series of elegies, is based on the Battle of Catraeth, now thought to be Catterick in Yorkshire, in the late fifth or early sixth century in which some 300 warriors from the Brittonic of Gododdin – an area which extended from southern Scotland to north-east England – were despatched to meet what turned out to be a much larger Saxon force including the Angles of Deira (Derwent) and Bernicia. As Kari Maund stresses, 'a considerable amount of later Welsh traditions surrounding the struggle of the Britons against the Saxons' originated in northern Britain and this ancestry became 'a badge of legitimacy and antiquity in Welsh pedigrees'.[1]

The line 'This is *Y Gododdin:* Aneirin sang it' would seem to suggest that at least part of the poem was composed by Aneirin in the sixth century, that he knew the warriors who went to meet the Saxons, and that he may well have taken part in the battle himself. However, the historian Alice Roberts reminds us that 'in the post-Roman period in Britain, contemporary written records all but disappear' and 'the historical record for the fifth to eighth centuries is patchy at best'.[2] Although originating in the sixth century, much of the Welsh-language text on which Clarke's version, *The Gododdin: Lament for the Fallen* (2021), is based probably dates to the thirteenth century. Clarke herself maintains that Aneirin's poem 'was passed, singer to listener, as word-music, for seven centuries before the making of a written text …

by two scribes, known as Scribe A and Scribe B'.³ Aneirin's original text was composed in recognition of a rarefied group of people who were caught up in a particular dramatic moment in history which they celebrated in song so that it would speak to their community. In her Introduction, Clarke suggests:

> It was originally sung, perhaps accompanied by the harp, in the house, hall and tavern, to be heard, memorised and passed on down the generations, from singer to singer, just as we, as children, learned nursery rhymes, playground games, and dipping and skipping songs.⁴

Thus, it is likely, as Clarke says, that the thirteenth-century version consists of various oral or lost written material derived from diverse traditions and events and, although it is important to be cautious given the length of time involved, includes something of a much older version probably dating back seven centuries to Aneirin's original poem.

At the time of working on *The Gododdin*, Clarke had access to, and consulted, a number of authoritative texts. In her journal dated 30 July 2018, two years after she began the project, Clarke recalls having 'been through my version of *Gododdin*, slowly reading aloud, listening, making adjustments. All translations by others are here on the table while I try to work out what I am doing, what I ought to do ... I think of it day and night.'⁵ Sir Ifor Williams's scholarly edition of *Canu Aneirin* was first published in 1938 and inspired a number of Welsh- and English-language Welsh works even years later including Anthony Conran's poem 'Elegy for the Welsh Dead, in the Falkland Islands, 1982' which invokes also those who died fighting the Anglo-Saxon invaders at Catraeth.⁶ Within three decades of Williams's volume, further important texts were published: Professor Kenneth Jackson's *The Gododdin: The Oldest Scottish Poem* (1969); A. O. H. Jarman, *Aneirin: Y Gododdin* (1988) and *Llyfr Aneirin: The Book of Aneirin* (National Library of Wales, 1989).

However, in some respects, the way toward this project was paved by new versions of two epics undertaken by two of Clarke's contemporaries: Seamus Heaney's translation of the Anglo-Saxon poem *Beowulf* (1999), which although written in England involves events that are set in Scandinavia, and Simon Armitage's highly acclaimed translation of *Sir Gawain and the Green Knight* (2009). In each text, as in Clarke's *The Gododdin*, poets many centuries apart imaginatively participate in the same mesmeric events and landscapes as their distant predecessors. Of the many aspects of Aneirin's *Y Gododdin* which chimes with Clarke's own writings, a significant similarity is the way in which they exploit the richness of the 'present', even if Aneirin's 'present' is located in the past and exists within a wider historical context that has to be unearthed. The short poem in which Clarke first expresses her interest in *Y Gododdin* begins with a line that suggests as much: 'Sorrow sharp as yesterday ...'[7] It is improbable that, consciously or unconsciously, this aspect of *Y Gododdin* would not have appealed to her. As Conran points out:

> It is rare that either Taliesin or Aneirin, the two poets of the sixth century whose works have come down to us, refer to anything except the immediate past. They seem to inhabit an immensely important present, which, with its troubles, has completely overwhelmed their memories. There are no meditations on the fall of Roman Britain; there is only one vague and possibly corrupt reference to Arthur ... It cannot be entirely that this utter preoccupation with the present is due to the selectiveness of the texts that have survived.[8]

The late Welsh novelist and poet Emyr Humphreys stresses how the poets of the Welsh princes during the centuries of struggle between the Welsh and the Normans were very conscious of their social role and what was expected of them.[9] He points out that poets 'used their special relationship with the prince to make sure that the greatest prestige of all belonged to their poetry' and this included, as Dafydd Benfras the court poet of Llywelyn the Great said, rendering 'praise as Aneirin did, the day he sang *Y Gododdin*'.[10]

In the Introduction to her version of *Y Gododdin*, Clarke not only recognises the role of the court poets but elaborates on it, seeing them in modern terms to some extent as 'historian, news-bearer, storyteller, genealogist and remembrancer' whose duty was 'to report, praise, sing and elegise'.[11] Humphreys maintains that they 'saw the struggle of the independent princes of Wales as an "action replay" of the sixth-century struggles of the Britons of the Old North' and 'were intent on recapturing the British Heroic Age'.[12] Clarke was obviously keenly aware when she embarked on her translation of Aneirin's poem that she, too, had lived through a period of struggle for Welsh independence. Although an independent Wales has yet to be achieved, Wales has attained a degree of independence from

Westminster with its own Senedd. After centuries during which the Welsh language was almost eradicated by the imposition of, and seemingly endless accommodation to, the English language and English culture as superior to Welsh, the Welsh-language has finally acquired legal status in Wales and is the subject of nationwide language policies and strategies. However, Clarke's *The Gododdin* reflects not only an interest in the way in which some aspects of Wales in the twentieth and twenty-first centuries resonates with the sixth-century opposition to the invasion of the Saxons but captures the changes in the concepts of emotional identity that occurred between the sixth- and thirteenth-century versions of *Y Gododdin*, which is the subject of the next section.

EMOTIONAL IDENTITY

In Clarke's short poem, 'The Book of Aneirin', Aneirin's grief for the young men slaughtered in the battle of Catraeth is conceived as having been penned on sheets laid down in layers, like sedimentary rock, an image which echoes her sequence 'The Stone Poems' (2004) (discussed in Chapter 5). Writing this short poem seems to have prompted Clarke to a contradiction at the heart of Aneirin's text evident in the contrast between what she perceives as the 'quires of quiet pages', with their implication of peace, and the 'blood-ballad / of the battlefield'.[13] It is a conundrum which Clarke seeks to unravel and resolve in her version of *Llyfr Aneirin* which is a war poem, a lament and a text about emotional community and identity.

In her version of *Y Gododdin*, Clarke extends her interest in the elegy beyond the tradition of the court poets and highlights emotional as much as heroic identity. Thus, while much of her poem reflects the role of the poets of the Welsh princes, and their obligations and responsibilities, its concern with emotional identity is honed to betray the influence of the later medieval concept of art on the link between human individuality and the history of the image.[14] Her version suggests that, according to the thirteenth-century document, Aneirin had a greater degree of freedom over the way traditional poetics is linked to private emotional identities than was generally customary among the sixth-century poets. She highlights a conflicting perspective in elegies and funereal portraits which by the thirteenth century had acquired a sharp focus. In ancient times, the elegy and the funereal portrait were approached differently in Roman to Greek culture which emphasised the individual as an ideal in which physical limits were transcended, while Roman culture valued the physical likeness of the individual.[15] Clarke's version of Aneirin's elegies highlights the contrast within them between the warriors as heroes on the battlefield, exemplifying what the historian Dipesh Chakrabarty (as discussed in Chapter 6) identifies as the march of physical aggrandisement and the centrality of humans to the larger scheme of things,[16] and their private lives with their families in a more intimate emotional community.

Clarke's translation of what was probably a largely thirteenth-century version of Aneirin's poem turns to a considerable extent on the amalgamation of the emotional needs of particular individuals and personalities with the wider heroic culture bringing the disparate nature of the community together. As Conran points out, 'in Wales the tragic hero does not seem to separate himself from his tribe to nearly the same extent as he normally does in Greece or England'.[17] Clarke's *The Gododdin* examines not simply the preparations for battle but the nature of the emotive community created in its slipstream by king Mynyddawg Mwynfawr who summoned men (probably chiefs) from various parts of the north, including north Wales, to Din Eydin (Edinburgh). In doing so, Clarke offers a new perspective on some of the more controversial aspects of Aneirin's text. The poet Carol Rumens, for example – using the English translation by the Welsh Scholar Daniel Silvan Evans (1818–1903) – questions 'whether the Gododdin were drunk when they went into battle' and draws attention to how Aneirin 'often emphasises the ill-effects of the mead'.[18] But, recognising that it was the custom for the King to feast his warrior chiefs royally for a year and that 'the nightly banquet was the means by which the king secured the men's fatal loyalty',[19] Rumens suggests that approaching the warrior life of Gododdin as an 'emotive community' (as defined in Chapter 1) might uncover a more positive reading of their preparation for battle than previous critics and historians have allowed. Clarke's version retains the way in which Aneirin at times sounds like 'a pious cleric',[20] often with the outspokenness which we find in Aneirin's text. For example, she describes the men, as in 'Son of Cian of Maen Gwyngwn', riding to Catraeth 'crazed with mead'.[21] But she readily acknowledges the practical nature of the nightly celebrations and the drinking of mead in the great hall as helping warrior chiefs of different personalities and from diverse parts to bond together as a community.

Conran points out that the provision of food, drink and gifts helped guarantee 'a loyal fighting force in wartime'[22] as Humphreys, too, recognises in his account of Gerald Cambrensis's much later *Hirlais Owain* (Owain's Drinking Horn) written upon the death of Owain, the son of Gruffudd ap Cynan. As Humphreys says, it was addressed to the heroes of a successful battle beyond the Long Mynd in Shropshire which 'was conceived in direct imitation of *Y Gododdin*'.[23] He reminds us that 'the cup-bearer at the feast is ordered to serve each hero generously in token of his valour in the expedition made the previous night to rescue a comrade taken prisoner', adding, although he himself was a pacifist, that 'the honour paid to them with the long blue drinking-horn was that much greater because of the deliberate echo of what took place in the Court of Mynyddog Mwynfawr in Edinburgh more than five centuries before'.[24]

The role of the drinking cup and the mead in creating the coherent Gododdin was especially important in the sixth century because the departure of the Romans from Britain in 410 CE left behind a power vacuum. Conran reminds us that the Welsh in the sixth century were in the 'process of undergoing the experience of Roman withdrawal, re-emergence of total tribalism, failure to keep their lands, mass migration and constant war'.[25] The difficulty of creating a coherent community in these circumstances is encapsulated in a single line in Clarke's translation in which the men are perceived as 'a rowdy troop; / band of brothers, a carousing crew'.[26] Her translation highlights the tension between the phrase 'band of brothers' – in which the consonance seems to confirm the emotional tightness that holds the warriors together as a unit – and the troops' rowdiness and carousing.

Elsewhere in the text, the warriors – albeit seen as a 'boisterous band' – are 'racing to war, their spears held high'.[27] The phrase 'boisterous band' once more has the brittleness implied in the phrase 'rowdy troop' but its consonance just about suggests – as in 'band of brothers' – that the individuality and singular interests of the warriors have blended so that 'band' implies in this context something nearer a community than a somewhat ribald grouping of convenience. The concept of 'brotherhood' has a singular significance in Welsh-language poetry that can be traced to the work of the Welsh poet Waldo Williams whom Clarke met in her childhood, which she recalls in a journal entry in 2019 written while she was working on *The Gododdin*:

One of my favourite Welsh poets is Waldo Williams. For some years, as head teacher of Dinas Cross Village School, Waldo lived close to my grandmother's farm, and my father knew him. Once, six years old and walking the farm track with my father, I was introduced to a man walking towards us: 'Mr Williams, the poet'. He shook my hand. A moment long-forgotten, to be remembered decades later, its significance at last understood. It was a revelation. Propped against a wall on a shelf in this room, where I write at the dining table, is a small oak block into which an artist has carved a line from one of Waldo's poems:

> Beth yw gweithio ond gwneud cân o'r coed a'r gwenith?
> (What is work but making a song of the wood and the wheat?)[28]

In his poem 'Brawdoliaeth' (Brotherhood), from the period 1938–46, Waldo writes that each of us 'alive is knit / Within God's secret net' – 'Mae rhwydwaith dirgel Duw / Yn cydio pob dyn byw' – and that 'Brotherhood old and simple / Is more than all the Temple' – 'Mae'r hen frawdgarwch syml / Tu hwnt i ffurfiau'r Deml'.[29]

In classical antiquity, as the French philosopher and historian of ideas Michel Foucault says, signs 'were the means of knowing and the keys to knowledge', they were 'co-extensive with representation, that is, with thought as a whole' and one representation was 'linked to another and represents that link within itself'.[30] Clarke's detail that the warriors 'held their spears high' when riding to war signifies pride, fearlessness and courage but, also, the emotional value system that constituted the communal culture to which they had committed themselves. Later in the poem, the raised spear, as a symbol of Gododdin – of the community it represents which, to employ Foucault's words, resides within it – is explicitly linked with the image of the carousing that helped bond the warriors together: 'spear upraised / as a wine-filled, gleaming cup'.[31] The small changes to this phrase, compared with similar wording used previously in Clarke's version – the spears are now said to be more defiantly and proudly 'upraised' and the cups of gleaming metal filled with wine rather than mead – suggests the subtlety of her text but also the ways in which the emotional community of Gododdin was itself forged through its signs and imagery.

It is important to remember that the depiction of warriors from about this time borrowed from Roman imperialist imagery. The spears and shields as necessary weapons of war are also creative and manipulative symbols, disrupting – and reshaping – the natural characteristics, impulses and behaviours of the men which their drunkenness reveals or, in some cases, no doubt distorts. An important aspect of Clarke's version of Aneirin's text is that this is largely achieved through the spectacle created by the images and the emotions which they embody, as in Owain's 'sword a blue-bright blade, / his armour burnished gold'[32] and in how Madog, Cadfannan and Gwefrfawr flaunted their brooches.[33] Clarke emphasises and pursues what the thirteenth-century text suggests, that the meaning embodied by signs, as Foucault maintains, 'cannot be anything more than the totality of signs arranged in their progression'.[34] But in highlighting, for example, the brooches in the way that she does, Clarke's text is distinguishable from *Llyfr Aneirin*. The brooches are invoked in Clarke's adaptation in a way that suggests that the functionality of signs, as Foucault says, 'is entirely on the side of what is signified'.[35]

However, the location of the brooch in connection with the wider sign system is problematic because its adoption by warriors and what it signified has a complicated and somewhat ambivalent history. Some historians suggest that the practice is of Germanic origin, implying the assimilation of that culture by others. In Gododdin, it may be evidence of the lingering influence of the Roman empire in northern Britain and may suggest the difficulty which northern Brittonic tribes had at that time in defining their own heroic sense of themselves. And there is the further complicating possibility that they were taken from the bodies of the defeated enemy.[36] The social and emotional dimension of brooches and weapons, as carried by the warrior elite, might suggest, as Roberts says, that 'post-Roman Britain was returning to an idea of itself that it had before it became part of the Empire'.[37] Indeed, Roberts interestingly suggests that we might 'even start to see Roman Britain as an aberration' with being part of the Empire in some ways having 'obscured long-standing connections between Britain and neighbouring politics and cultures'.[38]

While Clarke follows *Llyfr Aneirin*, consulting twentieth-century translations, versions and scholarly studies of the text, she is working in a complex, liminal space involving the changing nature of signs in the transition from Roman antiquity, a period subject to global influence, and the thirteenth century when different oral and written versions of Aneirin's sixth-century text were finally brought together and within frames of meaning which have survived from the Renaissance to the present day. Two concepts of the image come into tension in Clarke's version of *Llyfr Aneirin*, one in which signs, as Foucault says, occupied a 'teeming world throughout which the Renaissance had distributed them' and another in which signs are lodged in 'the interstices of ideas, in that narrow space in which they interact with themselves in a perpetual state of composition and recomposition'.[39]

Clarke's *The Gododdin* conceives of Aneirin's text as inevitably bringing different oral and written texts together over the seven centuries between Aneirin's sixth-century version and the scribes' thirteenth-century document. Within its different twentieth- and twenty-first century translations, and the various interpretations of its origins and contexts, Foucault's concept of 'a perpetual state of composition and recomposition' is significant. As Conran stresses, after the Battle of Catraeth, between the sixth and the ninth centuries, 'the centre of gravity in Britain moved steadily southwards: first Northumbria, then Mercia, then Wessex and finally Normandy. And with it went the decline of Celtic influence upon it.'[40] Increasingly, 'the Welsh were cut off from their countrymen in the North of England and in Cornwall' and were indeed the '"Welsh" – that is, strangers or foreigners in their own country'.[41] Not unnaturally, as Conran suggests, 'in their exile, they turned to the stories of their old homes, in Rheged, Elfed, Gododdin and the rich lands of Eastern Powys' – embracing Cumberland, Yorkshire, SE Scotland and Shropshire – and, although the prose and narrative of these sagas have been lost, their quality and character is discernible in the fragments of poetry and song that remain, which, he divulges, is 'stark in texture, tragic in conception'.[42] And Clarke's version of *Y Gododdin*, after all, was written at a time when the Welsh had achieved (and continue to have) international influence, Wales has its own government and there is extensive support for the Welsh language. Although Clarke's version betrays the influence of its twenty-first century context, it is rooted in the sixth century, in a particular community and historical 'present' which is unveiled by the late-twentieth-century and early-twenty-first-century history of emotions.

In translating and adapting Aneirin's text, Clarke recognises that, while its imagery is only comprehensible from the narrative of the battle, it occupies a space in intellectual history between the mnemonic techniques of antiquity and the way in which *historia* – the narrative – enables the imagery to recognise the warriors as emotional beings who at times rank higher than the historical narrative in which they are involved. The emphasis on knowing and appreciating another person – in Welsh 'adnabod' – in Clarke's *The Gododdin* is unsurprising given its importance to twentieth-century Welsh-language poetry. Again, it is traceable to the work of Waldo Williams who saw 'adnabod', as he says in his poem with that title written shortly after the Second World War, as meaning when 'Y mae rhin cydeneidiau'n ymagor' (the soul opens to soul its secret).[43] It is a notion that Welsh pacifist writing generally adopted, as in the essays of George Davies in *Pilgrimage of Peace* (1950) who incorporates it in his concept of 'personalism' which recognised 'the worth of individuals' as opposed to 'ideologies and slogans suited to the mass-mentality of hordes'.[44]

The attention which Clarke's version of Aneirin's poem pays to private emotions helps bring the warriors alive as individuals with their own characteristics. Owain we learn is shy with women; Rhys is a very different type of person – 'fickle, fitful, boisterous, brash, / moody, broody in the clash'; and Isag, an 'esteemed man of the south', has 'manners smooth as summer seas'.[45] Clarke seems especially entranced by the elegies in which the warrior is one thing on the battlefield and another in the community: Erthgi may be 'brutal in attack and plunder' but 'at court the quiet one'.[46] In Clarke's version, *Y Gododdin* is not as one-dimensional as the burnished shields and blue-bladed spears suggest, and, while the brutality, boisterousness and carousing of the men are admired, so is their more private side epitomised best perhaps by the celebrated Ceredig: 'loved life dearly, as his name tells – / favoured, favourite …'.[47] No disgrace as a warrior, he loved song and, like Owain, he is 'quiet and courteous'.[48]

In other words, Clarke is more prepared than even Aneirin, according to the thirteenth-century document, to overturn the way in which individuality in the elegy and the funereal portrait was replaced in antiquity by a *typos hieros* which played a part in the representation of the warriors. While the *typos hieros* points toward the order of ranking people in Roman times, Clarke's *The Gododdin* acknowledges that much of the Roman imagery associated with it is analogous to the cosmos, as well as empire, and is a symbol of the way in which the cosmos in pre- and early Christianity was represented, as indeed even today, in terms of circles which encapsulated not only its physical structure but its overall strength and awesomeness.

Clarke's version of *Llyfr Aneirin* draws attention to the way in which, as a largely thirteenth-century document, it incorporates the emotional identity of individual warriors but highlights, with the influence of medieval art in mind, how this content is transformed by an immaterial, akinetic aesthetic. Although Clarke follows Aneirin's text in describing the warrior's fighting ability and heroism, often in stock phrases, it develops the insights that Aneirin, through his feasting with and possibly fighting alongside the warriors of Gododdin, obtained into their individual characters, relationships and bonding. Of particular importance throughout Clarke's *The Gododdin* is the way in which the men's heroism, formal ritual and physical achievements are juxtaposed with emotions such as friendship, love, loyalty, grief and mental suffering – and that, in addition to the men, as Rumens reminds us, this includes the mourning women.[49] As such, *The Gododdin*, like the Welsh poet Waldo Williams, in his poem 'Pa Beth Yw Dyn?' (What is Man?), asks:

> Beth yw'r byd i'r nerthol mawr?
> Cylch yn treiglo
> Beth yw'r byd i blant y llawr?
> Crud yn siglo.
>
> What's the world to the strong?
> Hoop a-rolling.
> To the children of earth, what is it?
> A cradle rocking.[50]

The heroes who most overtly embody the warrior values and emotions are often those who have reputations for the warmth with which they relate to the non-combatants of the community in times of peace. For example, Gwenabwy's elegy says of him that while 'he fled no enemy breach in fear', 'his minstrel's never went unpaid; / tipped generously at the New Year'.[51] In this context, it is important to note what Conran says about Madog, from the elegy for Madog ap Maredudd, that he 'was the hope of minstrels for they loved him, yes; but also their hope because he stood for what they stood for, and his victims in battle were made theirs by the singing of them'.[52] And Gorthyn Hir, in one of the closing elegies of *The Gododdin*, who bravely 'rages' into battle is also a man who is inseparable from, and helps build, the community – one whom 'Any lord, any woman or girl / could approach.'[53]

CLARKE'S SHORTER ELEGIES

It must be noted at this point that Clarke experimented with elegies and poems confronting death in the 1970s and 1980s. One of her most well-known works is 'Cofiant' (published in *Letting in the Rumour*, 1989) which means biography and, as Clarke points out, many hundreds were written in the nineteenth century, mainly about preachers.[54] Several of these 'biographies' anticipate aspects of Clarke's *The Gododdin*. Two eleventh-century elegies, translated from the Welsh, 'Grufydd (1047)' and 'Bleddyn ap Cyfryn (1069)' resonate with *Y Gododdin* in that they record the deaths of noble warriors in battle. But 'Grufydd' begins to unpack this level of detail by suggesting that the narrative within the elegy is a story of treachery and revenge.

Even these elegies can be traced to Clarke's family tree and the majority of the poems are pithy biographies of her more immediate ancestors, presenting her genealogy, as in the Welsh Cofiant, as thumbnail emotional stories. The most detailed is of her father John Penry Williams (1899–1957) who comes alive as an individual who made notes in the margin of books, kept diaries and notebooks and used a Conway Stewart fountain pen. He was a chapel boy who became a radio engineer on board ships, sending Morse code messages during the Second World War (as discussed in Chapters 1 and 6) and, in an insight into the emotional life of the family, we are told that he was silenced by the news that his daughter was pregnant as she was later by news of his unexpected death in her teens.

The details within these biographies suggest how much is excluded from the tradition of elegies as is the case in *Y Gododdin* but also the significance that can be attached to even a single memory: for example, Clarke's aged aunt commenting on the train to Aberystwyth in the distance as she walked with her niece while holding on to her arm; Wil Williams (1851–1910) keeping a garden but disappointing his daughter with the condition of their home after his wife's death; and the family life of Thomas Williams (1800–1835) ripped apart by fever. In this respect, 'Cofiant' prepares us for the emphasis which Clarke places on the private, family life of the warriors in her adaptation of *Y Gododdin* but also the way in which the flow from one generation to another is a series of stops-and-starts suggested in singular details in 'Cofiant' such as Clarke's aunt 'stopped at the iron railings', the sudden death of a young child and capsized ships.[55] It is the emotional history encapsulated in such stories that, in more abbreviated terms, constitute the emotional undercurrent in *The Gododdin*.

The genealogy of the kind which was recorded in Welsh bibles which closes 'Cofiant' begins with Clarke's own place in her family ancestry – 'Daughter of Penri Williams, wireless engineer of

Carmarthenshire and Ceinwen Evans of Denbughshire'[56] – but, as in Welsh cofiant generally, there are few details about the women and how they contributed to families and communities. These are published later in 'The City'[57] and in poems in *The Silence* (2024). 'Gwenllian' in that volume returns, over many years later, to the conflicts within Clarke's childhood home between her father with a strong interest in the Welsh language, culture and myth, and her mother who 'cast off her story, her shame, / pretended not to be poor and Welsh'.[58]

Apart from 'Cofiant', Clarke's work, from its very beginnings, has included elegies and biographies such as 'Death of a Young Woman' (*The Sundial*, 1978) and 'Taid's Funeral' and 'Death of a Cat' (*Letter from a Far Country*, 1982) and each of them, like the cofiant, is rooted in a particular community. The later elegies that conclude *Zoology* (2017) also approach nation as community. These include two of her most striking elegies, 'Eisteddfod of the Black Chair' – to the shepherd poet Ellis Humphrey Evans (1887–1917), known by the bardic name Hedd Wyn ('Blessed Peace'), who was killed at Passchendaele only months before he was posthumously awarded the Eisteddfod Chair – and 'Madiba', an elegy to Nelson Mandela who achieved the status of being called the father of the South African nation. 'Madiba', introduced by two lines from Aneirin's *Y Gododdin*, is perceived as a warrior of peace. These elegies, written when Clarke had begun work on her version of *Y Gododdin*, point toward peace and generosity of spirit, elements of the lives of the most illustrious warriors of Gododdin.

ELEGIES AND THE EMOTIVE COMMUNITY

Clarke's version of Aneirin's poem emphasises how the Battle of Catraeth was structured around emotions as much as politics and how emotions determined the actions and behaviours prior to, during and after the fight. In the elegies, elation at the warriors' advent as heroes is sung alongside the sorrow of their death, each prompting equal although opposite emotions. In Clarke's version of *Y Gododdin*, as in Aneirin's original Welsh-language version, both are sung with similar dramatic expression. The elegies are constructed around a mesh of ambivalent feelings, recognising the courage of the Gododdin but also sorrowing in grief. In the singing of the elegies, both grief and joy reflect the dignity of the heroes. Throughout *The Gododdin*, the expression of loss is not compromised, focused often on the home as an emotional community that has been ripped apart – sometimes subtly as in the case of Owain whose elegy concludes 'Marro's / only son. Slain'[59] and, occasionally, as in the elegy for Gwlgod, unsparingly: 'I grieve to tell – unbearable sorrow – / their homes are bitter and childless now'.[60] Among the more emotionally intense moments in Clarke's *The Gododdin* are those which confront the appalling prospect of having to cope with the loss of someone who was most loved, admired and cherished. Few such moments are laid out as raw and as open as the grief for Cian: 'I grieve / for my lost friend, faithful, beloved, / fired-up for war – now I must live / without him who died too young.'[61] In a few lines the elegy shifts from pride in the warriors riding to war (albeit acknowledging once again that they were 'crazed with mead')[62] to the impossible countenance of the fate they met – 'O my heart breaks'[63] – to the private, honed love and friendship which the speaker has for Cain and finally the emptiness of their life to come without him. The way in which Clarke has translated and adapted *Y Gododdin* in these lines resonates with the fact, as Conran reminds us, that although tenderness is 'rare in old Welsh poetry. There is tragic grief, there is pride in people you love, there is fierce affection for the dead.'[64]

In the aftermath of the Saxon victory at Catraeth, the few warriors who lived to return and the men and women who remained at Mynyddawg Mwynfawr's court sing of how the community is brought low, shaken to its foundations. The joy and elation turn into a lament for the fallen and the joy and laughter of only a short time before are silenced. In Clarke's text, the two emotive communities, the warrior culture forged before the fire in the great hall where 'mead flowed free'[65] and the wider community in mourning – 'they knelt in church in penance, / the old, the young, the powerful, the penniless'[66] – are interwoven around the Battle of Catraeth with correspondingly dramatic shifts in emotional content and language. It is a matter of debate whether the Christian references, as to the mourners kneeling in the church in Gododdin, were a product of the sixth century or were a later insertion but certainly Christianity was establishing itself in fifth- and sixth-century Britain.

Although in Clarke's lament for the fallen, swords, symbols and armour are emotional symbols of glory and achievement in war, the realities of battle are not gainsaid, evident for example in how Owain becomes 'carrion for the crow, / sooner flesh to feed the raven'[67] and the warriors fight and die in 'mire and mud and blood'[68] – conditions resonant of the First World War trenches. In linking, albeit implicitly, the First World War and the Battle of Catraeth, Clarke is following a distinguished Welsh literary tradition in which the subject of war is approached with *Y Gododdin* in mind, including David Jones's *In Parenthesis* (1937) which makes extensive use of Aneirin and Conran's *Sir Galahad* about the soldiers burned to death under decks during the Falklands War, in which, as M. Wynn Thomas says, Conran's use of *Y Gododdin* 'allowed him to mingle heroic with mock-heroic in bringing out the obscene disparity between patriotic rhetoric and violent reality'.[69]

Viewed against twentieth- and twenty-first-century warfare and the writers whom Aneirin's poem influenced, Clarke's *The Gododdin* belongs to a wider Welsh tradition of peace.[70] Although the peace movement waxed and waned in Wales over the centuries, as elsewhere, the advocacy of peace has remained manifest in many aspects of Welsh society including eisteddfodau, religious and spiritual centres, political parties – especially Plaid Cymru – and educational institutions. It can be traced to Welsh literature from the late nineteenth century and the work of pacifist poets such as T. Gwynn Jones, D. Gwenallt Jones, T. E. Nicholas, Waldo Williams and Menna Elfyn, novelists such as Emyr Humphreys and major essayists such as George Davies and Iorwerth Peate. And it is evident in the key events associated with the Welsh peace movement including the astonishing 390,296 signatories to the Welsh Women's Peace Petition in 1923; the five-day procession of peacemakers through north Wales in June 1926, some of whom walked forward to a rally in Hyde Park; the march to Greenham Common over forty years ago; and, more recently, the protests in Wales over the Israeli bombardment of civilians and hospitals in the Gaza strip held by the Stop the War Coalition and other networks in, for example, Haverfordwest, Cardiff and London.[71]

In the First World War and the Battle of Catraeth, those sent to fight were killed with a vulnerability which their emotions and emotional symbols hid – as Clarke's English version of *Y Gododdin* says, 'in death they died defenceless'.[72] The transcendent symbolism and the grim reality of war are brought together in two lines from the elegy 'Son of Cian of Maen Gwyngwn': 'War-dogs battling in grim rows / with bloody blue-blade spears.'[73] The promise, hope and warrior values suggested by the spears and swords which they carried on their way to Catraeth are transformed so that they are more reflective of the horror of the battlefield. Now bloodshed dominates, captured in the repetition of 'bl' and the run of vowels which catch the sharp edge of the weapons.

Clarke's version follows Aneirin's *Y Gododdin* in that it is emotions that create the stimuli for action and judgement. But Clarke also recognises – as the historian Barbara Rosenwein points out in her study of the middle ages – that emotions, despite being guided by accepted modes of expression, have a dynamic of their own.[74] The elegy to Owain, making us think of the passion with which people enrolled to fight in the First World War, remembers him as 'on fire for the front, restless for war'.[75] Clarke seems intrigued as to what, in both cases, brought about this passion to fight. Her emphasis is not simply upon one set of emotions but the emotional choices that have been made: thus the elegy for Owain encourages the community to have 'praise for him / sooner gone to the battlefield / than to his marriage-bed'[76] and, in another elegy, Hyfaidd Hir is said to have sooner gone to be 'meat for the wolf than to his wedding'[77] – in each case betraying strong bewilderment. Clarke appears to want to suggest that the Gododdin went so willingly to fight not only because of the influence of the mead and of the emotional community in which they had been inculcated, but because, like those who went into the battles of the First World War, they did not know fully what to expect.

The allusions to later wars in Clarke's *The Gododdin* are not accidental or coincidental. As she says in her Introduction, 'the historical litany that begins with Catraeth is a long one: in the last century Ypres, the Somme, then Gaza, Helmand, Aleppo'.[78] She maintains that she chose to conclude her version with the poem 'Dinogad's Coat' – a poem which does not conclude the thirteenth-century manuscript version and might be regarded as an anomaly – because it might be seen to have been 'composed in the deadly hush that follows a terrible war, like a robin singing in the silence on the Somme'.[79] In her Introduction, Clarke invokes not only the diffused nature but the mediatisation of twentieth-century warfare (discussed in Chapter 6): 'We too easily imagine the slaughter, because the misery of war is brought to us daily in words and images almost as it is happening: deaths not of soldiers but civilians, not on battlefields but in the bombed ruins of besieged cities.'[80]

The way in which emotions in *The Gododdin* have been determined by, and in turn shape, the community is reflected in the widespread use of particular words and gestures, the importance of which to emotional communities Rosenwein has drawn attention.[81] In both Clarke's and Aneirin's versions of *Y Gododdin*, emotions are introduced and developed through particular words and in Clarke's version of the poem they include 'steadfastness', 'purposeful', 'fearlessness', 'steel-will', 'generosity', 'honesty' and 'integrity'.[82] The elegies present us with and blend what Rosenwein in another context eloquently refers to as a palette of emotions.[83] In this regard, we can see the challenge that a work like *Y Gododdin* would have presented Clarke as a poet working largely, but not exclusively, in a modern, isolated and isolating print culture and the inevitable difficulties in ensuring that her version does justice to the power of more collective and communal experiences. The elegies help fulfil the need in Gododdin as an emotional community for reinforcement through the repetition of emotion words, regularly invoking the kind of relationships that constituted the Gododdin, articulating core values and privileging expression of the community's key emotions.

The customs associated with the Gododdin, as unveiled in Clarke's version, are linked to codified behaviours in creating, validating and maintaining loyalties. Her text is especially interested in how emotional expression codified in a community's customs transforms relations. As she recognises, folk versions of emotions such as courage, loyalty and anger have much to do with how they are experienced as part of the wider community, and this is true especially of the way in which death is conceived. The elegies in Clarke's version of *Y Gododdin* frequently remind us that death is only one emotional moment in life and presents us with how death is confronted, as in Clarke's earlier poems about death, within traditions that had evolved and had been shaped by the community. In the later elegies of *The Gododdin*, grief is mitigated by the achievements of the warriors off as well as on the battlefield. As Conran says, Aneirin's 'sole emphasis is on the dual role of the chief – to be a brave leader in war, and to give generously to his warriors in time of peace'.[84] The final seven lines of the twenty-four-line elegy of Geraint, for example, stresses the gratitude of the community for the way he conducted himself and contributed to the lives of others, making it seem somewhat miserly to overindulge their grief at his death:

> He'd led us to a blazing hearth,
> a white-fleeced couch. Geraint,
>   his war-cry before men of the South.

> White-limed his shield, spear-lord,
> generous as the sea. I know his sort.
> I knew you, great-hearted Geraint.[85]

So much so that he seems to transcend death itself, as signified by his close association with his shield – rattled in time with the war-cry – and, as 'spear-lord', with his spear, the weapon raised and carried with gusto by the warriors throughout the poem. As a community, the Gododdin is defined not only by its battle symbols but the hearth and home. And not only the personal qualities associated with effective warriors, such as fearlessness and steadfastness, but those encouraged within and by peacetime communities such as generosity of spirit. As exemplified in the opening lines of the elegy to Gwaednerth, the later elegies become like prayers for release from grief: 'Heaven help us home to the land we yearn / from the pain, the grief, the mourning.'[86]

It almost goes without saying that the words used in particular emotional communities in connection with death reflect their normative values, emotional focus and propagated virtues. This was as true in sixth-century *Y Gododdin* as in the thirteenth-century. In *Y Gododdin*, one of the ways in which the community is bonded emotionally is by their collective perspectives on death, which helps those left behind cope with loss and in which the history of particular individuals becomes story which becomes myth. As is said in the elegy of Tudfwlch Hir, 'His courage lives in his people's mind.'[87] Thus, Clarke's version highlights stories and myths, for example, of Bradwen unarmed fighting with a wolf, Caradog hand-feeding wolves and grey eagles pecking food from Cyron's hand.[88] But such is the closeness of the Gododdin as a unit and their importance as an emotive community that the deeds and achievements of one in the people's imaginations stand for all, as in the second song to Llif:

> In border country they knew his story,
> gold-torqued soldier, paid in mead.
>
> They glowed in the glass of his glory,
> three hundred men in his company.[89]

But also important throughout *The Gododdin* is the way in which the battlefield is transformed at the moment of a warrior's death into paradise. Thus, the elegy to Ceredig prays that he might find his 'home in Paradise'; Cadfannan calls as he dies that the Lord will save them to heaven; and what Gwrfelling finds in death is the unbroken green grass of Paradise, signifying peace, over his grave.[90]

The elegies unveil how the virtues and values of Gododdin as an emotive community have been personalised, suggesting how it was modelled on particular human behaviours, obligations, ideals and even failings. No individual is isolated from his or her emotional context. Clarke's version sees *Y Gododdin* as Conran envisaged it: 'It is clearly a political poem, that tries to mitigate the futility of the exploit (and the more general defeatism of the times) by stressing its heroic glory.'[91] But her poem emphasises the values of the wider community. Each elegy takes as its title the name of a dead warrior and places him within his personal, emotional history in ways which have a wider relevance across different historical periods and geographies. They reflect the difference between Welsh-language and English-language tributes to the war dead, recalling individuals in the context of their lives and families rather than only the symbols of war.[92]

Afterword

Throughout Gillian Clarke's work, there is a strong sense of the beauty and the sublime at the heart of nature and the cosmos. And her poetry, essays and journals are flooded with insights that resonate with (and emerge from) the contemporary natural sciences. As one of the leading physicists of his generation, Lee Smolin (who might as well be speaking to Clarke's writings) says: 'The universe we live in is beautiful. And it is so at least partly ... because a multitude of phenomena are taking place on a vast array of different scales ... [and] it is interesting'.[1] But this book suggests that the more we read Clarke's work, the more we realise that this is only one part of the story.

In her August journal for 2007, as Chapter 3 observed, Clarke admitted that she was deeply troubled that 'nature, with flood, hurricane and earthquake, would shake us off the planet'.[2] As we have seen, changing weather patterns and the damage that humans have done to the environment are recurring themes in Clarke's work. Their impact on individual and collective consciousnesses has provided Clarke's work with a perspective that scholars and critics have often overlooked. And neither has due attention been given to the way in which Clarke's poetry examines the psychological impact of the continuous media coverage of conflict and its participation in the increasingly diffused nature of warfare. In pursuing the post-modern character of war, this book has suggested that Clarke's ambitious translation and adaptation of the sixth-century bard Aneirin's *Y Gododdin* should be included in her writings as a war poet and especially in the context of the tradition of Welsh pacifism and its commitment to peace. As Clarke herself says in 'The Starling', from her most recent volume of poetry *The Silence* (2024): '"There is enough evil" … from another time, another war.'[3]

In the course of this volume, discussions of these themes have highlighted the extent to which a sense of individual and collective emotional identity – and the extent to which they have evolved and changed over the last half-century – are important to Clarke's life, to her poetry and to her creativity in general. They are evidence that Clarke is very much a writer whose work is relevant to our times and who suggests (especially from the 1990s onwards) that the current environmental crisis is partly the result of our failure to imagine alternative ways of living and of conceiving the cosmos. Looking out from her life in rural west Wales, Clarke's work suggests that we need to assume a cosmology that recognises the importance of the relationality of all living and non-living forms to our universe and centres on planetary rather than human-centric thinking.

One of Clarke's most disturbing cosmological images is from one of her most recent poems, 'The Breath of Trees': 'Earth afloat in space / is burning.'[4] But the poem suggests that the Anthropocene does not have to end this way: 'four thousand young trees breathe / in their second summer.'[5] Invoking what is also Clarke's recurring concern with the amenability of the cosmos, Smolin argues that 'a universe complex enough to have clocks, and so describable by a quantum theory of cosmology, might also be a universe that is hospitable to life'.[6] On this basis, Smolin argues, as Clarke's *The Silence* suggests, that the universe may be special enough to 'avoid permanently the stasis of the universal heat death'.[7]

As Clarke's poems about the Great Silences suggest – from 'Blue Sky Thinking' (2012) to 'Spring Equinox, 2021' (2024), discussed in Chapter 2 – we need to create a new imaginary and develop our senses to align (or re-align) ourselves with a different cosmology that promotes a more stable planetary system. Not only is Clarke's life on her smallholding in west Wales, and the poetry which comes out of it, an argument against the exploitation of natural resources from dispersed local ecologies, but a case for a cosmology centred in multispecies communities. As she ponders in one of her essays, published in 2021: 'Is consciousness a special human thing? My hare looked just as alive, as aware as I.'[8]

Important threads throughout Clarke's work are the impact of uncertain futures on the public psyche and what it is that has brought us to this period of ecological and cosmological instability. But these themes run alongside others in which the relational universe of the new natural sciences is integrated with a less human-centred view of the cosmos and creativity is seen as enabling us to connect with different ways of thinking. Her emphasis upon creativity as a point of entry to a new scientific and cosmological awareness – 'The pen itself plumbs a poet's energy. It is a rod to touch the wire between brain and word. The electric flash it makes is the first spark of a poem'[9] – is rooted in the close relationship that she has enjoyed since the 1970s between the sky and her psyche. As she observes, 'To write poem or prose I need weather and sky. I look up, observe, think.'[10] This is not surprising, for creativity is an important element in Clarke's cosmology. The natural philosopher Paul Davies notes, as Clarke observes throughout much of her work, that the fact that nature has creative power may be, in Karl Popper's words, 'the great riddle of cosmology'.[11]

For Clarke, creativity enables difference in experiencing and making sense of the world, providing a space in which the imagination might be released and allowing thought systems and discourses to be reinvented. In numerous stories recorded in her journals, many of which become the subjects of poems and poem sequences, creative practice is perceived as a mode of (re)thinking and (re)performing knowledge.

While this book highlights some of the key themes in Clarke's work – underscoring its relevance to our times, its insights into cosmology and its contributions to Welsh writing and history – there are other related subjects that warrant scholarly and critical attention which this study has not had the space to pursue. Some of these I have touched upon in *Animals, Animality and Controversy in Modern Welsh Literature and Culture* (2022): non-human life in Clarke's poetry; the new awareness of multispecies communities; the environmental turn in Welsh writing, culture and the arts in connection with planetary ways of thinking; and the links between creativity and cosmology in contemporary English language- and Welsh-language writing. Each of these topics point to, or emanate from, key questions in contemporary cosmology, two of the most important of which the award-winning physicist and cosmologist John Barrow has highlighted: the extent to which the universe is essentially organised and the part that this plays in the relationship between consciousness and matter[12] – areas of enquiry important to Clarke's poetry and her own cosmological thinking.

NOTES

Introduction and Overview

1. Gillian Clarke, 'Cardiff', in Gillian Clarke, *At the Source* (Manchester: Carcanet, 2008), pp. 16–29, at p. 24.
2. Gillian Clarke, 'Beginning with Bendigeidfran', in Clarke, *At the Source*, pp. 8–15, at p. 10.
3. Gillian Clarke, 'Why I Write', *Roots Home: Essays and a Journal* (Manchester: Carcanet, 2021), pp. 5–11, at p. 8. Also, see Gillian Clarke, 'Cardiff', in Clarke, *At the Source*, p. 22.
4. Clarke, 'Cardiff', p. 20.
5. Clarke, 'Tramp. Nothing is until it has a word', in Clarke, *Roots Home: Essays and a Journal*, pp. 13–17, at p. 13.
6. Clarke, 'Tramp. Nothing is until it has a word', p. 20.
7. Clarke, 'Cardiff', p. 26.
8. Clarke, 'Cardiff', p. 26.
9. Susan Butler, 'An Interview with Gillian Clarke', in Susan Butler (ed.), *Common Ground: Poets in a Welsh Landscape* (Bridgend: Poetry Wales Press, 1985), p. 196.
10. David T. Lloyd, 'Interview with Gillian Clarke', in David T. Lloyd (ed.), *The Urgency of Identity: Contemporary English-Language Poetry from Wales* (Evanston, IL: Northwestern University Press, 1994), p. 29.
11. *Poetry Wales*, 6/1 (1970), 18–20. See, M. Wynn Thomas, 'Staying to mind things: Gillian Clarke's early poetry', in Menna Elfyn (ed.), *Trying the Line: A Volume of Tribute to Gillian Clarke* (Llandysul, Ceredigion: Gomer Press, 1997), pp. 44–68, at pp. 47–9.
12. Butler, 'An Interview with Gillian Clarke', p. 196.
13. Butler, 'An Interview with Gillian Clarke', p. 196.
14. Lloyd, 'Interview with Gillian Clarke', pp. 28–9.
15. Lloyd, 'Interview with Gillian Clarke', pp. 28–9.

16 Butler, 'An Interview with Gillian Clarke', p. 196.
17 Gillian Clarke, 'Voice of the Tribe', in Clarke, *At the Source*, pp. 55–63, at p. 59.
18 Clarke, 'Beginning with Bendigeidfran', p. 9.
19 Clarke, 'Beginning with Bendigeidfran', p. 9.
20 Clarke, 'Voice of the Tribe', p. 58.
21 Clarke, 'Beginning with Bendigeidfran', p. 9.
22 M. Wynn Thomas, *Corresponding Cultures: The Two Literatures of Wales* (Cardiff: University of Wales Press, 1999), p. 201.
23 Mary-Ann Constantine, 'Review: *The History of Wales in Twelve Poems by M. Wynn Thomas, with illustrations by Ruth Jên Evans*', Planet Digital, 245. Online.
24 Gillian Clarke, Review of Jan Morris, *Conundrum*, in *The Anglo-Welsh Review*, 53 (1974), 259.
25 Pedair, 'Mae 'na olau', sleeve notes, 5.
26 Gillian Clarke, 'Letter from a Far Country' (1982), in Gillian Clarke, *Selected Poems* (Manchester: Carcanet, 1985), pp. 52–64.
27 Gillian Clarke, 'The King of Britain's Daughter', in Gillian Clarke, *The King of Britain's Daughter* (Manchester: Carcanet, 1993), pp. 1–20.
28 Gillian Clarke, 'Concerto' and 'The City', in Clarke, *Five Fields*, pp. 61–8 and 52–60.
29 Gillian Clarke, 'Mumbai', in Gillian Clarke, *A Recipe for Water* (Manchester: Carcanet, 2009), pp. 30–3.
30 Gillian Clarke, 'Behind Glass', in Gillian Clarke, *Zoology* (Manchester: Carcanet, 2017), pp. 25–31.
31 A. Sclater (ed.), *The National Botanic Garden of Wales* (London: HarperCollins, 2000).
32 Gillian Clarke, *Making the Beds for the Dead* (Manchester: Carcanet, 2004), pp. 23–8 and Gillian Clarke, 'The Poetry of Stone: Pentre Ifan', in Clarke, *At the Source*, pp. 47–54.

1 Emotional Communities

1 See, for example, Barbara H. Rosenwein and Riccardo Cristiani, *What is the History of Emotions?* (Cambridge: Polity Press, 2021); Peter N. Stearns and Carol Z. Stearns, 'Emotionology: Clarifying the History of Emotions and Emotional Standards', *The American Historical Review*, 90/4 (October 1985), 813–36; William M. Reddy, *The Navigation of Feeling: A Framework for the History of Emotions* (Cambridge: Cambridge University Press, 2001); Jan Plamper, *The History of Emotions: An Introduction* (Oxford: Oxford University Press, 2015) (an English translation of J. Plamper, *Geschicte und Gefühl: Grundlagen der Emotionsgeschichte* (Munich: Siedler, 2012)); Rob Boddice, *The History of Emotions* (Manchester: Manchester University Press, 2018); and Sara Ahmed, *The Cultural Politics of Emotion* (2004; Edinburgh: Edinburgh University Press, 2014).
2 Rosenwein and Cristiani, *What is the History of Emotions?*, pp. 1–2.

NOTES

3. Barbara H. Rosenwein, *Emotional Communities in the Early Middle Ages* (New York: Cornell University Press, 2006), p. 2.
4. Rosenwein, *Emotional Communities in the Early Middle Ages*, p. 2.
5. See, 'Jan Plamper On the History of Emotions', posted on The History of Emotions Blog on 4 September 2017 by Helen Stark. Available at *www.qmul.ac.uk/emotions* (accessed 10 January 2021). (This interview with Plamper was originally published in *Kritika: Explorations in Russian and Eurasian History*, 18/3 (2017), 453–60.)
6. Reddy, *The Navigation of Feeling*, p. 129.
7. Ieuan Gwynedd Jones, *Communities: Essays in the Social History of Victorian Wales* (Llandysul, Dyfed: Gomer Press, 1987), p. 107.
8. Jones, *Communities*, p. 107.
9. Gillian Clarke, 'East Moors', in Gillian Clarke, *Selected Poems* (Manchester: Carcanet, 1985), p. 44.
10. Peter Finch, *Edging the City: A Journey Round the Border of Cardiff* (Bridgend: Seren, 2022), p. 194.
11. Dennis Morgan, *The Illustrated History of Cardiff's Suburbs* (2003; rpt Derby: The Beedon Books Publishing Co. Ltd, 2006), pp. 169–70.
12. Gillian Clarke, 'Tramp. Nothing is until it has a word', in Gillian Clarke, *Roots Home: Essays and a Journal* (Manchester: Carcanet, 2011), p. 8.
13. Clarke, 'Tramp. Nothing is until it has a word', p. 8.
14. Jones, *Communities*, p. 151.
15. Jones, *Communities*, p. 151.
16. Clarke, 'East Moors', p. 44.
17. Jones, *Communities*, p. 151.
18. Dan Evans, 'Reconstructing Welshness – Again', in Darren Chetty, Grug Muse, Hanan Issa and Iestyn Tyne (eds), *Welsh (Plural): Essays on the Future of Wales* (London: Repeater Books, 2022), pp. 214–30, at p. 218.
19. Jones, *Communities*, p. 150.
20. Gillian Clarke, 'Suicide on Pentwyn Bridge', in Clarke, *Selected Poems*, p. 72.
21. Clarke, 'Suicide on Pentwyn Bridge', p. 72.
22. Gillian Clarke, 'Taid's Funeral', in Clarke, *Selected Poems*, p. 51.
23. Gillian Clarke, 'Sunday', in Clarke, *Selected Poems*, p. 50.
24. Gillian Clarke, 'Blaen Cwrt', in Gillian Clarke, *The Sundial* (Llandysul: Gomer Press, 1978), p. 15.
25. Gillian Clarke, 'Death of a Young Woman', in Clarke, *The Sundial*, p. 14.
26. Clarke, 'Death of a Young Woman', p. 14.
27. Gillian Clarke, 'St Augustine's Penarth', in Clarke, *The Sundial*, p. 39.
28. Peter Finch, *Walking Cardiff* (Bridgend: Seren, 2019), p. 145.
29. Clarke, 'St Augustine's Penarth', p. 39.
30. Clarke, 'St Augustine's Penarth', p. 39.
31. Gillian Clarke, 'Why I Write', in Gillian Clarke, *Roots Home: Essays and a Journal* (Manchester: Carcanet, 2021), pp. 5–11, at p. 5.
32. Gillian Clarke, 'Beginning with Bendigeidfran', in Gillian Clarke, *At the Source* (Manchester: Carcanet, 2008), pp. 8–15, at p. 12.
33. Rosenwein and Cristiani, *What is the History of Emotions?*, pp. 89–90.
34. Jones, *Communities*, p. 155.

35 Gillian Clarke, 'Phoning Home', in Gillian Clarke, *Five Fields* (Manchester: Carcanet: 1998), p. 22.
36 Gillian Clarke, 'Siege', in Clarke, *Selected Poems*, p. 77.
37 Gillian Clarke, 'The City', in Clarke, *Five Fields*, pp. 52–60, at p. 54.
38 Clarke, 'The City', p. 54.
39 Clarke, 'The City', p. 54.
40 Clarke, 'A Box of Gloves', in Gillian Clarke, *The Silence* (Manchester: Carcanet, 2024), p. 52.
41 Rosenwein and Cristiani, *What is the History of Emotions?*, p. 124.
42 Gillian Clarke, 'Shopping', in Clarke, *Five Fields*, p. 24.
43 Gillian Clarke, 'The Habit of Light', in Clarke, *Five Fields*, p. 24.
44 Gillian Clarke, 'Migraine', in Clarke, *Five Fields*, p. 26.
45 Gillian Clarke, 'The Habit of Light', in Clarke, *Five Fields*, p. 24.
46 Gillian Clarke, 'Under the Stairs', in Clarke, *Five Fields*, p. 25.
47 Gillian Clarke, 'A Local Habitation and a Name', in Clarke, *At the Source*, pp. 2–7, at pp. 4–5.
48 Andri Snær Magnason, *On Time and Water: A History of Our Future*, trans. Lytton Smith (2020; rpt London: Serpent's Tale, 2021), p. 48.
49 Clarke, 'Journal', in Clarke, *Roots Home*, p. 71.
50 Clarke, 'Journal', *Roots Home*, p. 127.
51 M. Wynn Thomas, *Internal Difference: Twentieth Century Writing in Wales* (Cardiff: University of Wales Press, 1992), pp. xi–xii.
52 Rosenwein and Cristiani, *What is the History of Emotions?*, p. 126.
53 D. Parry-Jones, *Welsh Country Upbringing* (1948; rpt London and New York: B. T. Batsford, 1949), p. 61.
54 Parry-Jones, *Welsh Country Upbringing*, p. 61.
55 Parry-Jones, *Welsh Country Upbringing*, p. 61.
56 Clarke, 'East Moors', p. 44.
57 Clarke, 'East Moors', p. 44.
58 For a further discussion of the role of the body in the production, communication and performance of emotions within a community context, see Rosenwein and Cristiani, *What is the History of Emotions?*, p. 124.
59 Gillian Clarke, 'Notes about Letter from a Far Country'. Online. Available at *www.gillianclarke.co.uk* (accessed 31 May 2022).
60 Clarke, 'Notes about Letter from a Far Country'. Online.
61 Gillian Clarke, 'Letter from a Far Country', in Clarke, *Selected Poems*, pp. 52–64, at p. 61 .
62 Clarke, 'Letter from a Far Country', p. 61.
63 Rosenwein and Cristiani, *What is the History of Emotions?*, p. 86.
64 Clarke, 'Letter from a Far Country', p. 61.
65 Clarke, 'Letter from a Far Country', p. 63.
66 Clarke, 'Letter from a Far Country', p. 63.
67 Clarke, 'Letter from a Far Country', p. 56.
68 Clarke, 'Notes about Letter from a Far Country'. Online.
69 Clarke, 'Notes about Letter from a Far Country'. Online.
70 From 'An Interview with Gillian Clarke', in Susan Butler (ed.), *Common Ground: Poets in a Welsh Landscape* (Bridgend: Poetry Wales Press, 1985), p. 195.

NOTES

71. Clarke, 'Notes about Letter from a Far Country'. Online.
72. Samantha Walton, *Everybody Needs Beauty: In Search of the Nature Cure* (London and New York: Bloomsbury Publishing, 2021), pp. 32–3.
73. Walton, *Everybody Needs Beauty*, pp. 32–3.
74. Walton, *Everybody Needs Beauty*, p. 33.
75. Clarke, 'Letter from a Far Country', p. 56.
76. Gillian Clarke, 'Siege', in Clarke, *Selected Poems*, pp. 77–8, at p. 77.
77. Karen Armstrong, *A Short History of Myth* (Edinburgh: Canongate, 2005), p. 39.
78. Clarke, 'Notes about Letter from a Far Country'. Online.
79. Clarke, 'Journal', *Roots Home*, p. 157.
80. See, for example, Rosenwein and Cristiani, *What is the History of Emotions?*, p. 124.
81. Gillian Clarke, 'Plague', in Gillian Clarke, *Making the Beds for the Dead* (Manchester: Carcanet, 2004), pp. 61–2, at p. 61.
82. Linden Peach, *Animals, Animality and Controversy in Modern Welsh Literature and Culture* (Cardiff: University of Wales Press, 2022), p. 47.
83. Gillian Clarke, 'The Vet', in Clarke, *Making the Beds for the Dead*, p. 66.
84. See Linden Peach, *Animals, Animality and Controversy in Modern Welsh Literature and Culture*, pp. 179–88.
85. Gillian Clarke, 'Blackface', in Clarke, *Making the Beds for the Dead*, pp. 72–3, at p. 72.
86. Clarke, 'Blackface', p. 72.
87. Clarke, 'The Vet', pp. 66–7, at p. 66.
88. Clarke, 'The Vet', p. 67.
89. Clarke, 'The Vet', p. 66.
90. Clarke, 'The Vet', p. 66.
91. Ilse Pedler, 'The Importance of Air', in Ilse Pedler, *Auscultation* (Bridgend: Seren Books, 2021), pp. 16–17, at p. 16.
92. Pedler, 'The Importance of Air', p. 17.
93. Ilse Pedler, 'Castrating Calves', in Pedler, *Auscultation*, p. 18.
94. Clarke, 'The Vet', p. 66.
95. Clarke, 'The Vet', p. 66.
96. Clarke, 'The Vet', p. 66.
97. Ilse Pedler, 'All this Accumulation of Knowledge', in Pedler, *Auscultation*, p. 39.
98. Ilse Pedler, 'Teach Me To Kill', in Pedler, *Auscultation*, p. 10.
99. Ilse Pedler, 'Roadblock', in Pedler, *Auscultation*, p. 40.
100. Gillian Clarke, 'Wethers', in Clarke, *Making the Beds for the Dead*, pp. 53–4, at p. 54.
101. Gillian Clarke, 'First Lamb', in Clarke, *Making the Beds for the Dead*, p. 59.
102. Gillian Clarke, 'Woolmark', in Clarke, *Making the Beds for the Dead*, p. 65.
103. Gillian Clarke, 'On the Move', in Clarke, *Making the Beds for the Dead*, p. 58.
104. Gillian Clarke, 'Rumour', in Clarke, *Making the Beds for the Dead*, pp. 60–1, at p. 60.
105. Clarke, 'On the Move', p. 58.
106. Clarke, 'Tramp. Nothing is until it has a word', p. 16.
107. Clarke, 'Blackface', p. 72.

108 Clarke, 'Blackface', p. 72.
109 Clarke, 'Blackface', p. 72.
110 Clarke, 'Blackface', p. 72.
111 Clarke, 'Blackface', p. 73.
112 Pedler, 'Castrating Calves', p. 18.
113 Pedler, 'All this Accumulation of Knowledge', p. 39.

2 Cosmology in a Planetary Age

1 Audra Mitchell, *International Intervention in a Secular Age: Re-enchanting Humanity* (Abingdon: Routledge, 2014), p. 10. See, also, Milja Kurki, *International Relations in a Relational Universe* (Oxford: Oxford University Press, 2020), p. 14.
2 Kurki, *International Relations in a Relational Universe*, p. 68. Lee Smolin describes the core principles of relational cosmology in a number of texts: *The Life of the Cosmos* (London: Weidenfeld & Nicolson, 1997); *Three Roads to Quantum Gravity* (London: Phoenix, 2000); *The Trouble with Physics: The Rise of String Theory, The Fall of a Science and What Comes Next* (London: Penguin, 2008) and *Time Reborn: From the Crisis in Physics to the Future of the Universe* (Boston: Mariner Books, 2014). The salient work on natural philosophy based on the principles of a relational universe is Roberto Mangabeira Unger and Lee Smolin, *The Singular Universe and the Reality of Time* (Cambridge: Cambridge University Press, 2015). For a discussion of the impact of this new cosmology, see, for example, Smolin, *Three Roads to Quantum Gravity* and, for the need to see humans within the context of a wider non-hierarchical universe, see Smolin, *The Life of the Cosmos*.
3 Smolin, *The Life of the Cosmos*, p. 15.
4 Smolin, *The Life of the Cosmos*, p. 17.
5 Smolin, *The Life of the Cosmos*, p. 48.
6 Kurki, *International Relations in a Relational Universe*, p. 4.
7 Pierre Joris, 'The New Complexity', Foreword, in Allen Fisher, *Imperfect Fit: Aesthetic Function, Facture, and Perception in Art and Writing Since 1950* (Alabama: University of Alabama Press, 2016), p. xiv.
8 Gillian Clarke, 'Something Understood', in Gillian Clarke, *Roots Home: Essays and a Journal* (Manchester: Carcanet, 2021), pp. 37–46, at p. 40.
9 Clarke, 'Something Understood', p. 43.
10 Clarke, 'Something Understood', p. 40.
11 Clarke, 'Something Understood', p. 40.
12 Gillian Clarke, 'Islands', 'Journal', in Gillian Clarke, *At the Source* (Manchester: Carcanet, 2008), pp. 10–112, at p. 111.
13 W. P. Hodgkinson, *The Eloquent Silence* (1946; rpt. London: Hodder & Stoughton Ltd, for the English Universities Press Ltd, 1947), p. 99.
14 Hodgkinson, *The Eloquent Silence*, pp. 211 and 210.
15 Hodgkinson, *The Eloquent Silence*, pp. 210 and 213.
16 Hodgkinson, *The Eloquent Silence*, p. 213.
17 R. S. Thomas, 'Bravo!', in R. S. Thomas, *Collected Poems 1945–1990* (1993; rpt. London: Phoenix, 2000), p. 338.

NOTES

18 R. S. Thomas, 'At It', in Thomas, *Collected Poems*, p. 331.
19 Kurki, *International Relations in a Relational Universe*, p. 11.
20 J. P. Ward, *The Poetry of R. S. Thomas* (Bridgend: Poetry Wales Press, 1987), p. 100.
21 Smolin, *The Life of the Cosmos*, p. 24.
22 Smolin, *The Life of the Cosmos*, p. 19.
23 Molly Price-Owen, 'R. S. Thomas in conversation with Molly Price-Owen', *The David Jones Journal: R. S. Thomas Special Issue* (summer/autumn 2001), 93–110, at 93.
24 Ward, *The Poetry of R. S. Thomas*, p. 100.
25 Hodgkinson, *The Eloquent Silence*, p. 212.
26 Ward, *The Poetry of R. S. Thomas*, pp. 100–1.
27 Nicholas Campion, *Astrology and Cosmology in the World's Religions* (New York and London: New York University Press, 2012), pp. 4 and 5.
28 Campion; *Astrology and Cosmology in the World's Religions*, p. 6.
29 Gillian Clarke, 'Cynefin', in Gillian Clarke, *Zoology* (Manchester: Carcanet, 2017), p. 60.
30 Gillian Clarke, 'Labour', in Clarke, *Zoology*, p. 54.
31 Ilse Pedler, 'The Hill Ewe's Pasture', in Ilse Pedler, *Auscultation* (Bridgend: Seren, 2021), p. 28.
32 Karen Armstrong, *Sacred Nature: How We Can Recover Our Bond with the Natural World* (London: The Bodley Head, 2022), p. 18.
33 Richard Tarnas, 'Understanding the Modern Disenchantment of the Cosmos', in Nicholas Campion and Patrick Curry (eds), *Sky and Psyche: The Relationship Between Cosmos and Consciousness* (2006: rpt. Edinburgh: Floris Books, 2018), pp. 183–99, at p. 189.
34 Gillian Clarke, 'Blue Sky Thinking', in Gillian Clarke, *Ice* (Manchester: Carcanet, 2012), p. 48.
35 Clarke, 'Blue Sky Thinking', p. 48.
36 Gillian Clarke, 'Journal', in Clarke, *Roots Home*, p. 163.
37 Clarke, 'Journal', *Roots Home*, p. 164.
38 Clarke, 'Journal', *Roots Home*, p. 165.
39 Clarke, 'Journal', *Roots Home*, p. 165.
40 Gillian Clarke, 'Spring Equinox, 2020' and 'Spring Equinox, 2021', in Gillian Clarke, *The Silence* (Manchester: Carcanet, 2024), pp. 18 and 21. 'Spring Equinox, 2021' was first published as 'Spring Equinox, 2020', in Clarke, *Roots Home*, pp. 111–12. A different poem with the title 'Spring Equinox, 2020' is published in *The Silence*, p. 18.
41 Clarke, 'Spring Equinox, 2020', p. 18.
42 Clarke, 'Spring Equinox, 2020', p. 18.
43 Maev Kennedy, 'The lights go out across the UK to mark first world war's centenary', *The Guardian*, 10 July 2014. Online. Available at *https://www.theguardian.com/world/2014/jul/10/lights-out-lamps-mark-first-world-war-start* (accessed 26 November 2023).
44 Clarke, 'Spring Equinox, 2020', p. 18.
45 Clarke, 'Spring Equinox, 2020', p. 18.
46 Clarke, 'Spring Equinox, 2020', p. 18.

47 Carol Rumens, 'Poem of the Week: Spring Equinox, 2021 by Gillian Clarke', *The Guardian*, 26 February 2024. Online. Available at *https://www.theguardian.com/books/2024/feb/26/poem-of-the-week-spring-equinox-2021-by-gillian-clarke* (accessed 26 February 2024).
48 Clarke, 'Spring Equinox, 2021', p. 21.
49 Clarke, 'Spring Equinix, 2021', p. 21.
50 Clarke, 'Spring Equinox, 2021', p. 21.
51 Rumens, 'Poem of the Week: Spring Equinox, 2021 by Gillian Clarke'. Online.
52 Gillian Clarke, 'Wild Laburnum' and 'The Breath of Trees' in Clarke, *The Silence*, pp. 25 and 26.
53 Gillian Clarke, 'Bluebells', in Clarke, *The Silence*, p. 23.
54 Gillian Clarke, 'Sext', in Clarke, *The Silence*, p. 15.
55 Gillian Clarke, 'Song', in Clarke, *The Silence*, p. 17.
56 Clarke, 'Song', p. 17.
57 Gillian Clarke, 'A Spring Morning', in Clarke, *The Silence*, p. 19.
58 Clarke, 'Wild Laburnum', p. 25.
59 Smolin, *The Life of the Cosmos*, p. 176.
60 Smolin, *The Life of the Cosmos*, p. 176.
61 Dipesh Chakrabarty, *The Climate of History in a Planetary Age* (Chicago and London: The University of Chicago Press, 2021), p. 49.
62 Chakrabarty, *The Climate of History in a Planetary Age*, p. 47.
63 Clarke, 'Blue Sky Thinking', p. 48.
64 Cherry Gilchrist, 'The Russian Spirit of Place', in Campion and Curry (eds), *Sky and Psyche*, pp. 123–40, at p. 123.
65 Gillian Clarke, 'A Russian Woman in Tashkent, 1979', in Gillian Clarke, *The King of Britain's Daughter* (Manchester: Carcanet, 1993), p. 34.
66 Clarke, 'A Russian Woman in Tashkent, 1979', p. 34.
67 Chakrabarty, *The Climate of History in a Planetary Age*, p. 183 (Chakrabarty's italics).
68 Clarke, 'Scything', in Gillian Clarke, *Selected Poems* (Manchester: Carcanet, 1985), p. 45.
69 Gillian Clarke, 'The Brown Hairstreak Butterfly', 'Journal', in Clarke, *At the Source*, pp. 132–40, at p. 133.
70 Gillian Clarke, 'The Starling', in Clarke, *The Silence*, p. 68.
71 Gillian Clarke, 'The Honey Man', in Gillian Clarke, *Five Fields* (Manchester: Carcanet, 1998), p. 21.
72 Gillian Clarke, 'Kite, Buzzard, Crow', 'Journal', in Clarke, *At the Source*, pp. 122–31, at p. 122.
73 Clarke, 'Kite, Buzzard, Crow', p. 122.
74 Clarke, 'The Honey Man', p. 21.
75 Clarke, 'The Brown Hairstreak Butterfly', p. 133.
76 E. F. Linssen, *The Observer's Book of Insects of the British Isles, with a Section on Spiders* (1953; new edn London: Frederick Warne, 1978), p. 9.
77 Linssen, *The Observer's Book of Insects*, p. 8.
78 Gillian Clarke, 'Architect', in Clarke, *Five Fields*, p. 20.
79 Clarke, 'Architect', p. 20.
80 Clarke, 'Architect', p. 20.
81 Gillian Clarke, 'In Wren Graveyard', in Clarke, *Ice*, p. 34.

NOTES

82 R. S. Thomas, 'The Place', in Thomas, *Collected Poems 1945–1990*, p. 207.
83 See, for example, Melissa Mayntz, *Migration: Exploring the Remarkable Journeys of Birds* (London: Quadrant, 2020), p. 74.
84 Gillian Clarke, 'Osprey', in Clarke, *Ice*, p. 63.
85 Clarke, 'Osprey', p. 63.
86 Stuart Clark, *Beneath the Night: How the Stars Have Shaped the History of Humankind* (London: Guardian Faber, 2020), p. 251.
87 Clark, *Beneath the Night*, p. 223.
88 Clark, *Beneath the Night*, p. 224.
89 Clark, *Beneath the Night*, p. 194.
90 Clark, *Beneath the Night*, p. 195.
91 Clark, *Beneath the Night*, p. 190.
92 John Lubbock, *The Beauties of Nature and the Wonders of the World We Live In* (London: Macmillan and Co. Ltd, 1897), p. 418.
93 George Kimble and Raymond Bush, *The Weather* (Harmondsworth and New York: Penguin Books, 1943), pp. 24–5 and 170–1.
94 Sverre Petterssen, *Introduction to Meteorology* (1941; rev. London and New York: McGraw-Hill Book Co., Inc., 1958).
95 Petterssen, *Introduction to Meteorology*, p. 297.
96 Gillian Clarke, 'Cae Delyn', in Gillian Clarke, *A Recipe for Water* (Manchester: Carcanet, 2009), p. 77.
97 Gillian Clarke, 'Quayside', in Clarke, *A Recipe for Water*, p. 75.
98 Clarke, 'Quayside', p. 75.
99 Gillian Clarke, 'Library Chair', in Clarke, *A Recipe for Water*, p. 74.
100 Jules Cashford, 'Imagining Eternity: Weaving "The Heavens' Embroidered Cloths"', in Campion and Curry (eds), *Sky and Psyche*, pp. 83–104, at p. 85.
101 Gillian Clarke, 'Foghorns', in Gillian Clarke, *The Sundial* (Llandysul: Gomer Press, 1978), p. 31.
102 Clarke, 'Death of a Cat', in Clarke, *Selected Poems*, p. 74.
103 Gillian Clarke, 'Something Understood', p. 40.
104 Clarke, 'Journal', in *Roots Home*, p. 124.
105 Clarke, 'Something Understood', p. 40.
106 Neville Brown, 'Life Across the Cosmos', in Campion and Curry (eds), *Sky and Psyche*, pp. 77–82, at p. 78.
107 Cashford, 'Imagining Eternity', p. 94.
108 Clarke, 'Scything', p. 45.
109 Gillian Clarke, 'Siege', in Clarke, *Selected Poems*, pp. 77–8, at p. 78.
110 Clarke, 'Siege', p. 77.
111 Gillian Clarke, 'Miracle on St David's Day', in Clarke, *Selected Poems*, p. 41.
112 Gillian Clarke, 'The Water-Diviner', in Clarke, *Selected Poems*, p. 85.
113 Clarke, 'Siege', p. 78.
114 Hodgkinson, *The Eloquent Silence*, p. 213.
115 Hodgkinson, *The Eloquent Silence*, p. 213.
116 Reginald Lester, *The Observer's Book of Weather* (1955; rev. London and New York: Frederick Warne and Co. Ltd, 1964), p. 1.
117 Clark, *Beneath the Night*, p. 268.
118 Clarke, 'Journal', p. 160.
119 Clarke, 'Journal', p. 160.

120 Gillian Clarke, 'Looking', in Gillian Clarke, *Letting in the Rumour* (Manchester: Carcanet, 1989), p. 33.
121 D. W. Sciama, *Modern Cosmology* (1971; rpt Cambridge: Cambridge University Press, 1973), pp. 126–7.
122 Clarke, 'Looking', p. 33.
123 Noel Cobb, 'The Soul of the Sky', in Campion and Curry (eds), *Sky and Psyche*, pp. 105–21, at p. 118.
124 Gillian Clarke, 'Winter', in Clarke, *Ice*, p. 12.
125 Clarke, 'Winter', p. 12.
126 Clarke, 'Winter', p. 12.
127 Cobb, 'The Soul of the Sky', p. 119.
128 Cobb, 'The Soul of the Sky', p. 118.
129 Clarke, 'Winter', p. 12.
130 Cobb, 'The Soul of the Sky', p. 119.
131 Cobb, 'The Soul of the Sky', p. 119.
132 Gillian Clarke, 'The Year's Midnight', in Clarke, *Ice*, p. 76.
133 Gillian Clarke, 'The Hare', in Clarke, *Letting in the Rumour*, p. 37.
134 Clarke, 'The Hare', p. 37.
135 Cashford, 'Imagining Eternity', p. 85.
136 Rob Cowen, *Common Ground* (2015; rpt London: Windmill Books, 2016), pp. 87 and 88.
137 Cowen, *Common Ground*, p. 88.
138 Clarke, 'The Sundial', in Clarke, *The Sundial* (Llandysul: Gomer Press, 1978), p. 11.
139 Clarke, 'The Sundial', p. 11.
140 Karen Armstrong, *A Short History of Myth* (Edinburgh: Canongate, 2005), p. 15.
141 Gillian Clarke, 'The Water-Diviner' and 'Climbing Cader Idris', in Clarke, *Selected Poems*, pp. 85 and 95.
142 Armstrong, *Sacred Nature*, p. 135.
143 Gillian Clarke, 'Concerto', in Clarke, *Five Fields*, pp. 61–8, at p. 63.
144 Clarke, 'Concerto', pp. 62 and 63.
145 Nicholas Campion, 'Introduction', in Campion and Curry (eds), *Sky and Psyche*, pp. 9–14, at p. 9.
146 Campion, 'Introduction', *Sky and Psyche*, p. 12.
147 Clarke, 'Concerto', p. 61.
148 Robert R. Clewis, 'Introduction', in Robert R. Clewis (ed.) *The Sublime Reader* (London and New York: Bloomsbury Academic, 2019), pp. 1–13, at p. 1.
149 Clarke, 'Concerto', p. 61.
150 Clarke, 'Concerto', p. 62.
151 Reginald O. Morris, *The Structure of Music* (1935; Oxford: Oxford University Press, 1985), p. 63.
152 Tom McLeish, *The Poetry of Music and Science: Comparing Creativity in Science and Art* (2019: London and New York: Routledge, 2020), p. 75.
153 Clarke, 'Concerto', p. 63.
154 Clarke, 'Concerto', p. 65.
155 Timothy Morton, *Hyperobjects: Philosophy and Ecology after the End of the World* (Minneapolis: University of Minnesota Press, 2013), p. 164.

156 Morton, *Hyperobjects*, pp. 164 and 165.
157 Clarke, 'Concerto', p. 66.
158 Clarke, 'Concerto', p. 68.
159 Clarke, 'Concerto', p. 68.
160 Campion, *Astrology and Cosmology in the World's Religions*, p. 3.
161 Gillian Clarke, 'Estuary', in Clarke, *Five Fields*, p. 74.
162 Armstrong, *A Short History of Myth*, p. 20.
163 Armstrong, *A Short History of Myth*, p. 17.
164 Clarke, 'Concerto', p. 68.
165 Armstrong, *A Short History of Myth*, p. 16.
166 Armstrong, *A Short History of Myth*, p. 16.
167 Gillian Clarke, 'Chalk Pebble', in Clarke, *Selected Poems*, p. 43.

3 Climate and Weather in the Anthropocene

1 Tim Palmer, *The Primacy of Doubt* (Oxford: Oxford University Press, 2022), p. 11.
2 Gillian Clarke, 'Harvest Moon', in Gillian Clarke, *Ice* (Manchester: Carcanet, 2012), p. 65.
3 Gillian Clarke, 'Wild Plums', in Clarke, *Ice*, p. 64.
4 Clarke, 'Wild Plums', p. 64.
5 Lee Smolin, *The Life of the Cosmos* (London: Weidenfeld & Nicolson, 1997), p. 162.
6 James Gleick, *Chaos: Making a New Science* (London: William Heinemann Ltd, 1988), p. 5.
7 Annie Dillard, *Pilgrim at Tinker Creek* (1975; rpt London: Pan Books Ltd., 1976), p. 237.
8 Dillard, *Pilgrim at Tinker Creek*, p. 237.
9 Leonard Smith, *Chaos: A Very Short Introduction* (Oxford and New York: Oxford University Press, 2007), pp. 1–2.
10 Palmer, *The Primacy of Doubt*, p. 11.
11 Palmer, *The Primacy of Doubt*, p. 17.
12 W. P. Hodgkinson, *The Eloquent Silence* (1946; rpt London: Hodder and Stoughton Ltd, for the English Universities Press Ltd, 1947), p. 99.
13 Smith, *Chaos*, pp. 8 and 32.
14 Palmer, *The Primacy of Doubt*, p. 24.
15 Smith, *Chaos*, p. 3.
16 Smith, *Chaos*, p. 17.
17 Gillian Clarke, 'Kite, Buzzard, Crow', 'Journal', in Gillian Clarke, *At the Source* (Manchester: Carcanet, 2008), pp. 121–31, at p. 127.
18 Gillian Clarke, 'Storm Awst', in Gillian Clarke, *Selected Poems* (Manchester: Carcanet, 1985), p. 16.
19 Gillian Clarke, 'Storm', in Gillian Clarke, *Letting in the Rumour* (Manchester: Carcanet, 1989), p. 12.
20 Clarke, 'Storm', p. 12.
21 Gillian Clarke, 'Journal', in Gillian Clarke, *Roots Home: Essays and a Journal* (Manchester: Carcanet, 2021), p. 165.

22 Clarke, 'Journal', *Roots Home*, p. 158.
23 Gillian Clarke, 'Storwm Awst', in *The Silence* (Manchester: Carcanet 2024), p. 37.
24 Clarke, 'Storwm Awst', p, 37.
25 Clarke, 'Storwm Awst', p. 37.
26 Clarke, 'Storwm Awst', p. 37.
27 Clarke, 'Storwm Awst', p. 37.
28 D. Parry-Jones, *Welsh Country Characters* (London and New York: B. T. Batsford Ltd, 1952), p. 168.
29 Nicholas Campion, *Astrology and Cosmology in the World's Religions* (New York and London: New York University Press, 2012), p. 6.
30 Karen Armstrong, *A Short History of Myth* (Edinburgh: Canongate, 2005), p. 18.
31 Gleick, *Chaos*, pp. 7–8.
32 Daniel Butler, *The Owl House* (Bridgend: Seren, 2020), p. 82.
33 Butler, *The Owl House*, p. 83.
34 Sverre Petterssen, *Introduction to Meteorology* (1941; rpt London and New York: McGraw-Hill Book Co., Inc., 1958), p. 112.
35 Petterssen, *Introduction to Meteorology*, p. 113.
36 Petterssen, *Introduction to Meteorology*, p. 115.
37 Gillian Clarke, 'Cattle, Hayfield, Storm', in Gillian Clarke, *A Recipe for Water* (Manchester: Carcanet, 2009), p. 65.
38 Petterssen, *Introduction to Meteorology*, pp. 117–18.
39 Gillian Clarke, 'Storm-Snake', in Clarke, *Ice*, p, 52.
40 Gillian Clarke, 'Something Understood', in Clarke, *Roots Home*, pp. 37–46, at p. 42.
41 Butler, *The Owl House*, pp. 81–104.
42 Andri Snær Magnason, *On Time and Water: A History of Our Future* trans. Lytton Smith (2020; rpt London: Serpent's Tail, 2021), p. 254.
43 Reginald Lester, *The Observer's Book of Weather* (1955; rev. London and New York: Frederick Warne and Co. Ltd, 1964).
44 Lester, *The Observer's Book of Weather*, pp. 112 and 113.
45 Gillian Clarke, 'Flowers of the Mountain', in Gillian Clarke, *Zoology* (Manchester: Carcanet, 2017), p. 39.
46 Butler, *The Owl House*, p. 83.
47 Gillian Clarke, 'Chawton', in Clarke, *Zoology*, p. 68.
48 Gillian Clarke, 'White Lilies', in Clarke, *Zoology*, p. 93.
49 Lester, *The Observer's Book of Weather*, p. 114.
50 Lester, *The Observer's Book of Weather*, p. 1.
51 Clarke, 'Journal', in Clarke, *Roots Home*, p. 184.
52 Hywel Griffiths, 'Cyflwyniad' (Introduction), in Iestyn Hughes, *Tywydd Mawr* (Extreme Weather in Wales) (Talybont, Ceredigion: Y Lolfa Cyf, 2016), p. 7.
53 Griffiths, 'Cyflwyniad', *Tywydd Mawr*, p. 7.
54 Griffiths, 'Cyflwyniad', *Tywydd Mawr*, p. 7.
55 Clarke, 'Journal', *Roots Home*, p. 190.
56 Gillian Clarke, 'Cantre'r Gwaelod', in Clarke, *Roots Home*, pp. 192–3.
57 Gillian Clarke, 'Beginning with Bendigeidfran', in Clarke, *At the Source*, pp. 8–15, at p. 11.

58 Clarke, 'Beginning with Bendigeidfran', p. 11.
59 Karen Armstrong, *A Short History of Myth* (Edinburgh: Canongate, 2005), p. 23.
60 Clarke, 'Beginning with Bendigeidfran', p. 11.
61 Armstrong, *A Short History of Myth*, p. 148.
62 Armstrong, *A Short History of Myth*, p. 35.
63 Clarke, 'Journal', *Roots Home*, p. 190.
64 Clarke, 'Journal', *Roots Home*, p. 190.
65 Clarke's 'Journal', *Roots Home*, p. 191.
66 Clarke, 'Journal', *Roots Home*, p. 192.
67 Karen Armstrong, *Sacred Nature: How We Can Recover Our Bond with the Natural World* (London: The Bodley Head, 2022), p. 26.
68 Clarke, 'Journal', *Roots Home*, p. 193.
69 Clarke, 'Journal', *Roots Home*, p. 193.
70 Clarke, 'Journal', *Roots Home*, p. 193.
71 Clark, 'Journal', *Roots Home*, p. 193.
72 Samantha Wynne-Rhydderch, 'Floating Forest', *Planet: The Welsh Internationalist*, 248 (2022), 72–3, at 73.
73 Erica Gies, *Water Always Wins: Thriving in an Age of Drought and Deluge* (London: Head of Zeus Ltd, 2022), p. 289.
74 Timothy Morton, *Hyperobjects*: Philosophy and Ecology after the End of the World (Minneapolis: University of Minnesota Press, 2013), p. 1.
75 Morton, *Hyperobjects*, p. 1.
76 Morton, *Hyperobjects*, p. 2.
77 Morton, *Hyperobjects*, p. 2.
78 Morton, *Hyperobjects*, p. 172.
79 Morton, *Hyperobjects*, p. 160.
80 Morton, *Hyperobjects*, p. 160.
81 Morton, *Hyperobjects*, p. 181.
82 Morven Mckinnon, 'Climate change is harming my mental health', BBC Scotland news, 8 June 2023. Online. Available at *https://www.bbc.co.uk/news/uk-scotland-65633082* (accessed 7 June 2023).
83 Mckinnon, 'Climate change is harming my mental health'. Online.
84 Smith, *Chaos*, p. 22.
85 Smith, *Chaos*, p. 24.
86 Smith, *Chaos*, p. 144.
87 Gillian Clarke, 'The Rising Tide', in Gillian Clarke, *A Recipe for Water* (Manchester: Carcanet, 2009), p. 46.
88 Clarke, 'The Rising Tide', p. 46.
89 Gies, *Water Always Wins*, p. 289.
90 Clarke, 'The Rising Tide', p. 46.
91 Clarke, 'Cattle, Hayfield, Storm', p. 65.
92 Clarke, 'Cattle, Hayfield, Storm', p. 65.
93 Clarke, 'Something Understood', pp. 43–4.
94 Sophie Laniel-Musitelli, 'Still Life and Vital Matter in Gillian Clarke's Poetry', in Liliane Campos and Pierre-Louis Patoine (eds), *Life-Rescaled* (Open Book Publishers, 2022). Online. Available at *https://doi.org/10.11647/OBP.0303.03* (accessed 26 June 2023).

95 Morton, *Hyperobjects*, p. 48.
96 Morton, *Hyperobjects*, p. 2.
97 Clarke, 'Storm Awst', p. 16.
98 Clarke, 'Cattle, Hayfield, Storm', p. 65.
99 Clarke, 'Journal', *Roots Home*, p. 158.
100 Clarke, 'Journal', *Roots Home*, p. 165.
101 Clarke, 'Journal, *Roots Home*, p. 178.
102 Hughes, *Tywydd Mawr*, p. 9.
103 Hughes, *Tywydd Mawr*, p. 97.
104 Hughes, *Tywydd Mawr*, pp. 99, 116–18, 123–6.
105 Stuart Clark, *Beneath the Night: How the Stars Have Shaped the History of Humankind* (London: Guardian Faber, 2020), p. 265.
106 Gillian Clarke, 'Tawny Owl', in Clarke, *Selected Poems*, p. 106.
107 Clarke, 'Tawny Owl', p. 106.
108 Clarke, 'Tawny Owl', p. 106.
109 Smith, *Chaos*, p. 160.
110 Lubbock, *The Beauties of Nature and the Wonders of the World We Live In* (London: Macmillan and Co Ltd, 1897), pp. 254–5.
111 Gillian Clarke, 'Glacier', in Clarke, *A Recipe for Water*, p. 34.
112 Lubbock, *The Beauties of Nature*, pp. 258–9.
113 Clarke, 'Glacier', p. 34.
114 Clarke, 'Glacier', p. 34.
115 D. Densil Morgan notes: 'The 111-foot No. 7 Tip which was directly above the Pant-glas area of the village, had already suffered substantial slippage in 1963, yet despite local protests nothing was done either to secure it or to prevent further waste from being disposed on the site.' D. Densil Morgan, *The Span of the Cross: Christian Religion and Society in Wales 1914–2000* (Cardiff: University of Wales Press, 2011), pp. 230–1.
116 Ayesha Tandon and Roz Pidcock, 'Polar bears and climate change: What does the science say?', *CarbonBrief*, 08/12/22. Online. Available at *https://interactive.carbonbrief.org/polar-bears-climate-change-what-does-science-say/index.html* (accessed 28 July 2023).
117 'Arctic fox', *Centre for Biological Diversity*. Online. Available at *www.biologicaldiversity.org/species/mammals/Arctic_fox* (accessed 28 July 2022).
118 Gillian Clarke, 'Snow', in Clarke, *Ice*, p. 16.
119 Gillian Clarke, 'Ice Music', in Clarke, *Ice*, p. 14.
120 Gillian Clarke, 'White Nights', in Clarke, *Ice*, p. 17.
121 Gillian Clarke, 'Freeze 1947', in Clarke, *Ice*, p. 21.
122 Clarke, 'White Nights', p. 17.
123 Samantha Walton, *Everybody Needs Beauty: In Search of the Nature Cure* (London and New York: Bloomsbury Publishing, 2023), p. 122.
124 Clarke, 'Ice Music', p. 14.
125 Clarke, 'Ice Music', p. 14.
126 Richard Fortey, *Trilobite! Eyewitness to Evolution* (London: HarperCollins Publishers, 2001), p. 176.
127 Clarke, 'Snow', p. 16.
128 Clarke, 'Snow', p. 16.
129 Clarke, 'Snow', p. 16.

NOTES   197

130 Gillian Clarke, 'In the Bleak Midwinter', in Clarke, *Ice*, p. 18.
131 Gillian Clarke, 'Carol of the Birds', in Clarke, *Ice*, p. 20.
132 Clarke, 'In the Bleak Midwinter', p. 18.
133 Robert R. Clewis, 'Introduction', in *The Sublime Reader*, ed. Robert R. Clewis (London and New York: Bloomsbury Academic, 2019), pp. 1–13, at p. 3.
134 Walton, *Everybody Needs Beauty*, p. 54.
135 Walton, *Everybody Needs Beauty*, p. 54.
136 Clewis, 'Introduction', *The Sublime Reader*, p. 1.
137 Clewis, 'Introduction', *The Sublime Reader*, p. 1.
138 Clarke, 'Ice Music', p. 14.
139 James Gleick, *Chaos: Making a New Science* (London: William Heinemann Ltd, 1988), pp. 314 and 313.
140 Neville Brown, 'Life Across the Cosmos' in Nicholas Campion and Patrick Curry (eds), *Sky and Psyche: The Relationship Between Cosmos and Consciousness* (2006; rpt Edinburgh: Floris Books, 2018), pp. 77–82, at pp. 78–9.
141 Jules Cashford, 'Imagining Eternity: Weaving "The Heavens' Embroidered Cloths"', in Campion and Curry (eds), *Sky and Psyche*, pp. 83–104, at p. 85.
142 Clarke, 'Journal', *Roots Home*, p. 73.
143 Gillian Clarke, 'Polar', in Clarke, *Ice*, p. 9.
144 Gleick, *Chaos*, pp. 314 and 313.
145 Clarke, 'Polar', p. 9.
146 Dipesh Chakrabarty, *The Climate of History in a Plenary Age* (Chicago and London: The University of Chicago Press, 2021), p. 185.
147 Clarke, 'Polar', p. 9.
148 Clarke, 'Polar', p. 9.
149 Clarke, 'Freeze 1947', p. 21.
150 Gillian Clarke, 'Freeze 2010', *Ice*, p. 22.
151 Magnason, *On Time and Water*, p. 198.
152 Brown, 'Life Across the Cosmos', p. 77.
153 Clarke, 'Kite, Buzzard, Crow', p. 127.
154 Clarke, 'Kite, Buzzard, Crow', pp. 130–1.
155 Gies, *Water Always Wins*, p. 289.
156 Clarke, 'Journal', *Roots Home*, p. 146.
157 Clarke, 'Journal', *Roots Home*, p. 87.
158 Clarke, 'Journal', *Roots Home*, p. 212.
159 Clarke, 'Journal', *Roots Home*, p. 213.
160 Clarke, 'Journal', *Roots Home*, p. 213.
161 Clarke, 'Journal', *Roots Home*, p. 69.

4 Sound, Water, Blackness and Cosmogenesis

1 Brian Thomas Swimme, *Cosmogenesis: An Unveiling of the Expanding Universe* (Berkeley, CA: Counterpoint, 2022), p. 3.
2 Swimme, *Cosmogenesis*, p. 3.
3 Swimme, *Cosmogenesis*, p. 4.
4 Swimme, *Cosmogenesis*, p. 4.

5. Swimme, *Cosmogenesis*, p. 5.
6. Gillian Clarke, 'The City', in Gillian Clarke, *Five Fields* (Manchester: Carcanet, 1998), p. 58.
7. Clarke, 'The City', p. 58.
8. Clarke, 'The City', p. 58.
9. Clarke, 'The City', p. 57.
10. Clarke, 'The City', p. 58.
11. Brian Greene, *The Elegant Universe* (1999; rpt London: Vintage Books, 2000), p. 15.
12. Greene, *The Elegant Universe*, p. 15.
13. Clarke, 'The City', p. 58.
14. Greene, *The Elegant Universe*, p. 16.
15. Swimme, *Cosmogenesis*, p. 25.
16. Greene, *The Elegant Universe*, pp. 15–16.
17. The publishing company Common Ground was formed in 1983 to pioneer imaginative work 'on nature, culture and place' in order to 'link people, landscape, wild life, buildings, history and customs, as well as bridging philosophy and practice, environment and the arts': Angela King and Susan Clifford (eds), *The River's Voice: An Anthology of Poetry* (Totnes: Green Books Ltd, 2000), p. 421.
18. Gillian Clarke, 'A Recipe for Water', in Gillian Clarke, *A Recipe for Water* (Manchester: Carcanet, 2009), pp. 20–3, at p. 20.
19. Sophie Laniel-Musitelli, 'Still Life and Vital Matter in Gillian Clarke's Poetry', in Liliane Compos and Pierre-Louis Patoine (eds), *Life-Rescaled: The Biological Imagination in Twenty-First Century Literature and Performance* (Cambridge: Open Books, 2022), pp. 69–91, at pp. 73–4. Available online at *https://doi.org/10.11647/OBP.0303.03* (accessed 26 June 2023).
20. Clarke, 'A Recipe for Water', p. 20.
21. Clarke, 'A Recipe for Water', p. 20.
22. Clarke, 'A Recipe for Water', p. 21.
23. Swimme, *Cosmogenesis*, p. 17.
24. Swimme, *Cosmogenesis*, p. 17.
25. Gillian Clarke, 'Something Understood', in Gillian Clarke, *Roots Home: Essays and a Journal* (Manchester: Carcanet, 2021), pp. 37–46, at p. 43.
26. Clarke, 'A Recipe for Water', p. 23.
27. Andri Snær Magnason, *On Time and Water: A History of Our Future*, trans. Lytton Smith (2020; rpt London: Serpent's Tail, 2021), p. 68.
28. Samantha Walton, *Everybody Needs Beauty: In Search of the Nature Cure* (2021; London and New York: Bloomsfield Publishing, 2022), p. 32.
29. Gillian Clarke, 'Severn', in Clarke, *A Recipe for Water*, pp. 24–9, at p. 25.
30. Clarke, 'Severn', p. 25.
31. Walton, *Everybody Needs Beauty*, pp. 26–7.
32. Walton, *Everybody Needs Beauty*, p. 27.
33. Clarke, 'Severn', p. 25.
34. Clarke, 'Severn', pp. 25–6.
35. King and Clifford, *The River's Voice*, p. 13.
36. Clarke, 'Severn', p. 26.
37. Clarke, 'Severn', p. 26.

38 John Lubbock, *The Beauties of Nature and the Wonders of the World We Live In* (1892; rpt London: Macmillan and Co. Ltd, 1897), pp. 253–4.
39 Robert Gibbings, *Coming Down the Wye* (1942; rpt London: The Travel Book Club, 1945), p. 104.
40 Gibbings, *Coming Down the Wye*, p. 16.
41 Walton, *Everybody Needs Beauty*, p. 29.
42 Clarke, 'Severn', p. 26.
43 Clarke, 'Severn', p. 27.
44 Clarke, 'Severn', p. 27.
45 Gillian Clarke, 'Slate', in Clarke, *Roots Home*, pp. 29–36, at p. 35.
46 Clarke, 'Slate', p. 36.
47 Clarke, 'Slate', p. 36.
48 Clarke, 'Slate', p. 36.
49 King and Clifford, *The River's Voice*, p. 13.
50 R. S. Thomas, 'Reservoirs', *Not That He Brought Flowers* (1968), *Collected Poems 1945–1990* (London: Phoenix, 2000), p. 194.
51 King and Clifford, *The River's Voice*, p. 13.
52 King and Clifford, *The River's Voice*, p. 14.
53 Walton, *Everybody Needs Beauty*, pp. 40 and 36.
54 Gillian Clarke, 'Mumbai', in Clarke, *A Recipe for Water*, pp. 30–3, at p. 30.
55 Erica Gies, *Water Always Wins: Thriving in an Age of Drought and Deluge* (London: Head of Zeus Ltd, 2022), p. 289.
56 Walton, *Everybody Needs Beauty*, p. 28.
57 Walton, *Everybody Needs Beauty*, p. 28.
58 Walton, *Everybody Needs Beauty*, p. 29.
59 Walton, *Everybody Needs Beauty*, p. 33.
60 Magnason, *On Time and Water*, p. 287.
61 Clarke, 'East Moors', in Gillian Clarke, *Selected Poems* (Manchester: Carcanet, 1985), p. 44. Originally published in *Letter from a Far Country* (1982).
62 Clarke, 'Mumbai', p. 33.
63 Richard Tarnas, 'Understanding the Modern Disenchantment of the Cosmos', in Nicholas Campion and Patrick Curry (eds), *Sky and Psyche: The Relationship Between Cosmos and Consciousness* (2006: rpt Edinburgh: Floris Books, 2018), pp. 183–99, at p. 191.
64 Tarnas, 'Understanding the Modern Disenchantment of the Cosmos', p. 192.
65 Tarnas, 'Understanding the Modern Disenchantment of the Cosmos', p. 196.
66 Tarnas, 'Understanding the Modern Disenchantment of the Cosmos', p. 192.
67 Clarke, 'Valley', in Clarke, *Five Fields*, p. 43.
68 Swimme, *Cosmogenesis*, p. 236.
69 Swimme, *Cosmogenesis*, p. 236.
70 Swimme, *Cosmogenesis*, p. 236. The concept that matter is not simply inert but has some kind of 'intelligence' is to be found in areas of science, especially 'popular' science, philosophy and spirituality. It has been open to several areas of interpretation, principally that the physical and chemical processes in cosmogenesis and the expansion of the universe constitute a 'life force' or that there is a connection between the so-called intelligence of matter and the 'consciousness' of life forms including our own. See, also, Dumitru Constantin

Dulcan, *The Intelligence of Matter* (1981; trans. Vasile Andreica; Romania: Editura Scoala Ardekeana, 2023) in which he traces the path of matter from the first waves of light to the moment when the human mind becomes self-consciously aware.

71 Kathryn Simon, 'Poetics of Black', A Dissertation Submitted to the Division of Media and Communications of the European Graduate School in Candidacy for the Degree of Doctor of Philosophy, Magna Cum Laude, October 2013, p. 9.
72 Simon, 'Poetics of Black', pp. 9 and 13.
73 Simon, 'Poetics of Black', p. 14.
74 Clarke, 'Journey', in Clarke, *Selected Poems*, p. 8.
75 Simon, 'Poetics of Black', p. 29.
76 Karen Armstrong, *A Short History of Myth* (Edinburgh: Canongate, 2005), p. 37.
77 Armstrong, *A Short History of Myth*, pp. 33 and 37.
78 Gillian Clarke, 'Snow on the Mountain' and 'Journey', in Clarke, *Selected Poems*, pp. 9 and 8.
79 Tarnas, 'Understanding the Modern Disenchantment of the Cosmos', p. 197.
80 Clarke, 'God's Eye', in Clarke, *Five Fields*, p. 36.
81 Swimme, *Cosmogenesis*, p. 236,
82 Simon, 'Poetics of Black', p. 12.
83 Simon, 'Poetics of Black', p. 37.
84 Rob Cowen, *Common Ground* (2015; rpt London: Windmill Books, 2016), p. 281.
85 Gillian Clarke, 'The Lineage of Bees', 'Journal', in Gillian Clarke, *At the Source* (Manchester: Carcanet, 2008), pp. 141–9, at p. 145.
86 Simon, 'Poetics of Black', p. 24.
87 Simon, 'Poetics of Black', p. 24.
88 For a fuller discussion of light and dark in Western Platonic metaphysics, see Simon, 'Poetics of Black', pp. 24–6.
89 Swimme, *Cosmogenesis*, p. 17.
90 Simon, 'Poetics of Black', p. 28.
91 Gillian Clarke, 'Ode to Winter', in Gillian Clarke, *Ice* (Manchester: Carcanet, 2012), p. 75.
92 Simon, 'Poetics of Black', p. 27.
93 Simon, 'Poetics of Black', p. 17.
94 Simon, 'Poetics of Black', p. 17.
95 Simon, 'Poetics of Black', p. 17.
96 Gillian Clarke, 'Nightride', in Clarke, *Selected Poems*, p. 13.
97 Simon, 'Poetics of Black', p. 17.
98 Simon, 'Poetics of Black', p. 17.
99 Gillian Clarke, 'Hunting the Wren', in Clarke, *Ice*, p. 19.
100 Simon, 'Poetics of Black', p. 23.
101 Clarke, 'Hunting the Wren', p. 19.
102 Simon, 'Poetics of Black', pp. 23 and 24.
103 Swimme, *Cosmogenesis*, p. 236.
104 Simon, 'Poetics of Black', p. 37.

105 Cowen, *Common Ground*, p. 91.
106 Cowen, *Common Ground*, pp. 88–91.
107 Gillian Clarke, 'The Hare', in Clarke, *Selected Poems*, pp. 99–100, at p. 99.
108 Clarke, 'The Hare', pp. 99–100.
109 Parry-Jones, *Welsh Country Characters*, p. 168.
110 Simon, 'Poetics of Black', p. 27.
111 Simon, 'Poetics of Black', p. 27.
112 Simon, 'Poetics of Black', p. 27.

5 Geology, Human Development and the Anthropocene

1 Clarke, 'Beginning with Bendigeidfran', in Gillian Clarke, *At the Source* (Manchester: Carcanet, 2008), pp. 8–15, at p. 14.
2 Gillian Clarke, 'The Poetry of Stone: Pentre Ifan', in Clarke, *At the Source*, pp. 47–54, at p. 49.
3 W. R. Hamilton, A. R. Woolley and A. C. Bishop, *The Hamlyn Guide to Minerals, Rocks and Fossils* (London: Hamlyn, 1974).
4 Thomas Richard Owen, *Geology Explained in South Wales* (Cardiff: David and Charles, 1973) and *The Upper Palaeozoic and Post-Palaeozoic Rocks of Wales* (Cardiff: University of Wales Press, 1974).
5 I. O. Evans, *The Observer's Book of Geology* (London and New York: Frederick Warne & Co. Ltd, 1968), p. 27.
6 Clarke, 'The City', in Gillian Clarke, *Five Fields* (Manchester: Carcanet, 1998), pp. 52–60, at p. 52.
7 Clarke, 'The City', p. 53.
8 Clarke, 'The City', p. 52.
9 Clarke, 'The City', p. 52.
10 Evans, *The Observer's Book of Geology*, p. 32.
11 Clarke, 'The Poetry of Stone', p. 49.
12 D. W. Sciama, *Modern Cosmology* (1971; rpt Cambridge: Cambridge University Press, 1973), p. 126.
13 Clarke, 'The City', p. 52.
14 Gillian Clarke, 'Rock', 'The Stone Poems', in Gillian Clarke, *Making the Beds for the Dead* (Manchester: Carcanet, 2004), pp. 23–8, at p. 23.
15 Clarke, 'The Poetry of Stone', p. 47.
16 Clarke, 'The Poetry of Stone', p. 47.
17 Albert S. Seward, *Geology for Everyman* (1943; rpt Cambridge: Cambridge University Press, 2011), p. 259.
18 Sophie Laniel-Musitelli, 'Still Life and Vital Matter in Gillian Clarke's Poetry', in Liliane Compos and Pierre-Louis Patoine (eds), *Life-Rescaled: The Biological Imagination in Twenty-First Century Literature and Performance* (Cambridge: Open Books, 2022), pp. 69–91, at p. 70. Available online at *https://doi.org/10.11647/OBP.0303.03* (accessed 26 June 2023).
19 Gillian Clarke, 'Kite, Buzzard, Crow', 'Journal', in Clarke, *At the Source*, pp. 122–31, at p. 127.
20 Richard Fortey, *The Earth: An Intimate History* (London: Harper Perennial, 2005), p. 25.

21. Dipesh Chakrabarty, *The Climate of History in a Planetary Age* (Chicago and London: The University of Chicago Press, 2021), pp. 30–2.
22. Clarke, 'Rock', p. 23.
23. Gillian Clarke, 'Hay', 'The Stone Poems', in Clarke, *Making the Beds for the Dead*, p. 23.
24. Clarke, 'Rock', p. 23.
25. Laniel-Musitelli, 'Still Life and Vital Matter in Gillian Clarke's Poetry', p. 77.
26. Clarke, 'Granite', 'The Stone Poems', in Clarke, *Making the Beds for the Dead*, p. 49.
27. Fortey, *The Earth*, p. 298.
28. Clarke, 'Into the Mountain', in Clarke, *Five Fields*, p. 44.
29. Gillian Clarke, 'Slate', in Gillian Clarke, *Roots Home: Essays and a Journal* (Manchester: Carcanet, 2021), pp. 29–36, at p. 35.
30. Gillian Clarke, 'Slate', 'The Stone Poems', in Clarke, *Making the Beds for the Dead*, p. 24.
31. Gillian Clarke, 'Woman Washing her Hair', 'The Stone Poems', in Clarke, *Making the Beds for the Dead*, p. 26.
32. Clarke, 'Woman Washing her Hair', p. 26.
33. Gillian Clarke, 'The Stone Hare', 'The Stone Poems', in Clarke, *Making the Beds for the Dead*, p. 26.
34. Clarke, 'The Poetry of Stone', p. 48.
35. Clarke, 'The Stone Hare', p. 27.
36. Laniel-Musitelli, 'Still Life and Vital Matter in Gillian Clarke's Poetry', p. 82.
37. Laniel-Musitelli, 'Still Life and Vital Matter in Gillian Clarke's Poetry', p. 72.
38. James Gleick, *Chaos: Making a New Science* (London: William Heinemann Ltd, 1988), p. 314.
39. Clarke, 'The Stone Hare', p. 27.
40. Clarke, 'The Stone Hare', p. 27.
41. Clarke, 'Slate', p. 35.
42. Clarke, 'Slate', p. 35.
43. Gillian Clarke, 'Edward Llwyd and the Trilobite', 'The Stone Poems', in Clarke, *Making the Beds for the Dead*, p. 25.
44. Seward, *Geology for Everyman*, p. 254.
45. Richard Fortey, *Trilobite! Eyewitness to Evolution* (London: HarperCollins Publishers, 2001), pp. 43–4.
46. Fortey, *Trilobite!*, p. 82.
47. Fortey, *Trilobite!*, p. 96.
48. Seward, *Geology for Everyman*, p. 132.
49. Jamie Woodward, *The Ice Age: A Very Short Introduction* (Oxford: Oxford University Press, 2014).
50. Woodward, *The Ice Age*, p. 132.
51. Woodward, *The Ice Age*, p. 132.
52. Robert Minhinnick, 'The Dinosaur Park', in Robert Minhinnick, *The Dinosaur Park* (Bridgend: Poetry Wales, 1985), pp. 7–8, at p. 8.
53. Minhinnick, 'The Dinosaur Park', p. 8.
54. Clarke, 'Mesozoic', 'The Stone Poems', in Clarke, *Making the Beds for the Dead*, p. 28.
55. Evans, *The Observer's Book of Geology*, p. 264.

NOTES 203

56 Chakrabarty, *The Climate of History in a Planetary Age*, p. 31.
57 Clarke, 'The City', p. 53.
58 Laniel-Musitelli, 'Still Life and Vital Matter in Gillian Clarke's Poetry', p. 70.
59 Douglas Palmer, *Fossils* (2006; rev. London: Collins, 2012), p. 112.
60 Gillian Clarke, 'Archaeopteryx', 'Behind Glass', in Gillian Clarke, *Zoology* (Manchester: Carcanet, 2017), p. 26.
61 Clarke, 'Archaeopteryx', p. 26.
62 Clarke, 'Archaeopteryx', p. 26.
63 Clarke, 'Archaeopteryx', p. 26.
64 Clarke, 'Archaeopteryx', p. 26.
65 Palmer, *Fossils*, p. 14.
66 Clarke, 'Archaeopteryx', p. 26.
67 Palmer, *Fossils*, pp. 14–15.
68 Palmer, *Fossils*, p. 112.
69 Gillian Clarke, 'Ichthyosaur' in Clarke, *Zoology*, p. 27. The poem was first published in Gillian Clarke, *Letting in the Rumour* (Manchester: Carcanet, 1989).
70 See Linden Peach, *Animals, Animality and Controversy in Modern Welsh Literature and Culture* (Cardiff: University of Wales Press, 2022), pp. 86–7.
71 Palmer, *Fossils*, p. 109.
72 Clarke, 'Ichthyosaur', p. 27.
73 Gillian Clarke, 'The Company of Bones', 'Behind the Glass', in Clarke, *Zoology*, p. 28.
74 Clarke, 'The Company of Bones', p. 28.
75 Clarke, 'The Company of Bones', p. 28.
76 Gillian Clarke, 'The Snowdon Rainbow Beetle', 'Behind the Glass', in Clarke, *Zoology*, p. 31.
77 Clarke, 'The Snowdon Rainbow Beetle', p. 31.
78 Gillian Clarke, 'Marsh Fritillaries', 'Behind the Glass', in Clarke, *Zoology*, p. 30.

6 *War and Peace (Part One)*

1 Dipesh Chakrabarty, *The Climate of History in a Planetary Age* (Chicago and London: The University of Chicago Press, 2021), pp. 184 and 185.
2 Chakrabarty, *The Climate of History in a Planetary Age*, p. 185.
3 Gillian Clarke, 'Beginning with Bendigeidfran', in Gillian Clarke, *At the Source* (Manchester: Carcanet, 2008), pp. 8–15, at p. 11.
4 Tony Curtis (ed.), *After the First Death: An Anthology of Wales and War in the Twentieth Century* (Bridgend: Seren, 1997), p. 10.
5 Curtis, *After the First Death*.
6 Tony Curtis (ed.), *Wales at War: Critical Essays on Literature and Art* (Bridgend: Seren, 2007).
7 Gillian Clarke, 'Journal', in Gillian Clarke, *Roots Home: Essays and a Journal* (Manchester: Carcanet, 2021), p. 131.
8 Clarke, 'Journal', *Roots Home*, p. 132.
9 Annie Dillard, *Pilgrim at Tinker Creek* (1975; rpt London: Pan Books Ltd, 1976), p. 235.

10. Clarke, 'Journal', *Roots Home*, p. 132.
11. Clarke, 'Journal', *Roots Home*, p. 74.
12. Clarke, 'Journal', *Roots Home*, p. 74.
13. Clarke, 'Journal', *Roots Home*, p. 74.
14. Gillian Clarke, 'Letter from a Far Country', in Gillian Clarke, *Selected Poems* (Manchester, Carcanet, 1985), pp. 52–64, at p. 59.
15. Gillian Clarke, 'The Dead after the Thaw', in Gillian Clarke, *Ice* (Manchester: Carcanet, 2012), p. 24.
16. Tony Curtis, 'Art in Wales during and from the Second World War', in Curtis (ed.), *Wales at War*, pp. 55–74, at p. 72.
17. Curtis, 'Art in Wales during and from the Second World War', pp. 69 and 70.
18. R. S. Thomas, *Neb*, gol Gwenno Hywyn (Caernarfon: Gwasg Gwynydd, 1985). See also M. Wynn Thomas, '"The Stones of the Field" and the Power of the Sword: R. S. Thomas as War Poet', in Curtis (ed.) *Wales at War*, pp. 142–64.
19. Clarke, 'Beginning with Bendigeidfran', p. 11.
20. R. S. Thomas, *The Echoes Return Slow* (London: Macmillan, 1988), p. 19.
21. Clarke, 'Beginning with Bendigeidfran', pp. 11–12.
22. Clarke, 'Journal', *Roots Home*, p. 167.
23. Clarke, 'Beginning with Bendigeidfran', p. 12.
24. Clarke, 'Beginning with Bendigeidfran', p. 12.
25. Gillian Clarke, 'Poet's Introduction', in Judith Kinsman (ed.), *Six Women Poets* (Oxford: Oxford University Press, 1992), pp. 1–3, at p. 2.
26. Clarke, 'Poet's Introduction', p. 2.
27. Gillian Clarke, 'Siege', in Gillian Clarke, *Selected Poems* (Manchester: Carcanet, 1985), pp. 77–8.
28. Clarke, 'Poet's Introduction', p. 2.
29. Clarke, 'Siege', p. 78.
30. Clarke, 'Siege', p. 78.
31. Katie Gramich, 'Welsh Women Writers and War', in Curtis (ed.), *Wales at War*, pp. 122–41, at pp. 137–8.
32. Gillian Clarke, 'The King of Britain's Daughter', in Gillian Clarke, *The King of Britain's Daughter* (Manchester: Carcanet, 1993), p. 6.
33. Gillian Clarke, 'Gorse', in Gillian Clarke, *The Silence* (Manchester: Carcanet, 2024), p. 72.
34. Clarke, 'Gorse', p. 72.
35. Clarke, 'Gorse', p. 72.
36. Manfred B. Steger, *Globalization: A Very Short Introduction* (Oxford: Oxford University Press, 2009), p. 36.
37. Steger, *Globalization*, p. 78.
38. Andrew Hoskins and Ben O'Loughlin, *War and Media: The Emergence of Diffused War* (London: Polity Press, 2010), p. 1.
39. Hoskins and O'Loughlin, *War and Media*, pp. 17–18.
40. Hoskins and O'Loughlin, *War and Media*, pp. 6–7.
41. Hoskins and O'Loughlin, *War and Media*, p. 17.
42. Clarke, *At the Source*, p. 127.
43. Clarke, *At the Source*, p. 111.

NOTES

44 Gillian Clarke, 'Times Like These', in Nigel Jenkins and Menna Elfyn (eds), *Glas-Nos: Cerddi Dros Heddwch/Poems for Peace* (Machynlleth, Powys: CND Cymru, 1987), p. 14. The poem was subsequently published in Gillian Clarke, *Letting in the Rumour* (Manchester: Carcanet, 1989), p. 49.
45 Clarke, 'Times Like These', p. 14.
46 Rhodri Glyn Thomas, 'Rhagymadrodd/Preface', in Nigel Jenkins and Menna Elfyn (eds), *Glas-Nos*, p. xii.
47 Curtis, *After the First Death*, pp. 204, 254 and 256.
48 Gillian Clarke, 'The Night War Broke', in Curtis (ed.), *After the First Death*, p. 254.
49 Gillian Clarke, 'The Field-Mouse', in Curtis (ed.), *After the First Death*, p. 256.
50 Gillian Clarke, 'Notes: The Field Mouse'. Online. Available at *https://www.gillianclarke.co.uk/gc2017/the-field-mouse/* (accessed 25 August 2022).
51 Clarke, 'The Field-Mouse', p. 256.
52 Clarke, 'Notes: The Field Mouse'. Online.
53 Clarke, 'Notes: The Field Mouse'. Online.
54 Clarke, 'The Field-Mouse', p. 254.
55 Tony Curtis, 'Crane Flies', in Curtis (ed.), *After the First Death*, pp. 255–6, at p. 255.
56 Curtis, 'Crane Flies', p. 256.
57 Hoskins and O'Loughlin, *War and Media*, p. 186.
58 Hoskins and O'Loughlin, *War and Media*, p. 186.
59 Hoskins and O'Loughlin, *War and Media*, p. 187.
60 For further discussion of this subject see, for example, Hoskins and O'Loughlin, *War and Media*, p. 172.
61 Hoskins and O'Loughlin, *War and Media*, p. 172.
62 Gillian Clarke, 'Listen', in Clarke, *Ice*, p. 69.
63 Clarke, 'Listen', p. 69.
64 Jane Aaron and M. Wynn Thomas, '"Pulling You Through Changes": Welsh writing before, between and after two Referenda', in M. Wynn Thomas (ed.), *A Guide to Welsh Literature: Welsh Writing in English v.7: Welsh Writing in English* (Cardiff: University of Wales Press, 2003), pp. 278–309, at p. 290.
65 Aaron and Thomas, '"Pulling You Through Changes"', pp. 290–1.
66 Milja Kurki, *International Relations in a Relational Universe* (Oxford: Oxford University Press, 2020), p. 186.
67 Gillian Clarke, 'Birthday', in Gillian Clarke, *Making the Beds for the Dead* (Manchester: Carcanet, 2004), p. 75.
68 Clarke, 'Birthday', p. 75.
69 Clarke, 'Birthday', p. 75.
70 Gillian Clarke, 'Aftermath', in Clarke, *Making the Beds for the Dead*, p. 76.
71 Clarke, 'Aftermath', p. 76.
72 Clarke, 'Aftermath', p. 76.
73 Anthony Burke, Stefanie Fishel, Audra Mitchell, Simon Dalby and Daniel Levine, 'Planet Politics: a Manifesto from the end of IR [International Relations]', *Millennium: Journal of International Studies*, 44/3 (2016), 499–523, at 500. Cit. Kurki, *International Relations in a Relational Universe*, p. 170.
74 Burke et al., 'Planet Politics', 500. Cit. Kurki, *International Relations in a Relational Universe*, p. 170.

75. Kurki, *International Relations in a Relational Universe*, p. 186.
76. Kurki, *International Relations in a Relational Universe*, p. 186.
77. Gillian Clarke, 'Tomatoes', in Clarke, *Making the Beds for the Dead*, p. 52.
78. Clarke, 'Tomatoes', p. 52.
79. See, Linden Peach, 'When Wales Said No: Palestine, Parch and Personalism', *Planet: The Welsh Internationalist*, 253 (2024), 23–31, at 26 and 30.
80. Kurki, *International Relations in a Relational Universe*, p. 180.
81. Kurki, *International Relations in a Relational Universe*, p. 134.
82. Steger, *Globalization*, pp. 134–5.
83. Cit. Kurki, *International Relations in a Relational Universe*, p. 180.
84. Kurki, *International Relations in a Relational Universe*, p. 180.
85. Gillian Clarke, 'Mercury', in Gillian Clarke, *A Recipe for Water* (Manchester: Carcanet, 2009), p. 54.
86. Clarke, 'Mercury', p. 54.
87. Clarke, 'Mercury', p. 54.
88. Gillian Clarke, 'Journal', *Roots Home: Essays and a Journal*, p. 105.
89. Clarke, 'Journal', *Roots Home*, p. 105.
90. Gillian Clarke, 'A Difficult Birth', in Clarke, *Roots Home*, pp. 105–6, at p. 105.
91. Clarke, 'A Difficult Birth', p. 105.
92. Gillian Clarke, 'The Silence', in Clarke, *The Silence*, p. 20.
93. Helen Briggs, 'Coronavirus: Bat scientists find new evidence'. Online. Available at BBC *https://www.bbc.co.uk/news/science-environment-55998157* (accessed 10 April 2023).
94. Gillian Clarke, 'Today', in Clarke, *The Silence*, p. 22.
95. Clarke, 'Letter from a Far Country', p. 59.
96. Clarke, 'Journal', *Roots Home*, p. 187.
97. Clarke, 'Journal', *Roots Home*, p. 187.
98. Clarke, 'Journal', *Roots Home*, p. 187.
99. Clarke, 'Six Bells', in Clarke, *Ice*, p. 57.
100. Clarke, 'Six Bells', p. 57.
101. Clarke, 'Six Bells', p. 57.
102. Gillian Clarke, 'Letters from Bosnia', in Gillian Clarke, *Five Fields* (Manchester: Carcanet, 1998), p. 76.
103. Clarke, 'Letters from Bosnia', p. 76.
104. Clarke, 'Journal', *Roots Home*, p. 75.
105. *Hatimura* was a British merchant steamship torpedoed by a German U-boat in 1942.
106. Gillian Clarke, 'The Listeners', in Gillian Clarke, *The King of Britain's Daughter* (Manchester: Carcanet, 1993), p. 27.
107. Clarke, 'The Listeners', p. 27.
108. Clarke, 'The Listeners', p. 27.
109. Chakrabarty, *The Climate of History in a Planetary Age*, p. 187.
110. Gillian Clarke, 'Oradour-sur-Glane', in Clarke, *A Recipe for Water*, p. 59.
111. Clarke, 'Oradour-sur-Glane', p. 59.
112. Clarke, 'Oradour-sur-Glane', p. 59.
113. Clarke, 'Oradour-sur-Glane', p. 59.
114. Gillian Clarke, 'European Fields', in Clarke, *Five Fields*, p. 48.
115. Clarke, 'European Fields', p. 48.

116 Clarke, 'European Fields', p. 48.
117 Reginald O. Morris, *The Structure of Music* (1935; rpt Oxford: Oxford University Press, 1985), p. 63.
118 Morris, *The Structure of Music*, p. 64.
119 Tom McLeish, *The Poetry and Music of Science: Comparing Creativity in Science and Art* (2019; rpt Oxford: Oxford University Press, 2020), p. 2. See also Karl Popper, *Unended Quest: An Intellectual Autobiography* (1976; rpt London and New York: Routledge, 2002).
120 Gillian Clarke, 'The City', in Clarke, *Five Fields*, p. 52.
121 Brian Greene, *The Elegant Universe* (1999; rpt London: Vintage Books, 2000), p. 368.
122 Morris, *The Structure of Music*, p. 68.
123 Morris, *The Structure of Music*, p. 55.
124 Clarke, 'The City', p. 53.
125 Clarke, 'The City', p. 59.
126 Clarke, 'The City', p. 59.
127 Clarke, 'The City', pp. 55, 57, 58 and 59.
128 Clarke, 'The City', p. 59.
129 Tim Palmer, *The Primacy of Doubt* (Oxford: Oxford University Press, 2022), p. 11.
130 Palmer, *The Primacy of Doubt*, p. 17.
131 Clarke, 'The City', p. 59.
132 Clarke, 'The City', p. 59.
133 Clarke, 'The City', p. 59.
134 Clarke, 'The City', p. 59.
135 Clarke, 'The City', p. 60.
136 Greene, *The Elegant Universe*, p. 15.
137 Greene, *The Elegant Universe*, p. 16.
138 Kurki, *International Relations in a Relational Universe*, p. 135.
139 Kurki, *International Relations in a Relational Universe*, p. 135.

7 War and Peace (Part Two)

1 Kari Maund, *The Welsh Kings: Warriors, Warlords and Princes* (Stroud: The History Press, 2006), p. 30.
2 Alice Roberts, *Buried: An Alternative History of the First Millennium in Britain* (London: Simon & Schuster, 2022), p. xiii.
3 Gillian Clarke, 'Introduction', *The Gododdin: Lament for the Fallen* (London: Faber, 2021), p. viii.
4 Clarke, 'Introduction', p. vii.
5 Gillian Clarke, *Roots Home: Essays and a Journal* (Manchester: Carcanet, 2021), p. 140.
6 Jane Aaron and M. Wynn Thomas, '"Pulling You Through Changes": Welsh writing before, between and after two Referenda', in M. Wynn Thomas (ed.), *A Guide to Welsh Literature: Welsh Writing in English v.7: Welsh Writing in English* (Cardiff: University of Wales Press, 2003), pp. 278–309, at p. 291.

7 Gillian Clarke, 'The Book of Aneirin', in Gillian Clarke, *Ice* (Manchester, Carcanet, 2012), p. 72.
8 Anthony Conran, 'Introduction', *The Penguin Book of Welsh Verse*, trans. Anthony Conran (Harmondsworth: Penguin, 1967), p. 21.
9 Emyr Humphreys, *The Taliesin Tradition: A Quest for Welsh Identity* (Bridgend: Seren Books, 1989), p. 18.
10 Humphreys, *The Taliesin Tradition*, p. 13.
11 Clarke, 'Introduction', *The Gododdin*, p. viii.
12 Humphreys, *The Taliesin Tradition*, p. 13.
13 Clarke, 'The Book of Aneirin', p. 72.
14 Hans Belting, *Likeness and Presence: A History of the Image before the Era of Art*, trans. Edmund Jephcott (1994; rpt Chicago and London: The University of Chicago Press, 1996), p. 16.
15 Belting, *Likeness and Presence*, p. 98.
16 Dipesh Chakrabarty, *The Climate of History in a Planetary Age* (Chicago and London: The University of Chicago Press, 2021), pp. 184 and 185.
17 Conran, 'Introduction', *The Penguin Book of Welsh Verse*, p. 28.
18 Carol Rumens, 'Poem of the Week: from The Gododdin by Aneirin', *The Guardian*, 9 July 2018. Online. Available at *https://www.theguardian.com/books/booksblog/2018/jul/09/poem-of-the-week-from-the-gododdin-by-aneirin* (accessed 22 January 2023).
19 Rumens, 'Poem of the Week: from The Gododdin by Aneirin'. Online.
20 Rumens, 'Poem of the Week: from The Gododdin by Aneirin'. Online.
21 Clarke, *The Gododdin*, p. 19.
22 Conran, 'Introduction', *The Penguin Book of Welsh Verse*, p. 23.
23 Humphreys, *The Taliesin Tradition*, p. 15.
24 Humphreys, *the Taliesin Tradition*, p. 15.
25 Conran, 'Introduction', *The Penguin Book of Welsh Verse*, p. 22.
26 Clarke, *The Gododdin*, p. 17.
27 Clarke, *The Gododdin*, p. 7.
28 Clarke, 'Journal', *Roots Home*, p. 94.
29 Tony Conran (ed. and trans.), *The Peacemakers: Waldo Williams* (1997; rpt Talybont, Ceredigion: Y Lolfa, 2023), pp. 88 and 89.
30 Michel Foucault, *The Order of Things: An Archaeology of the Human Sciences* (1970; rpt London: Routledge), p. 72.
31 Clarke, *The Gododdin*, p. 113.
32 Clarke, *The Gododdin*, p. 5.
33 Clarke, *The Gododdin*, pp. 7, 9 and 11.
34 Foucault, *The Order of Things*, p. 73.
35 Foucault, *The Order of Things*, p. 73.
36 For a lengthier discussion of this subject, see Roberts, *Buried*, pp. 141–78.
37 Roberts, *Buried*, p. 177.
38 Roberts, *Buried*, p. 177.
39 Foucault, *The Order of Things*, p. 74.
40 Conran, 'Introduction', *The Penguin Book of Welsh Verse*, p. 26.
41 Conran, 'Introduction', *The Penguin Book of Welsh Verse*, p. 25.
42 Conran, 'Introduction', *The Penguin Book of Welsh Verse*, p. 26.
43 Conran, *The Peacemakers*, pp. 108 and 109.

NOTES

44 George M. Ll. Davies, 'Big-Enders or Little-Enders?' (1945) and 'The Politics of Personality' (1947), in George M. Ll. Davies, *Pilgrimage of Peace* (London: The Fellowship of Reconciliation, 1950), pp. 70 and 87.
45 Clarke, *The Gododdin*, pp. 5, 91 and 55.
46 Clarke, *The Gododdin*, p. 27.
47 Clarke, *The Gododdin*, p. 57.
48 Clarke, *The Gododdin*, p. 57.
49 Rumens, 'Poem of the Week: from The Gododdin by Aneirin'. Online.
50 Conran, *The Peacemakers*, pp. 130 and 131.
51 Clarke, *The Gododdin*, p. 51.
52 Conran, 'Introduction', *The Penguin Book of Welsh Verse*, p. 35.
53 Clarke, *The Gododdin*, p. 151.
54 Gillian Clarke, 'Cofiant', in Gillian Clarke, *Letting in the Rumour* (Manchester: Carcanet, 1989), pp. 63–79, at p. 64.
55 Clarke, 'Cofiant', pp. 70, 73 and 74.
56 Clarke, 'Cofiant', p. 79.
57 Gillian Clarke, 'The City', in Gillian Clarke, *Five Fields* (Manchester: Carcanet, 1998), pp. 52–60.
58 Gillian Clarke, 'Gwenllian', in Gillian Clarke, *The Silence* (Manchester: Carcanet 2024), p. 54.
59 Clarke, *The Gododdin*, p. 5.
60 Clarke, *The Gododdin*, p. 63.
61 Clarke, *The Gododdin*, p. 19.
62 Clarke, *The Gododdin*, p. 19.
63 Clarke, *The Gododdin*, p. 19.
64 Conran, 'Introduction', *The Penguin Book of Welsh Verse*, p. 22.
65 Clarke, *The Gododdin*, p. 13.
66 Clarke, *The Gododdin*, p. 15.
67 Clarke, *The Gododdin*, p. 5.
68 Clarke, *The Gododdin*, p. 13.
69 M. Wynn Thomas, *Internal Difference: Twentieth-century Writing in Wales* (Cardiff: University of Wales Press, 1992), p. 54. For a succinct discussion of how Welsh- and English-language Welsh writers drew on *Y Gododdin*, see Thomas, *Internal Difference*, pp. 54–7.
70 See, Linden Peach, *Pacifism, Peace and Modern Welsh Writing* (Cardiff: University of Wales Press, 2019).
71 See, Linden Peach, 'When Wales Said No: Palestine, Parch and Personalism', *Planet: The Welsh Internationalist*, 253 (2024), 23–31.
72 Clarke, *The Gododdin*, p. 15.
73 Clarke, *The Gododdin*, p. 19.
74 Barbara H. Rosenwein, *Emotional Communities in the Early Middle Ages* (2006; rpt Ithaca and London: Cornell University Press, 2007), p. 199.
75 Clarke, *The Gododdin*, p. 5.
76 Clarke, *The Gododdin*, p. 5.
77 Clarke, *The Gododdin*, p, 13.
78 Clarke, 'Introduction', *The Gododdin*, p. ix.
79 Clarke, 'Introduction', *The Gododdin*, p. xvi.
80 Clarke, 'Introduction', *The Gododdin*, p. ix.

81. Rosenwein, *Emotional Communities in the Early Middle* Ages, p. 175.
82. Such concepts pervade Clarke, *The Gododdin*. See, for example, pp. 7, 9, 19, 23, 55 and 69.
83. Rosenwein, *Emotional Communities in the Early Middle Ages*, p. 194.
84. Conran, 'Introduction', *The Penguin Book of Welsh Verse*, p. 23.
85. Clarke, *The Gododdin*, pp. 145–7.
86. Clarke, *The Gododdin*, p. 159.
87. Clarke, *The Gododdin*, p. 25.
88. Clarke, *The Gododdin*, pp. 81, 59 and 115.
89. Clarke, *The Gododdin*, p. 45.
90. Clarke, *The Gododdin*, pp. 57, 77 and 33.
91. Conran, 'Introduction', *The Penguin Book of Welsh Verse*, pp. 23–4.
92. See, 'How Welsh language communities remembered their war dead differently', *Nation.Cymru*, 11 Nov 2018.

Afterword

1. Lee Smolin, *The Life of the Cosmos* (London: Weidenfeld & Nicolson, 1997), p. 163.
2. Gillian Clarke, 'Kite, Buzzard, Crow', 'Journal', in Gillian Clarke, *At the Source* (Manchester: Carcanet, 2008), pp. 121–31, at p. 127.
3. Gillian Clarke, 'The Starling', in Gillian Clarke, *The Silence* (Manchester: Carcanet, 2024), p. 68.
4. Gillian Clarke, 'The Breath of Trees', in Clarke, *The Silence*, p. 26.
5. Clarke, 'The Breath of Trees', p. 26.
6. Smolin, *The Life of the Cosmos*, p. 292.
7. Smolin, *The Life of the Cosmos*, p. 292.
8. Gillian Clarke, 'Why I Write', in Gillian Clarke, *Roots Home: Essays and a Journal* (Manchester: Carcanet, 2021), pp. 5–11, at p. 10.
9. Clarke, 'Why I Write', p. 11.
10. Clarke, 'Why I Write', p. 11.
11. Paul Davies, *The Cosmic Blueprint: Order and Complexity and the Edge of Chaos* (London: Penguin, 1995), p. 5. Citing Karl Popper and John Eccles, *The Self and its Brain* (Berlin: Springer International, 1977), p. 61. See also, Nicholas Campion, 'Introduction: Sky Psyche – Heaven and Soul', in Nicholas Campion and Patrick Curry (eds), *Sky and Psyche: The Relationship Between Cosmos and Consciousness* (2006; rpt Edinburgh: Floris Books, 2018), pp. 9–14, at p. 12.
12. See, for example, John Barrow and Frank Tipler, *The Anthropic Cosmological Principle* (Oxford: Oxford University Press, 1996). See, also, Nicholas Campion, 'Introduction', in Campion and Curry (eds), *Sky and Consciousness*, p. 12.

Select Bibliography

Primary Texts

Butler, D., *The Owl House* (Bridgend: Seren, 2020).
Butler, S., 'An Interview with Gillian Clarke', in Susan Butler (ed.), *Common Ground: Poets in a Welsh Landscape* (Bridgend: Poetry Wales Press, 1985).
Clarke, G., *The Silence* (Manchester: Carcanet, 2024).
Clarke, G., *The Gododdin: Lament for the Fallen* (London: Faber, 2021).
Clarke, G., *Roots Home: Essays and a Journal* (Manchester: Carcanet, 2021).
Clarke, G., *Zoology* (Manchester: Carcanet, 2017).
Clarke, G., *Ice* (Manchester: Carcanet, 2012).
Clarke, G., *A Recipe for Water* (Manchester: Carcanet, 2009).
Clarke, G., *At the Source* (Manchester: Carcanet, 2008).
Clarke, G., *Making the Beds for the Dead* (Manchester: Carcanet, 2004).
Clarke, G., *Nine Green Gardens* (Llandysul: Gomer Press, 2000).
Clarke, G., *Five Fields* (Manchester: Carcanet, 1998).
Clarke, G., 'The Night War Broke', in Tony Curtis T. (ed.), *After the First Death: An Anthology of Wales and War in the Twentieth Century* (Bridgend: Seren, 1997).
Clarke, G., 'The Field-Mouse', in Tony Curtis T. (ed.), *After the First Death: An Anthology of Wales and War in the Twentieth Century* (Bridgend: Seren, 1997).
Clarke, G., *The King of Britain's Daughter* (Manchester: Carcanet, 1993).
Clarke, G., *Letting in the Rumour* (Manchester: Carcanet, 1989).
Clarke, G., *Selected Poems* (Manchester: Carcanet, 1985).

Clarke, G., Review of Jan Morris, *Conundrum*, in *The Anglo-Welsh Review*, 53 (1974), 259.
Clarke, G., *Snow on the Mountain* (Swansea: Christopher Davies, 1971).
Clarke, G., Four Poems, *Poetry Wales*, 6/1 (1970), 18–20.
Conran, A. (ed. and trans.), *The Peacemakers: Waldo Williams* (1997; rpt Talybont, Ceredigion: Y Lolfa, 2023).
Conran, A. (ed. and trans.), *The Penguin Book of Welsh Verse* (Harmondsworth: Penguin, 1967).
Cowen, R., *Common Ground* (2015; rpt London: Windmill Books, 2016).
Curtis T. (ed.), *After the First Death: An Anthology of Wales and War in the Twentieth Century* (Bridgend: Seren, 1997).
Davies, G. M. Ll., *Pilgrimage of Peace* (London: The Fellowship of Reconciliation, 1950).
Dillard, A., *Pilgrim at Tinker Creek* (1975; rpt London: Pan Books Ltd, 1976).
Finch, P., *Edging the City: A Journey Round the Border of Cardiff* (Bridgend: Seren, 2022).
Finch, P., *Walking Cardiff* (Bridgend: Seren, 2019).
Gibbings, R., *Coming Down the Wye* (1942; rpt London: The Travel Book Club, 1945).
Hodgkinson, W. P., *The Eloquent Silence* (1946; rpt London: Hodder & Stoughton Ltd, for the English Universities Press Ltd, 1947).
Huws, D. (ed.), *Llyfr Aneirin: The Book of Aneirin* (National Library of Wales, 1989).
Jackson, K., *The Gododdin: The Oldest Scottish Poem* (Edinburgh: Edinburgh University Press, 1969).
Jarman, A. O. H., *Aneirin: Y Gododdin* (Cardiff: Welsh Classics, 1988).
Jenkins, N. and Elfyn, M. (eds), *Glas-Nos: Cerddi Dros Heddwch / Glas-Nos: Poems for Peace* (Machynlleth, Powys: CND Cymru, 1987).
Lloyd, D. T., 'Interview with Gillian Clarke', in D. T. Lloyd (ed.), *The Urgency of Identity: Contemporary English-Language Poetry from Wales* (Evanston, IL: Northwestern University Press, 1994).
Lubbock, J., *The Beauties of Nature and the Wonders of the World We Live In* (London: Macmillan and Co. Ltd, 1897).
Minhinnick, R., *The Dinosaur Park* (Bridgend: Poetry Wales, 1985).
Parry-Jones, D., *Welsh Country Characters* (London and New York: B. T. Batsford Ltd, 1952).
Parry-Jones, D., *Welsh Country Upbringing* (1948; rpt London and New York: B. T. Batsford, 1949).
Pedler, I., *Auscultation* (Bridgend: Seren Books, 2021).

Price-Owen, M., 'R. S. Thomas in conversation with Molly Price-Owen', *The David Jones Journal: R. S. Thomas Special Issue* (summer/autumn 2001).
Thomas, R. S., *Collected Poems 1945–1990* (1993; rpt London: Phoenix, 2000).
Thomas, R. S., *The Echoes Return Slow* (London: Macmillan, 1988).
Wynne-Rhydderch, S., 'Floating Forest', *Planet: The Welsh Internationalist*, 248 (2022), 72–3.

Online Sources

'Arctic fox', *Centre for Biological Diversity*. Online. Available at *www.biologicaldiversity.org* (accessed 28 July 2022).
Clarke, G., 'Notes: The Field Mouse'. Online. Available at *https://www.gillianclarke.co.uk/gc2017/the-field-mouse/* (accessed 25 August 2022).
Clarke, G., 'Notes about Letter from a Far Country', available at *www.gillianclarke.co.uk* (accessed 31 May 2022).
Laniel-Musitelli, S., 'Still Life and Vital Matter in Gillian Clarke's Poetry', in Liliane Compos and Pierre-Louis Patoine (eds), *Life-Rescaled: The Biological Imagination in Twenty-First Century Literature and Performance* (Cambridge: Open Books, 2022). Available at *https://doi.org/10.11647/OBP.0303.03* (accessed 26 June 2023).
Rannard, G., 'Climate change: UK sea level rise speeding up – Met Office', BBC Climate & Science, 28 July 2022. Online. Available at *https://www.bbc.co.uk/news/science-environment-62322574* (accessed 28 July 2022).
Rumens, C., 'Poem of the Week: from The Gododdin by Aneirin', *The Guardian*, 9 July 2018. Online. Available at *https://www.theguardian.com/books/booksblog/2018/jul/09/poem-of-the-week-from-the-gododdin-by-aneirin* (accessed 22 January 2023).
Tandon, A. and Pidcock, R., 'Polar bears and climate change: What does the science say?', *CarbonBrief*, 8 December 2022. Online. Available at *https://interactive.carbonbrief.org/polar-bears-climate-change-what-does-science-say/index.html* (accessed 28 July 2023).

Secondary Sources

Aaron, J. and Thomas, M. W., '"Pulling You Through Changes": Welsh writing before, between and after two Referenda', in M. Wynn Thomas (ed.), *A Guide to Welsh Literature: Welsh Writing in English v.7: Welsh Writing in English* (Cardiff: University of Wales Press, 2003).
Ahmed, S., *The Cultural Politics of Emotion* (2004; Edinburgh: Edinburgh University Press, 2014).

Armstrong, K., *Sacred Nature: How We Can Recover Our Bond with the Natural World* (London: The Bodley Head, 2022).

Armstrong, K., *A Short History of Myth* (Edinburgh: Canongate, 2005).

Barrow, J. and Tipler, F., *The Anthropic Cosmological Principle* (Oxford: Oxford University Press, 1996).

Belting, H., *Likeness and Presence: A History of the Image before the Era of Art*, trans. Edmund Jephcott (1994; rpt Chicago and London: University of Chicago Press, 1996).

Boddice, R., *The History of Emotions* (Manchester: Manchester University Press, 2024).

Brown, N., 'Life Across the Cosmos', in N. Campion and P. Curry (eds), *Sky and Psyche: The Relationship Between Cosmos and Consciousness* (2006; rpt Edinburgh: Floris Books, 2018).

Campion, N., *Astrology and Cosmology in the World's Religions* (New York and London: New York University Press, 2012).

Campion, N. and Curry, P. (eds), *Sky and Psyche: The Relationship Between Cosmos and Consciousness* (2006; rpt Edinburgh: Floris Books, 2018).

Cashford, J., 'Imagining Eternity: Weaving "The Heavens' Embroidered Cloths"', in N. Campion and P. Curry (eds), *Sky and Psyche: The Relationship Between Cosmos and Consciousness* (2006: rpt Edinburgh: Floris Books, 2018).

Chakrabarty, D., *The Climate of History in a Planetary Age* (Chicago and London: University of Chicago Press, 2021).

Chetty, D., Issa, H., Muse, G. and Tyne, I. (eds), *Essays on the Future of Wales* (London: Repeater Books, 2022).

Clark, S., *Beneath the Night: How the Stars Have Shaped the History of Humankind* (London: Guardian Faber, 2020).

Clewis, R. R. (ed.), *The Sublime Reader* (London and New York: Bloomsbury Academic, 2019).

Conran, A. (ed. and trans.), Introduction, *The Penguin Book of Welsh Verse* (Harmondsworth: Penguin, 1967).

Curtis, T. (ed.), *Wales at War: Critical Essays on Literature and Art* (Bridgend: Seren, 2007).

Curtis, T., 'Art in Wales during and from the Second World War', in T. Curtis (ed.), *Wales at War: Critical Essays on Literature and Art* (Bridgend: Seren, 2007).

Davies, P., *The Cosmic Blueprint: Order and Complexity and the Edge of Chaos* (London: Penguin, 1995).

Elfyn, M., *Trying the Line: A Volume of Tribute to Gillian Clarke* (Llandysul, Ceredigion: Gomer Press, 1997).

Entwistle, A., *Poetry, Geography, Gender: Women Rewriting Contemporary Wales* (Cardiff: University of Wales Press, 2013).

Evans, D., 'Reconstructing Welshness – Again', in D. Chetty, H. Issa, G. Muse and I. Tyne, *Essays on the Future of Wales* (London: Repeater Books, 2022).

Evans, I. O., *The Observer's Book of Geology* (London and New York: Frederick Warne & Co. Ltd, 1968).

Fortey, R., *The Earth: An Intimate History* (2004; rpt London: Harper Perennial, 2005).

Fortey, R., *Trilobite! Eyewitness to Evolution* (London: HarperCollins Publishers, 2001).

Foucault, M., *The Order of Things: An Archaeology of the Human Sciences* (1970; rpt London: Routledge, 2023).

Gies, E., *Water Always Wins; Thriving in an Age of Drought and Deluge* (London: Head of Zeus Ltd, 2022).

Gilchrist, C., 'The Russian Spirit of Place', in N. Campion and P. Curry (eds), *Sky and Psyche: The Relationship Between Cosmos and Consciousness* (2006; rpt Edinburgh: Floris Books, 2018).

Gleick, J., *Chaos: Making a New Science* (London: William Heinemann Ltd, 1988).

Gramich, K., 'Welsh Women Writers and War', in T. Curtis (ed.), *Wales at War: Critical Essays on Literature and Art* (Bridgend: Seren, 2007).

Greene, B., *The Elegant Universe* (1999; rpt London: Vintage Books, 2000).

Griffiths, H., 'Cyflwyniad' (Introduction), in I. Hughes, *Tywydd Mawr* (Extreme Weather in Wales) (Talybont, Ceredigion: Y Lolfa Cyf, 2016).

Hamilton, W. R., Woolley, A. R. and Bishop, A. C., *The Hamlyn Guide to Minerals, Rocks and Fossils* (London: Hamlyn, 1974).

Hoskins, A., and O'Loughlin, B., *War and Media: The Emergence of Diffused War* (London: Polity Press, 2010).

Hughes, I., *Tywydd Mawr* (Extreme Weather in Wales) (Talybont, Ceredigion: Y Lolfa Cyf, 2016).

Humphreys, E., *The Taliesin Tradition: A Quest for the Welsh Identity* (1983; rpt Bridgend: Seren Books, 1989).

Jarvis, M., *Welsh Environments in Contemporary Poetry* (Cardiff: University of Wales Press, 2008).

Kimble, G. and Bush, R., *The Weather* (Harmondsworth and New York: Penguin Books, 1943).

Kurki, M., *International Relations in a Relational Universe* (Oxford: Oxford University Press, 2020).

Lester, R., *The Observer's Book of Weather* (1955; rev. London and New York: Frederick Warne and Co. Ltd, 1964).

Linssen, E. F., *The Observer's Book of Insects of the British Isles, with a Section on Spiders* (1953; new edition. London: Frederick Warne, 1978).

Magnason, A. S., *On Time and Water: A History of Our Future*, trans. L. Smith (2020; rpt London: Serpent's Tale, 2021).

Maund, K., *The Welsh Kings: Warriors, Warlords and Princes* (Stroud: The History Press, 2006).

Mayntz, M., *Migration: Exploring the Remarkable Journeys of Birds* (London: Quadrant, 2020).

McLeish, T., *The Poetry and Music of Science: Comparing Creativity in Science and Art* (2019; rpt Oxford: Oxford University Press, 2020).

Mitchell, A., *International Intervention in a Secular Age: Re-enchanting Humanity* (Abingdon: Routledge, 2014).

Morgan, D., *The Illustrated History of Cardiff Suburbs* (2002; rpt Derby: The Beedon Books Publishing Co. Ltd, 2006).

Morgan, D. D., *The Span of the Cross: Christian Religion and Society in Wales 1914–2000* (Cardiff: University of Wales Press, 2011).

Morris, R. O., *The Structure of Music* (1935; rpt Oxford: Oxford University Press, 1985).

Morton, T., *Hyperobjects: Philosophy and Ecology after the End of the World* (Minneapolis: University of Minnesota Press, 2013).

Owen, T. R., *The Upper Palaeozoic and Post-Palaeozoic Rocks of Wales* (Cardiff: University of Wales Press, 1974).

Owen, T. R., *Geology Explained in South Wales* (Cardiff: David and Charles, 1973).

Palmer, D., *Fossils* (2006; rev. London: Collins, 2012).

Palmer, T., *The Primacy of Doubt* (Oxford: Oxford University Press, 2022).

Peach, L., 'When Wales Said No: Palestine, Parch and Personalism', *Planet: The Welsh Internationalist*, 253 (2024), 23–31.

Peach, L., *Animals, Animality and Controversy in Modern Welsh Literature and Culture* (Cardiff: University of Wales Press, 2022).

Peach, L., *Pacifism, Peace and Modern Welsh Writing* (Cardiff: University of Wales Press, 2019).

Petterssen, S., *Introduction to Meteorology* (1941; rev. London and New York: McGraw-Hill Book Co., Inc., 1958).

Plamper, J., *The History of Emotions: An Introduction* (Oxford: Oxford University Press, 2015). [An English translation of J. Plamper, *Geschicte und Gefühl: Grundlagen der Emotionsgeschichte* (Munich: Siedler, 2012).]

Reddy, W. N., *The Navigation of Feeling: A Framework for the History of Emotions* (Cambridge: Cambridge University Press, 2001).
Roberts, A., *Buried: An Alternative History of the First Millennium in Britain* (London: Simon & Schuster, 2022).
Rosenwein, B. H. and Cristiani, R., *What is the History of Emotions?* (Cambridge: Polity Press, 2021).
Sciama, D. W., *Modern Cosmology* (1971 rpt. Cambridge: Cambridge University Press, 1973).
Seward, A. C., *Geology for Everyman* (Cambridge: Cambridge University Press, 2011).
Simon, K., 'Poetics of Black', A Dissertation Submitted to the Division of Media and Communications of the European Graduate School in Candidacy for the Degree of Doctor of Philosophy, Magna Cum Laude', October 2013.
Smith, L., *Chaos: A Very Short Introduction* (Oxford and New York: Oxford University Press, 2007).
Smolin, L., *Time Reborn: From the Crisis in Physics to the Future of the Universe* (Boston: Mariner Books, 2014).
Smolin, L., *The Trouble with Physics: The Rise of String Theory, The Fall of a Science and What Comes Next* (London: Penguin, 2008).
Smolin, L., *Three Roads to Quantum Gravity* (London: Phoenix, 2000).
Smolin, L., *The Life of the Cosmos* (London: Weidenfeld & Nicolson, 1997).
Sparks, B. W., *Geomorphology* (1960; rpt London: Longmans, 1969).
Stearns, P. N. and Stearns, C. Z., 'Emotionology: Clarifying the History of Emotions and Emotional Standards', *The American Historical Review*, 90/4 (October 1985), 813–36.
Steger, M. B., *Globalization: A Very Short Introduction* (Oxford: Oxford University Press, 2009).
Tarnas, R., 'Understanding the Modern Disenchantment of the Cosmos', in N. Campion and P. Curry (eds), *Sky and Psyche: The Relationship Between Cosmos and Consciousness* (2006; rpt Edinburgh: Floris Books, 2018).
Thomas, M. W., *Corresponding Cultures: The Two Literatures of Wales* (Cardiff: University of Wales Press, 1999).
Thomas, M. W., 'Staying to mind things: Gillian Clarke's early poetry', in M. Elfyn (ed.), *Trying The Line: A Volume of Tribute to Gillian Clarke* (Llandysul, Ceredigion: Gomer Press, 1997).
Thomas, M. W., *Internal Difference: Twentieth Century Writing in Wales* (Cardiff: University of Wales Press, 1992).

Unger, R. M. and Smolin, L., *The Singular Universe and the Reality of Time* (Cambridge: Cambridge University Press, 2015).
Wallace-Wells, D., *The Uninhabitable Earth: A Story of the Future* (London: Allen Lane, 2019).
Walton, S., *Everybody Needs Beauty: In Search of the Nature Cure* (London and New York: Bloomsbury Publishing, 2021).
Ward, J. P., *The Poetry of R. S. Thomas* (Bridgend: Poetry Wales Press, 1987).
Williams, I., *Canu Aneirin* (1938; new edn Cardiff: University of Wales Press, 1961).
Woodward, J., *The Ice Age: A Very Short Introduction* (Oxford: Oxford University Press, 2014).

INDEX

A
Aaron, Jane 144
Aberfan (Aber-fan) 73, 83–4, 123
Abertillery *see* Six Bells colliery
Aberystwyth 73–4, 82, 87, 170
Afghanistan 141, 143, 150
Africa(n) 51, 55
Aneirin 10, 158–63, 166–9, 171–5,
    159, 175–6, 179
    see also Gododdin, Y
Anglo-Saxons (Saxons, Angles,
    Deira, Bernicia) 117, 159–60,
    162, 173
Anglo-Welsh Review 4, 5
Anthropocene 45–7, 62, 65–92, 101,
    115–31, 180
archaeopteryx 128–9
arctic fox 84
Arctic regions 84
Armitage, Simon 160
    Sir Gawain and the Green Knight
    (trans.) 160
Armstrong, Karen 25, 41, 56, 59–61,
    63, 69, 75–6, 109
Arup 60

Atlantic 26, 68, 73, 75, 81–2, 145
Australia 91

B
Baghdad 146
Barrow, John 181
Barry 3, 89, 134
Basset, Douglas 116
Bavaria 128
Belfast 148
Bethlehem 145
Bidgood, Ruth 5
Bielski, Alison 5
Big Bang 96, 157
bio-cosmology 42–7, 49
bird migration 50–1
Birmingham 104
Bishop, A. C. 116
    Guide to Minerals, Rocks and
    Fossils 116
Black Death 27
Blaen Cwrt 20–1, 43, 81
    see also Clarke, Gillian: *poems*,
    'Blaen Cwrt'

Blake, William 45
  'Jerusalem' 45
Blaser, Robin 37
Blyton, Enid 74
Borth, and Borth storm 74, 77
  see also Clarke, Gillian: poems
  'Cantre'r Gwaelod'
Bosnia 141–3, 151–2
Boveri, Theodor 39
Bradwen (figure in *The Gododdin*)
  176
Branwen (myth) 8, 138
Brexit 91
Bridgewater Hall 8, 59–60, 94–5
Bristol Channel 102
British Council 8
Brown, John 53
Brown, Neville 54, 88, 90
Burke, Anthony 145
Bush, Raymond 52
Butler, Daniel 69, 71, 72

C
Cage, John 62
Cambrian mountains 71
Cambridge, Museum of Zoology 8, 128
Campion, Nicholas 41, 60, 62–3, 69
Canada 84
Capel Celyn 79, 104, 152
  see also Cwm Tryweryn
Caradog (figure in *The Gododdin*)
  176
Cardiff 1–4, 6, 12–13, 15, 18–19, 21, 69, 79, 85, 107, 134, 174
  Capital Poet 1
  Cyncoed 15
  East Moors Steelworks 12–14, 107; see also Clarke, Gillian: poems, 'East Moors'
  Ely 85
  Roath 13
  Rumney 13
  Splott 13, 16
  Taf 102
  Tremorfa 13
Carmarthenshire 2, 171
Cashford, Jules 53–4, 58, 88
Catraeth, battle of 159–60, 162, 163, 167, 171–5
  see also Catterick
Catterick 159
Cadfannan (figure in *The Gododdin*)
  166, 176
census (1870) 22
Ceredig (figure in *The Gododdin*)
  176
Ceredigion 4, 6, 74, 75, 141
Chakrabarty, Dipesh 47–8, 89, 118, 127, 133, 135–6, 138–9, 151, 152, 158, 163
Chamberlain, Brenda 135
China 1, 150
Clark, Stuart 51, 55, 82

Clarke, Gillian
childhood 3, 7, 10, 16, 18, 38, 45, 52, 83, 115, 120, 128, 133–9, 143, 147, 164, 171
family relations 2–3, 5, 6, 14, 16–20, 23, 25, 45, 46, 48, 53, 65, 75, 89, 108, 110, 115, 120, 133–5, 137, 147, 148, 151, 165, 170–1

INDEX

essays and journals
'Beginning with Bendigeidfran' 2, 6, 16
'Cardiff' 3
'For seven years Cardiff became The Weekend and The Holidays' 2
'Slate' 103, 120, 124
'Something Understood' 37, 53, 71
'The Drowned Forest' 75
'The Poetry of Stone: Pentre Ifan' 9, 115
'Tramp. Nothing is until it has a word' 3
'Voice of the Tribe' 6

poems and elegies
'A Barge on the Severn' 98–9
'A Difficult Birth' 148
'A Recipe for Water' 97–8, 100
'A Russian Woman in Tashkent, 1979' 47
'A Spring Morning' 46
'Aftermath' 145, 146
'Archaeopteryx' 129
'Architect' 50
'At the Banganga Tank' 105
'Barrage' 104
'Beach Buds' 5
'Behind Glass' (poem sequence) 8, 10, 123
'Birthday' 145, 146
'Blackface' 28
'Blaen Cwrt' 15
'Bleddyn ap Cyfryn (1069)' 170
'Blue Sky Thinking' 42–5, 47, 149, 180
'Bluebells' 45
'Cae Delyn' 52–3
'Cantre'r Gwaelod' 73, 74–7

'Capel Celyn' 152
'Carols of the Birds' 86
'Cattle, Hayfield, Storm' 70–1, 79–81
'Chalk Pebble' 63
'Chawton' 72
'Coal (Upper Carboniferous)' 122, 123, 124
'Cofiant' 170–1
'Concerto' 8, 9. 60–3, 94, 155
'Death of a Cat' 53, 54, 171
'Death of a Young Woman' 15, 171
'December' (poem sequence) 52
'Dinogad's Coat' 174
'East Moors' 12–14, 107
'Edward Llwyd and the Trilobite (Ordovician)' 124
'Eisteddfod of the Black Chair' 171
'Estuary' 62
'European Field' 153–5
'First Lamb' 31
'Flowers of the Mountain' 72
'Foghorns' 53–4
'Freeze 1947' 85, 87, 89, 90
'Freeze 2010' 87, 90
'Glacier' 83–4, 123
'Glass' (poem sequence) 18–20
'God's Eye' 109
'Gorse' 139
'Granite (Pre-Cambrian)' 120
'Grufydd (1047)' 170
'Gwenllian' 171
'Hands' 107
'Hare in July' 113
'Harvest Moon' 65
'Hay' 119
'Hunting the Wren' 111
'Ice' 100
'Ice Music' 85

'Ichthyosaur' 129
'In the Bleak Midwinter' 86–7
'In the Taj' 106
'Into the Mountain' 120
'Journey' 108, 109, 111
'Labour' 41
'Language Act' 6
'Laundry' 106
'Letter from a Far Country' 8, 9, 12, 15, 19, 20, 22–7, 33, 90, 94, 135, 149
'Letters from Bosnia' 151–2
'Library Chair' 53
'Listen' 143, 150
'Looking' 55–6
'Madiba' 171
'Making the Beds for the Dead' (poem sequence) 9, 12, 27–30, 32–3, 84
'Man in a Shower' 105
'Marsh Fritillaries' 130
'Mercury' 147
'Mesozoic' 125–7
'Migraine' 19
'Miracle on St David's Day' 54
'Mumbai' (poem sequence) 8, 10, 105–7
'Nightride' 5, 111
'Not' 17
'Ode to Winter' 111
'One Year' (poem sequence) 8, 28
'Oradour-sur-Glane' 152
'Oranges' 140
'Orangutan, Chimpanzee, Gorilla, Man' 130
'Osprey' 50
'Phoning Home' 18
'Plague' 27
'Polar' 89

'Post Script' 107
'Post-War, Cold War, New Wars' 141
'Quayside' 53
'Red' 45
'Rock' 119
'Sabrina' 99–100
'Sailing' 5
'Scything' 48, 54
'Severn' (poem sequence) 80, 98, 100
'Sext' 46
'Shopping' 19
'Siege' 18, 25, 54, 137
'Six Bells' 150–3
'Slate (Cambrian)' 121
'Snow' 51, 86
'Son of Cian of Maen Gwyngwn' 163, 173
'Song' 46
'Source' 98
'Spring Equinox, 2020' 43–4
'Spring Equinox, 2021' 43–4 , 53, 149, 180
'St Augustine's, Penarth' 15
'St Winefride's Well' 97
'Storm' 67
'Storm Awst' (1978) / 'Storwm Awst' (2024) 67–8, 70, 80, 81, 87
'Storm-Snake' 71
'Suicide on Pentwyn Bridge' 14
'Sunday' 15
'Taid's Funeral' 14, 171
'Tawny Owl' 82
'The Book of Aneirin' 162
'The Breath of Trees' 45, 180
'The City' (poem sequence) 2, 8, 10, 17–18, 94–6, 116–17, 127, 155–6, 171
'The Company of Bones' 130

'The Dead after the Thaw' 87, 90, 135
'The Field-Mouse' / 'The Field Mouse' 141–3
'The Fox' 5
'The Great Silence' 43
'The Habit of Life' 19
'The Hare' 58, 113
'The Honey Man' 49–50
'The Hours' (poem sequence) 46
'The King of Britain's Daughter: an Oratorio' (poem sequence) 8, 138
'The Lacemaker' 26
'The Listeners' 151–2
'The Night War Broke' 140–1, 143
'The Place' 50
'The Rising Tide' 79–80
'The Silence' 149
'The Snowdon Rainbow Beetle' 130
'The Starling' 48, 179
'The Stone Hare (Lower Carboniferous)' 122
'The Stone Poems' (poem sequence) 8, 10, 100, 117–26, 162
'The Sundial' 58–9, 62
'The Tide' 100
'The Vet' 28
'The Water-Diviner' 54
'The Year's Midnight' 57
'Times Like These' 140
'Tomatoes' 146
'Valley' 97, 108
'White Nights' 85–7
'Why I Write' 4, 16
'Wild Laburnum' 45–6
'Winter' 56–7
'Woman Washing her Hair (Devonian)' 121–3

poetry collections
A Recipe for Water 8, 10, 17, 46, 52, 70, 79, 83, 84, 98, 105, 115, 128, 147
At the Source 20, 102, 115, 117, 137
Bioverse: Poems for the National Botanic Gardens of Wales 8
Five Fields 6, 18–19, 26, 49, 50, 51, 60, 62–3, 94, 108, 115, 116, 120, 141, 151, 153
Glas-Nos: Cerddi Dros Heddwch/ Poems for Peace 144
Ice 10, 50, 56, 57, 66, 71, 84, 85–7, 88–90, 100, 111, 115, 128, 143, 149, 150
Letter from a Far County 12, 14, 15, 16, 18, 54, 59, 63, 119, 137, 171
Letting in the Rumour 55, 58, 67–8, 113, 140, 170
Making the Beds for the Dead 8, 100, 115, 117, 127, 140, 145–6
Roots Home 75, 141, 147
Selected Poems 16, 59, 82, 112–13
The Gododdin: Lament for the Fallen 10, 159–64, 167–9, 170–7
The King of Britain's Daughter 47, 144, 151
The Sundial 15, 16, 51, 53, 58–9, 62, 108, 119, 171
Zoology 28, 123, 128, 171

Clewis, Robert 60, 86–7
CND 140
Cobb, Noel 35, 56–8, 63
colour theory 10, 44, 45, 72, 108, 110–11, 112, 113
Common Ground (charity) 96

Conran, Anthony 160, 161, 163–4, 167, 169, 172, 173, 175, 177
  'Elegy for the Welsh Dead, in the Falkland Islands, 1982' 160
  Sir Galahad 173
Constantine, Mary-Ann 7
Cornwall 167
cosmology and microcosmology 9–10, 33–4, 35–64, 65–9, 72, 75–6, 88–92, 93–5, 99–100, 103, 107–8, 111–12, 115, 121–7, 129, 133, 135, 139, 142–3, 145, 147, 149, 156, 158, 159, 180–1
cosmos ('beautiful order') 9, 35–42, 44–54, 56–64, 65–6, 69–72, 75–6, 80, 82, 87, 88–91, 94–6, 98–9, 101–3, 105–7, 109, 110, 114, 118–19, 122–3, 125, 127, 136, 139–40, 142–3, 145, 147, 149, 152, 155–6, 168, 179–81
Covid-19 pandemic 43, 45–6, 127, 149–50
Cowen, Rob 58, 110–12
Crick, Francis 39
Cristiani, Riccardo 11, 19, 21, 23
Cumberland 167
Curtis, Tony 4, 133, 135–6, 140–3
  'Crane Flies' 141–3
  After the First Death 143
  War Voices 141
Cwm Elan 73, 104
Cwm Tryweryn 73, 79, 104
Cwmreglwys 73
Cynefin 41
Cyron (figure in *The Gododdin*) 176

D
Dafydd Benfras 161
Darwin, Charles 128
  Origin of Species 128
Davies, George 168, 173
  Pilgrimage of Peace 168
Davies, Paul 181
Denbighshire 2
'desacralization' 107
Dillard, Annie 66, 69, 134
  Pilgrim at Tinker Creek 66, 134
Din Eydin *see* Edinburgh
Dinas Cross 165
Dinorwic 103
Dolgarrog 73–4
Dordogne 50
Dowlais Iron Company 12

E
Earth 3–7, 43, 50, 52, 54–9, 66, 71, 76, 78, 80, 83, 88–9, 90, 94–6, 99, 108, 110, 117, 118–20, 122–5, 133, 145, 151, 180
Eckersley, Robyn 146
'eco-anxiety' and 'eco-grief' 78
Eden 46
Egan, Kate 60
  'Space Piece' 60
Elan Valley reservoir 104
  see also Cwm Elan
Elfed 167
Elfyn, Menna 144, 173
Elidir Fawr 103
emotional communities 9, 10, 11–34, 35, 159, 162–3, 165, 172, 175–7
energeia 49

INDEX

England 116, 159, 160, 163, 167
   English Lake District
   North of England 116, 159, 167
   see also Cornwall
Evans, Ceinwen (mother) *see* family relations
Evans, Dan 14
Evans, Daniel Silvan 163
Evans, Ellis Humphrey *see* Hedd Wyn
Evans, I. O. 116–17
   The Observer's Book of Geology 116
extreme weather 71, 73, 74, 78–84, 86
   see also Clarke, Gillian: *poems*, 'Storwm Awst'; Hughes, Iestyn; 'tywydd mawr'

F

Farmer's Weekly 23
farming 2, 7, 8, 12, 17, 21–2, 26, 27, 28–9, 30–3, 41, 103–4, 108, 124, 146, 149, 165, 171
   see also Hughes, Anne
'feminine values' 5–6, 14, 22, 58, 144
Finch, Peter 13, 16
Fisher, Allen 37
Flanders 144
Fortey, Richard 86, 118, 120, 124–5
   The Earth: An Intimate History 118, 120
   Trilobite! Eyewitness to Evolution 124
Foucault, Michel 165–7

G

Ganges 106
general theory of relativity 93
geological periods
   Cambrian 116, 121; *see also* Clarke, Gillian: *poems*, 'Slate'
   Ordovician 116, 124; *see also* Clarke, Gillian: *poems*, 'Edward Llwyd and the Trilobite'
   Pre-Cambrian 116, 118, 120
   Silurian 116, 124
   see also Clarke, Gillian: *poems*, 'The Stone Poems'
Gerald (Giraldus) Cambrensis 164
Gibbings, Robert 101–2
   Coming Down the Wye 101
Gies, Erica 77, 106
Gilchrist, Cherry 47
Gleick, James 66, 69, 88–9, 123
global warming 67, 75, 78, 81, 98, 125
   see also extreme weather
Glyndŵr Award 1
Gododdin (people and region) 159, 163–7, 169, 171–3, 175–7
Gododdin, Y 10, 158, 159–64, 167–9, 170–7, 179
   see also Clarke, Gillian: *poetry collections*, *The Gododdin: Lament for the Fallen*
Gogynfeirdd see Poets of the Princes
Good Friday Agreement 147–9
Gormley, Antony 153–4
   European Field 153
Gorsedd of Bards 1
Gramich, Katie 138
Great Silence 43–4, 45, 127, 180
   see also Clarke, Gillian: *poems*, 'Blue Sky Thinking', 'Spring Equinox' and
Greene, Brian 95–6, 101, 155, 158
Greenham Common 144, 173

Greenland/Denmark 83, 84, 123
  see also Clarke, Gillian: *poems*, 'Glacier'
Grey, Edward 44
Griffiths, Hywel 73–4
Grove Park Grammar School 2
Guardian, The 74, 150
Gwaednerth (figure in *The Gododdin*) 176
Gwefrfawr (figure in *The Gododdin*) 166
Gwenabwy (figure in *The Gododdin*) 169
Gwrfelling (figure in *The Gododdin*) 177

H

Haverfordwest 173
Hay-on-Wye 8
Heaney, Seamus 6, 160
  Beowulf (trans.) 160
Hedd Wyn 171
Henry Reed 43
  'Lessons of the War: 1: Naming of Parts' 43
Hinduism 106
history of emotions 2, 9, 11–12, 14, 33, 35, 167
Hodgkinson, W. P. 38, 40, 54, 66
Horovitz, Frances 113
Hoskins, Andrew 139, 143
Hughes, Anne 23
  The Diary of a Farmer's Wife 1796–1797 23
Hughes, Iestyn 73, 78, 82, 87
  Tywydd Mawr 73, 78, 82, 87
Hughes, Ted 6
Humphreys, Emyr 161, 164, 173

Huxley, Thomas Henry 128
Hyde Park 173
Hyfaidd Hir (figure in *The Gododdin*) 175
hyperobjects 78, 81
  see also Morton, Timothy
Hywel Dda, The Laws of 49

I

Iceland 20, 43, 71, 85, 127
India 8, 105–6
  see also Clarke, Gillian: *poems*, 'Mumbai'
industrial pollution (and industrialisation) 12–13, 29, 80, 84, 100, 104, 106–7, 127, 156
IRA 148, 155
Iran (Iranian Embassy) 138
  Zhuzestan (province) 138

J

Jackson, Professor Kenneth 160
  The Gododdin: The Oldest Scottish Poem 160
Jarman, A. O. H. 160
  Aneirin: Y Gododdin 160
  Llyfr Aneirin: The Book of Aneirin 160
Jenkins, Nigel 144
  'Brawdy' 144
Jones, Colin 98
Jones, D. Gwenallt 173
Jones, David 173
  In Parenthesis 173
Jones, Ieuan Gwynedd 12–14, 17, 26
Jones, T. Gwynn 173
Joris, Pierre 37

K

Kan Yasuda 60–1
Kant, Immanuel 48
   Critique of Judgment 48
Kimble, George 52
Kurki, Milja 35, 36, 39, 133, 144–6, 158
   International Relations in a Relational Universe 133

L

Laniel-Musitelli, Sophie 81, 97, 118, 119, 122, 127
Lapland 50
Lester, Reginald 55, 71, 72
   The Observer's Book of Weather 55, 71, 72
Lewis, Alun 135
Linssen, E. F. 49
Liverpool and Wirral 79, 104, 136, 152
Llandeilo 124
Llanelli Grammar School 2
Llanidloes 151
Llif (figure in *The Gododdin*) 176
Llyn Peris 103
Llywelyn the Great 161
London 3, 138, 174
Lubbock, John 52, 83, 101
   The Beauties of Nature and the Wonders of the World We Live In 101

M

Mabinogion 75
Machynlleth 1
Madog (figure in *The Gododdin*) 166
Madog ap Maredudd (mythical figure) 169
Maeterlinck, Maurice 49
   The Life of the Bee 49
Magnason, Andri Snær 20, 71, 80, 90, 98, 106
Malmö 153
Manchester 8, 60, 94, 116, 155–6
Mandela, Nelson *see* Clarke, Gillian: *poems* 'Madiba'
Marchlyn reservoir 103
Marconi company 2
Marged, Blaen Cwrt 20–1, 86
   see also Blaen Cwrt
Maund, Kari 159
McLeish, Tom 61, 155
Mead, Margaret 37
Mercia 167
mercury 86, 147
   see also Clarke, Gillian: *poems*, 'Mercury'
Mercury 147
   see also Clarke, Gillian: *poems*, 'Mercury'
Meredith, Christopher 4
Merthyr Tydfil 12
Milky Way 37, 93
Milton, John 44
   Paradise Lost 44
Minhinnick, Robert 126, 144
   Life Sentences 144
   'The Dinosaur Park' 126
Mitchell, Audra 35
Morgan, Dennis 13
Morris, Reginald O. 61, 155
Morrison, Toni 26
Morton, Timothy 62, 78, 81
Mumbai 105–7
   see also Clarke, Gillian: *poems*, 'Mumbai'

'mutuality' concept 48, 133, 135, 136, 138, 151, 148
  see also Chakrabarty, Dipesh
Mynyddawg (Mynyddog) Mwynfawr 163–4, 172
  see also Gododdin, Y

N
National Coal Board 84
National Museum of Wales 116
National Poet of Wales 1
National Theatre of Wales 8
National Trust 8
nature 2, 9, 18, 25, 26, 36, 38, 41–6, 48–9, 51, 53, 54, 59, 62, 64, 65–8, 69, 71–2, 80, 83, 87–8, 90, 93, 96, 100, 102, 105–6, 107, 115, 120, 122, 126–7, 136, 138, 140, 149, 157, 179, 181
  see also Butler, Daniel; Clarke, Gillian: *poems*, 'Harvest Moon', 'Miracle on St David's Day', 'Storm Awst'; Cowen, Rob; Hodgkinson, W. P.; Lubbock, John
New IRA *see* IRA
New York Times 66
Newport College of Art 4
Newton, Isaac 67, 36, 39, 42
Nicholas, T. E. 173
Nonconformism 7
Normandy 167
Northumbria 167
Norway 84

O
O'Loughlin, Ben 139, 143

Old North 161
  see also Catraeth; Catterick; England; *Gododdin, Y*
Östra Grevie 153
Owain, son of Gruffudd ap Cynan 164, 166, 168, 172, 173, 174, 175
  Hirlais Owain 164
Owen, Thomas Richard 116
  Geology Explained in South Wales 116
  The Upper Palaeozoic and Post-Palaeozoic Rocks of Wales 116

P
Palmer, Douglas 128–9
Palmer, Tim 65–7, 157
Paradise 176–7
Parry-Jones, D. 21–2, 68, 113
  Welsh Country Characters 69, 113
  Welsh Country Upbringing 21–2
Peach, Linden 28, 181
  Animals, Animality and Controversy in Modern Welsh Literature and Culture 28, 181
  Pacifism, Peace and Modern Welsh Writing ix
Peate, Iorwerth 173
Pedair (folk-music group) 7
Pedler, Ilse 29, 30, 33, 41
  Auscultation 29
  'All this Accumulation of Knowledge' 33
  'Castrating Calves' 29, 33
  'Culling' 29
Pembrokeshire 2

Penarth 3, 15–16
  St Augustine's Church 15–16
  see also Clarke, Gillian: *poems*,
    'St Augustine's, Penarth'
Penrhyn 117
Perigord 50
Petterssen, Sverre 52, 70
  Introduction to Meteorology 52
phenology 72
Plaid Cymru 173
plate tectonics 93
Plath, Sylvia 5
Poetry Wales 1, 5
Popper, Karl 155, 181
Porthcawl 2
Powys 167
Preston, Jeanne 23
Psychogeography 13, 89
Pugh, Sheenagh 4

Q
quantum mechanics 93, 180

R
Reddy, William 12
relational universe 35–6, 104, 131,
    133, 146, 158, 181
Renaissance 166
Rheged 167
Rhondda 21
Richards, Ceri 135–6, 142
  Desolate Landscape 136
  *The Force That Drives the Water
    Through the Rocks* 136
Roberts, Alice 159, 166
Roberts, Lynette 135
Roberts, Sally 5

Rosenwein, Barbara H. 11, 16, 19,
    21, 23, 174, 175
Rovelli, Carlo 35
Rumens, Carol 44–5, 163, 169
Russia 15, 47, 84, 150

S
Sachdeva, Sonya 106
Samarkand 143–4
Sciama, Dennis W. 56, 117
Sclater, A. 8
  *The National Botanic Garden of
    Wales* 8
Scotland 159, 167
Severn (river, valley, bore, estuary)
    38, 55, 66, 80, 98–103, 104, 105
  see also Clarke, Gillian: *poems*,
    'Severn'
Seward, Albert S. 118, 124, 125
Sexton, Anne 5
Shakespeare, William 3
  King Lear 3
Shropshire 164, 167
Simon, Kathryn 10, 108–14
Six Bells colliery, Abertillery 150
  see also Clarke, Gillian: *poems*,
    'Six Bells'
Smith, Leonard 66–7, 78–9, 83
Smolin, Lee 35–6, 40–1, 46, 65,
    179–80
Snowdon *see* Wyddfa, Yr
Snowdon beetle 130
  see also Clarke, Gillian: *poems*,
    'The Snowdon Rainbow
    Beetle'
Snowdon Lily 72, 124
  see also Clarke, Gillian: *poems*,
    'Flowers of the Mountain'

South Africa 171
Steger, Manfred 139, 146
Stephens, Meic 5
Stevenson, Anne 5
Stop the War Coalition 173
string theory 95, 158
Sutton, Walter 39
Sweden 55, 153
Swimme, Brian 93–4, 96, 98, 108–10, 112
   Cosmogenesis: An Unveiling of the Expanding Universe 93

T
Taj Mahal 106
Taj Mahal Hotel 106
   see also Clarke, Gillian: *poems*, 'In the Taj'
Taoism 112
Tarnas, Richard 42, 107, 109
Tennant, J. R. 90
thermodynamics, second law of 93
Thomas Jones, Owen 116
Thomas, Dylan 136, 142
   'The force that through the green fuse drives the flower' 136, 142
Thomas, M. Wynn 7, 21, 144, 173
Thomas, R. S. 6, 38, 39, 40, 50, 54, 104, 136, 137, 141
   'At It' 39
   'Bravo!' 38
   Frequencies 38, 39, 40
   Neb 136
   'Reservoirs' 104
   The Echoes Return Slow 136
   'The Place' 50
Thompson, James 39

Tryweryn *see* Cwm Tryweryn
Tudfwlch Hir (mythical figure) 176
Tulsi Pipe Road 106
   see also Clarke, Gillian: *poems*, 'At the Taj', 'Laundry'
Tŷ Newydd (writers' centre) 4
typos hieros 168
   see also Gododdin, Y
'tywydd mawr' 74
   see also extreme weather; Hughes, Iestyn

U
Unger, Roberto Mangabeira 35
United States of America 1, 84
University of Glamorgan (now University of South Wales) 4
University of Salford 60
Uzbekistan 143

V
Vaughan, Henry 38
Vitos 151

W
Wales
   anglicised aspirations 3, 19
   geography 9, 10, 21, 33, 75, 88–9, 103, 116, 119, 127, 177
   historical, cultural, linguistic differences 9, 21, 25, 28, 59, 100, 116, 137, 177
   history 6–7, 9, 11–12, 17, 20–7, 33, 35, 73–4, 75, 77, 79, 99–100, 119, 152–3, 161, 181

myths and stories 2, 73, 74–6, 88, 89, 99–100, 102, 138, 153, 171, 177
nationalism 104
pacifism and peace 10, 144, 146, 164, 168, 174, 179
Welsh assembly/Senedd 6, 162
Walton, Samantha 24–5, 85, 87, 98, 99, 102, 105–6
war and conflict, zones of
   Afghanistan 141, 143, 150
   Aleppo 174
   Bosnia 141, 142, 143, 151; *see also* Clarke, Gillian: *poems*, 'Letters from Bosnia'
   D-Day 134–5
   Falklands War 160, 173; *see also* Conran, Anthony
   First World War 32, 44, 133, 143, 144, 173–4
   Gaza 173, 174
   Gulf 140–1, 143, 146
   Helmand 174
   Iraq 141
   Kosovo 140–1
   Middle East 141
   Second World War 2, 8, 32, 34, 44, 52, 54–5, 70, 72, 101, 116, 133, 135–6, 150, 155, 168, 170
   Somme 174
   Vietnam 140
   Ypres 174
   see also Catraeth; *Gododdin, Y*
Ward, J. P. 39–40
Watkins, Vernon 135
Watson, James 39
Watts, Meic 122

waves (oscillatory patterns) 18, 80, 82, 94–5, 102, 127, 157
Welsh language 2–3, 6–7, 17, 50, 53, 104, 159, 162, 164, 167–8, 171, 172, 177, 181
   banned Welsh 2
   Welsh-language communities 2
Welsh Women's Peace Petition 173
Welsh writing in English (Anglo-Welsh Writing) 1, 4
Wessex 167
Westminster 28, 162
Wildlife and Conservation Act (1981) 43
Wilfred Owen Association 1
Williams, Adrian 8
Williams, Alwyn 116
Williams, Ifor 160
   Canu Aneirin 160
Williams, John Penry (father) *see* family relations
Williams, Waldo 53, 164–5, 168, 169, 173
   'Brawdoliaeth' 165
   'Pa Beth Yw Dyn?' 169
Williams Parry, R. 50
   'Y Llwynog' 50
Winnicott, Donald 24
Woodward, James 126
Wrexham 2
Wyddfa, Yr (Snowdon) 8
Wye 97, 102
   see also Gibbings, Robert
Wynne-Rhydderch, Samantha 77

Y
Yorkshire 159, 167
   see also Catterick; *Gododdin, Y*